EMPIRE *and* LIBERTY

EMPIRE *and* LIBERTY

The Tied Histories of Two American Landmarks

VANEESA COOK

BEACON PRESS, BOSTON

BEACON PRESS
24 Farnsworth Street
Boston, Massachusetts
www.beacon.org

Beacon Press books
are published under the auspices of
the Unitarian Universalist Association of Congregations.

Printed in the United States of America

29 28 27 26 8 7 6 5 4 3 2 1

This book is printed on acid-free paper that meets the uncoated paper ANSI/NISO specifications for permanence as revised in 1992.

Text design and composition by Kim Arney

Library of Congress Cataloguing-in-Publication Data is available for this title.
Hardcover ISBN: 978-0-8070-1968-9
E-book ISBN: 978-0-8070-1970-2
Audiobook: 978-0-8070-2455-3

The authorized representative in the EU for product safety and compliance is Easy Access System Europe 16879218, Mustamäe tee 50, 10621 Tallinn, Estonia: https://beacon.org/eu-contact.

To Michael D. Gambone,
the truest American I know

CONTENTS

PREFACE

The fog had not yet lifted on Saturday morning, July 28, 1945, when Lieutenant Colonel William Franklin Smith Jr. requested clearance to land at Newark (Liberty) Airport in the B-25 Mitchell bomber he was piloting from Bedford Air Field in Massachusetts. Smith was not new to the B-25 aircraft. A World War II veteran with over five hundred combat hours, he had served as a lead pilot of Eighth Air Force missions in the European theater, enough to earn him the Flying Cross and an Air Medal. The war in the Pacific was not quite over, but the Allied advance against Japan was intensifying, and plans to use atomic weapons were finalizing that summer.

Smith's responsibility on July 28 involved transporting personnel on a routine flight made difficult and dangerous by the surrounding fog in New York City. At 9:40 a.m., Smith became disoriented and crashed the plane directly into the north side of the Empire State Building, between the seventy-eighth and eightieth floors, causing a massive fire, structural damage, and the death of fourteen people, including himself and two others on board. The building, however, ultimately survived.

Colorful stories such as these have made their way into the lore of the Empire State Building, a world landmark and cultural icon. But in 1945, the 102-story Art Deco skyscraper located at Fifth Avenue and Thirty-Fourth Street in Midtown Manhattan was only fourteen years old. Conceived by a group of New York elites, the immense silver tower was constructed to be the world's tallest building (1,454 feet tall with antenna), and it achieved this lofty goal in 1931, even as Americans struggled in the depths of the Great Depression. Tourism to the Empire State Building rivaled and then surpassed visitation to New York City's other monumental attraction, the Statue of Liberty, visible on clear days from the observation deck of the new skyscraper. By the early 1930s, the once-copper-colored Lady Liberty, erected in 1886, had eroded to a shade of green, and the statue was in need of renovation.

Most people in the United States and around the world have heard of the Empire State Building, and many have taken a trip to its top to view the city from the building's 86th or 102nd floors. The same holds true for the Statue of Liberty, standing three-hundred-feet tall, just south of Manhattan. Visitors to Liberty Island perceive the monument as an enduring symbol of freedom, but they are less likely to know about the debates surrounding the concept of liberty that have made the meaning of the statue murky since the late 1800s. Likewise, few connect the name of the most famous American skyscraper to the imperial power it was meant to evoke. Despite seeing their images in countless media outlets, the public knows little about the conception and reception of these two landmarks, and millions of people around the world have a limited understanding of them as hallmarks of American identity.

The names of the monuments indicate their symbolism: "empire" and "liberty," each endorsing seemingly incompatible missions of control vs. freedom. Yet the concepts of empire and liberty have been intertwined throughout US history. In 1785, George Washington referred to New York as the "seat of the empire," which gave the state its moniker and, eventually, the skyscraper its name. Washington had just fought to secure liberty for a nation, and he was already proclaiming an empire.

The Statue of Liberty, since the late 1800s, aided US empire by beckoning immigrants and resources from around the world and by enhancing the image of the United States as a liberating force. Gifted by France and dedicated officially in October 1886, the statue was intended to seal the bond of republicanism that the United States and France both fought to secure in their respective countries in the late eighteenth century. In the late nineteenth century, a republic was still rare, and the French wanted to celebrate a form of government derived from the people rather than from a monarch or tyrant, as was the case for most of the world. Édouard Laboulaye, the French intellectual who proposed the idea behind the statue, also wanted to commemorate the emancipation of slaves following the US Civil War. Liberty, he hoped, had finally triumphed in America in 1865. However, Americans unwilling to let liberty loose from the bounds of imperial control limited the freedom of millions across the US continent and around the world.

The Statue of Liberty and the Empire State Building were built by thousands of individuals working together for a common cause. Workers spanned the spectrum of class and ethnicity, from high-end architects to unskilled laborers, but they all likely registered the sense of hope and optimism that the structures represented. Many recently arrived immigrants who helped construct the tallest skyscraper in the world in 1930 had been greeted by the Statue of Liberty when they reached the shores of the United States. During the Cold War, US officials fortified the connection between the two symbols in people's minds and hearts by highlighting their shared role in representing the United States as a benevolent power. Empire and liberty have been endlessly, if uneasily, integrated.

There is no doubt that the Empire State Building and Statue of Liberty have achieved iconic status. Icons, however, are not born ready-made; they develop over time through public reception. The emotional meaning accrued is crucial in forging the image. Millions of visitors to the Empire State Building's observatory, for example, have felt the thrill of seeing the city from a thousand feet up. On the open-air deck, one can faintly hear the bustle from the streets below, and a sense of calm and quiet prevails, unbroken except for the gusts of wind that whip around the parapet. The perspective is vast and truly awesome, imparting a rare combination of peace, freedom, and power. Likewise, anyone who has stood at the base of the Statue of Liberty has gazed at the resolute countenance of a queen secure in her convictions. The graceful curves and light-green hues of the statue soften the effect, invoking an amalgam of emotions that also resonate peace, freedom, and empowerment across generations.

Despite their proximity, about five miles apart, the two landmarks are typically considered separately. When studied in tandem, however, it becomes clear that they represent twin touchpoints for American identity and ideals. The story of these two landmarks, therefore, is essentially about the American people and their experiences—how they construed the structures as symbols of empire and liberty and how they instilled them with spirit and character. After all, the reception was not always a warm one. Women and people of color have put pressure on the meaning of the Statue of Liberty, calling out the shortcomings of freedom in the United States for minority citizens.

The United States' role as an empire has also sparked controversy. Back in the late 1700s, George Washington and the founders realized they needed to protect newfound liberties against future attacks, and many Americans aspired to join the ranks of rival powers by extending US rule across the continent. Over the course of the twentieth century, the relatively young nation acquired colonies and established itself as a major economic power. Yet the term "empire," which is typically used to describe the conquering of widespread territories, was fraught with complications for a republic and its people priding themselves on liberty.

Americans have grappled with the tensions between empire and liberty since the nation's founding and continue to do so today. International observers have also struggled to reconcile the contradictions inherent in US identity, an ongoing issue that has sparked resentment and retaliation. Lieutenant Colonel Smith crashed his B-25 into the Empire State Building by accident. Fifty-six years later, two commercial jet airliners would strike the World Trade Center, another symbol of US empire, on purpose. The 9/11 attack and the subsequent War on Terror are a testament to the limits of the United States' ability to project a positive image as an "empire of liberty" for everyone around the world.

The Empire State Building and Statue of Liberty have stood bearing witness to these developments over time, from the immigration surge of the nineteenth century to the tragedy of 9/11 in the twenty-first century. At the heart of this narrative is the struggle of Americans who faced the challenges posed by each of these monumental structures and the values they represent. The Empire State Building and the Statue of Liberty are each founded on the optimism of those convinced they could overcome all obstacles, including economic disasters, war, social crises, racism, the limits of technology, and all the gaps between idealism and realism. We should remember that they were both created with the sincere hope that America would set a shining example for the rest of the world.

Liberty in fog

CHAPTER 1

LIBERTY ENLIGHTENING THE WORLD—1865

Frédéric Auguste Bartholdi dreamed of creating a monumental sculpture well before he knew what form it would take or what purpose it would serve. "When I discover a subject grand enough, I will honor that subject by building the tallest statue in the world," he supposedly informed a friend in 1856.[1]

The French-born artist had returned from a half year's journey around Egypt in search of a reason worthy enough to fulfill his vision. He was summoned home before he found it. In Colmar, France, that summer, his most recent creation honoring Napoleonic-war General Count Jean Rapp was ready to be presented at an unveiling ceremony in the town square, and Bartholdi's mother had insisted he cut his trip short to attend the event. Bartholdi showed up, but his thoughts were elsewhere, cycling through plans for his masterpiece, an ambitious venture to draw interest from the entire world rather than a particular patron.

Nearly ten years later, in 1865, Bartholdi met the man whose idealism could match the colossal scale of the sculptor's vision. The fateful encounter arose from a rather mundane request for Bartholdi to craft a bust rendering of Édouard René Lefèbvre de Laboulaye, a lecturer and legal expert long fascinated with the arc of democracy since the French and American Revolutions. It broke Laboulaye's heart to know the much-lauded experiment for republican values, including voting rights, freedom, the rule of law, and balance of power, teetered on shaky ground in both France and the United States. In the mid-1860s, Emperor Napoleon III reigned over the French populace and the French Second Empire overseas. His public projects gained popular support, especially his investment in parks and infrastructure throughout Paris. But political theorists like Laboulaye longed for a return to the spirit of "Liberté, Égalité, Fraternité" that had marked the Revolution a century earlier. Across the Atlantic in the spring of 1865, Americans were reeling from the chaos of the Civil War and the assassination of President Lincoln. Laboulaye, a staunch abolitionist, celebrated the Union victory and the emancipation of slaves. He hoped for a renewed commitment to republican principles in France and the United States and a renewed partnership for advancing liberty in both nations. "I have no need to tell you how happy I am in this victory of liberty and humanity," he wrote to the US consul to France as the Civil War was ending.[2]

During a dinner party hosted by Laboulaye in 1865 at his home near Versailles, Bartholdi heard the French scholar praise the American republic firsthand. The guests, mostly pro-American and antislavery advocates like their host, made their way into the conservatory of Laboulaye's country mansion to smoke and mingle after finishing their meal. As Bartholdi remembered the scene in his memoir, someone speculated whether nations, collectively, could maintain bonds of gratitude and friendship across time. Laboulaye answered yes, if the people shared a "community of thoughts and of struggles, sustained with common aspirations" and a "fraternity of feelings."[3] He was referring to the passionate republicanism that had once tied together American and French fates and fueled their revolutionary momentum in the late eighteenth century. Though many decades had passed and the paths of the two countries had since diverged, Laboulaye believed that Americans still esteemed the courage of French volunteers who fought with the Continental Army for the cause of American independence. The Marquis de Lafayette, he pointed out, remained honored across the United States in statues and buildings bearing his name. In his memory, the spirit of republicanism lived on in the United States where rights had been extended to Black men.

Laboulaye had championed American republicans all his life. He translated the biography of Benjamin Franklin and the sermons of Unitarian abolitionist William Ellery Channing, and he served as an unofficial representative of the Union cause in France. The death of Abraham Lincoln prompted an outpouring of condolences, which he sent to ambassador John Bigelow; the succeeding president, Andrew Johnson; and later, the widow Mary Todd Lincoln. In a letter to Bigelow dated April 29, 1865, Laboulaye expressed how "overwhelmed" he was by the news of the assassination, but he vowed to keep the late president's legacy alive through his lectures and writings. "You ought to see how great is the emotion in Paris," he reported, concluding with an open-ended offer to help the nation weather the storm. "Count me as one of yourselves."[4]

Days later, the French Committee of Emancipation, which Laboulaye founded and presided over, addressed President Johnson with a retrospective of Lincoln's merits. The Committee, as "faithful friends of the United States, sons of the French nation who fought for the independence of your nation," encouraged Americans to honor Lincoln's memory by shunning revenge, reminding the new president that "crimes are isolated, glories are national." After all, they continued, Lincoln had fought wars on multiple fronts with "no protector but liberty" save his two "great weapons—conscience and patience" which "formed [his] whole strength." From the French perspective, the United States had deftly avoided the tempting swing toward monarchy that had plagued their own recent past. "Europe did not expect to see a commercial people become warlike, without the military spirit lapsing into despotism," the Committee wrote. Yet the US Constitution and the moral fortitude of leaders like Washington and Lincoln had preserved the republic. "But spare us more surprises," the French Committee pleaded.[5]

Words of sympathy, however, weren't enough for Laboulaye. Over the next several months, he helped manage a fundraising campaign to send an engraved medallion to Lincoln's widow, Mary Todd. The seemingly innocent gesture caught the attention of the French emperor, who considered it a critique of his illiberal rule. Funds collected by the committee from forty thousand republican-loving contributors, each giving their two cents, were confiscated by Napoleon III, a move that further demonstrated the suppression of liberties under the Second Empire. Undeterred, Laboulaye and his friends launched a second effort, more clandestine and ultimately successful. They smuggled the minted gold coin from the "heart of France" to diplomat John Bigelow, who sent it to Mary Todd in December 1866. In an inscription etched into the medal, the French democrats referred to Lincoln as an "honest" man who had "saved the Republic, without veiling the statue of liberty."[6]

Clearly, Laboulaye felt a tremendous loss. He had considered President Lincoln a kindred spirit who fought the war to preserve the Union on moral grounds. In the Gettysburg Address, delivered by the president in November 1863, Lincoln connected the nation's founding, which had been "conceived in Liberty," to the present "testing" of republican ideals. "This nation, under God," Lincoln envisaged, "shall have a new birth of freedom," sanctified by the soldiers who had given their lives for that "great task."[7] Like his American hero, Laboulaye also dared to hope that the devastating war would engender more widespread freedoms. The same year Lincoln visited Gettysburg, Laboulaye wrote an optimistic introduction in his novel about French-American relations, *Paris en Amerique*:

> One day, perhaps, by the light of my lamp, thou wilt see all the deformity of the idols which thou adorest today; perhaps, too, beyond the decreasing shadows, thou wilt perceive, in all the charm of her immortal smile, Liberty, the daughter of the Gospel, the sister of justice and pity, the mother of equality, abundance and peace.

In descriptive language that anticipated the design of the Statue of Liberty a decade later, Laboulaye called upon the current generation to protect those hard-won freedoms for the future. "On that day, friendly reader, do not suffer the flame which I confide to thee to die out; enlighten, enlighten that youth which already presses on our footsteps and urges us forward," he wrote.[8]

The word "liberty," derived from the Latin word *libertas*, refers to the name of the Roman goddess who personified the meaning of freedom in the late Roman Republic. Often displayed on coins and plaques, Libertas was recognizable as a robed female figure holding a spear and wearing a conical cap that could resemble a crown or diadem. The symbolism surrounding Libertas (and her American doppelgänger Columbia) became more pronounced during the Age of Enlightenment in the eighteenth century, and theories of liberty were discussed by the learned elite in France and the United States. Revolutionary leaders from Samuel Adams to Alexander Hamilton, Ben Franklin to Thomas Jefferson spoke in terms of liberty as a rallying point for their cause, and they often referred to the writings of French republicans such as Montesquieu, Rousseau, Diderot, and Voltaire. Patrick Henry famously declared: "Give me liberty or give me death!" The nuances between liberty, democracy, and a functioning republic would take time to work out, especially in the US Constitution. However, liberty was the lingua franca of republicans in the United States and Europe.

Laboulaye believed that liberty, the most vital principle in human history, deserved immortalization in a sculpture, gifted in friendship, dedicated to its honor. That is the idea he pitched to his dinner guests at his home, Glatigny, on that notable evening in the summer of 1865. Most pointedly, perhaps, he directed his idea to the sculptor F. Auguste Bartholdi. The two republicans, however, were not yet on the same page. While Laboulaye looked west to the promise of America, Bartholdi turned east to Egypt. But the dinner party at Glatigny set Bartholdi on a decades-long journey that would eventually prompt him to follow the path of fellow Frenchmen Marquis de Lafayette and Alexis de Tocqueville to the United States.

IIIIIIIIIII

Both Laboulaye and Bartholdi grew up in an era of empire, not a land of liberty. In 1804, Napoleon Bonaparte launched the First Empire, embarking upon battles to expand or defend French territory. Since the Age of

Discovery in the 1600s, the French had established footholds of imperial control all over the world, in Asia, Africa, and the Western Hemisphere; but in the early 1800s, Napoleon and his forces secured hegemony over most of continental Europe, stretching to the eastern edges of Poland. After an ill-fated invasion of Russia in 1812 and a brutal retreat from Moscow that winter, counterforces across Europe began to push the French army back west. Laboulaye was born in Paris during this war-torn time, in 1811.

Throughout his career as a law professor and public intellectual, Laboulaye had to tailor his topics and his tone to the oft-changing whims of the French government as power changed hands from emperors to revolutionaries to monarchs. Even the royal families switched back and forth. The house of Bourbon was restored after Napoleon's first and then final exile, but the Orléans monarchy overthrew the Bourbons in 1830 to place Louis-Philippe on the throne. Not long after Laboulaye achieved admission to the bar in 1842, the most significant revolutionary movements of the nineteenth century exploded across Europe. The 1848 rebellions for republican reforms affected every country and everyone, regardless of class, occupation, or nationality. In Italy, Sicilians revolted against the ensconced Bourbon monarchy. In France, bloody clashes pitted middle-class liberals against more-radical workers. Similar strife occurred in Germany, Hungary, Denmark, Sweden, and Romania throughout the spring and summer. A perfect storm of changes and subsequent problems sparked the discontent: industrialization, migration, unemployment, food shortages, and the repression of rights and representation. The lives of millions hung in the balance.

These turbulent years made a profound impact on the young law professor's thinking, directing his attention away from ancient Greek democracies to stable contemporary systems like the United States. "These revolutions made a political writer of me," Laboulaye stated, "and overturned all of my ideas."[9] Laboulaye was familiar with Alexis de Tocqueville's famous travelogue *Democracy in America*, but until this turning point in 1848, he could not have predicted that he would become one of France's premier interpreters of American political culture. He performed the job well. Besides the Ben Franklin and Reverend Channing translations, Laboulaye published a three-volume history of US politics and a thorough study of French-US relations.

He also maintained friendships with American travelers and officials such as John Bigelow, Lincoln's appointed minister to France. Soon after arriving in Paris, in 1861, Bigelow wrote a note of introduction to the constitutional expert and supporter of the Union, hoping to forge an "alliance." Laboulaye replied that he would be "happy to serve in any way . . . the cause of liberty and justice." Bigelow followed up, meeting the scholar for the first time at his Paris residence in the early 1860s when Laboulaye was fifty years old. As Bigelow recalled, the Frenchman welcomed him into "spacious rooms" crowded with stacks of books befitting an avid reader. "His voice was gentle and low, though clear and admirably modulated," the ambassador remembered, describing the "black frock-coat" he wore "buttoned close to the chin." Bigelow immediately thanked Laboulaye for his "brave" republican stance, which was not appreciated by the prevailing imperial establishment in France. The meeting proved beneficial for Bigelow's purposes, as Laboulaye promised to continue to support the cause of liberty. "From that time forth his pen and his influence were always at our service," the American minister wrote.[10]

When news of Abraham Lincoln's violent death reached Paris, Laboulaye lectured at the College de France about the late president and his higher purpose before releasing the students to march with a group of about 1,500 youth from the Latin Quarter to the office of Minister Bigelow. Police barricaded the US embassy to prevent the crowd from addressing Bigelow, though some men made it through to deliver their condolences and comradery, shouting "Long live the great American Republic." Bigelow received them cordially and asked the police to stop harassing the demonstrators, whom the French authorities accused of stirring up another anti-imperialist rebellion. A correspondent for the *New York Times* reported, "the speeches of the students have been published in part, but they are too revolutionary for publication entire."[11] Republican ideals were dangerous ideas in France in 1865.

IIIIIIIIIII

As insurrections erupted periodically to oust the Orléans monarchs, Bartholdi was born in 1834 in the Alsatian town of Colmar just west of the Rhine River. He and his mother and one sibling, Jean-Charles, lived off and on in Colmar and in Paris, where the aspiring artist attended the Lycée Louis-le-Grand. His studies were interrupted by the revolutionary activity of 1848, but Bartholdi and his mother were able to network with wealthy patrons. His career path, like Laboulaye's, followed the trajectory of political opinion as he received commissions from the elites of the day. After completing his first major work in 1855, the heroic General Rapp statue in Colmar, Bartholdi continued to seek civic projects, but he craved a grand undertaking to capture the world's attention.

His photographic tour of Egypt and Yemen in the 1850s with a group of artists studying the masters of antiquity introduced him to a region rich with monumental wonders. Before it collapsed during an earthquake in 226 BCE, the Colossus of Rhodes had towered 108 feet above the landscape of its Greek island home, and centuries later, it continued to challenge artists and engineers to match its legendary height. Bartholdi was able to visit the Great Sphinx and Pyramids of Giza, the massive Luxor and Abu Simbel temples, and the twin Colossi of Memnon. The sites struck him with awe. "These granite beings, in their imperturbable majesty, seem to be still listening to the most remote antiquity," Bartholdi observed. "Their kindly and impassable glance seems to ignore the present and to be fixed upon an unlimited future."[12] Bartholdi picked up ideas in Egypt that eventually made their way into his design for his own colossal statue, but he also found inspiration closer to home.

At Laboulaye's dinner party in 1865, the seed for a statue dedicated to liberty took root, as the Glatigny host dreamed aloud about a "memorial to [American] independence" that could unite the two nations once again. "This conversation interested me so deeply that it remained fixed in my memory," Bartholdi recalled.[13] The artist, however, needed more time to act upon the idea. It's not difficult to discern the reasons for Bartholdi's delayed response to Laboulaye's proposition. The American people were recovering from the physical and social wounds of the Civil War, and the battle-weary, bankrupt nation was not ripe for major artistic investment. Neither was France. The atmosphere in Paris in 1865 crackled in anticipation of another mass uprising or imperial conflict, and expressions of republicanism were suppressed. For the time being, Bartholdi found safer subjects in the distant past.

At the 1867 Paris Universal Expo on the grounds of the Champ de Mars, Bartholdi made his way through the crowds to view the displays of the Egyptian contingent, which featured plans for the Suez Canal being built as a gateway for trade ships from around the world. The thirty-three-year-old sculptor was searching for someone: Ismail Pasha, the khedive ruler of Egypt, who was in Paris to help raise money for the ongoing canal construction. Bartholdi wanted to submit an idea he had for a monumental statue called *Egypt Carrying the Light to Asia*, which he hoped the Muhammad Ali dynasty would agree to commission.

Bartholdi's neoclassical design for *Egypt Carrying the Light to Asia* portrayed an enormous female figure robed in the garb of a fellah, the Arab equivalent of a peasant, holding a torch toward the heavens in an outstretched arm. Bartholdi planned to build the statue 130 feet tall, including a pedestal, high enough to surpass the Colossus of Rhodes. As for the symbolism of the piece, the French artist assured the khedive it would reflect Egypt's expanding territory, industrial progress, and modern marvels, such as the new canal, connecting the world from east to west. The concept of "liberty," notably, was not emphasized in this rendering. In Egypt as well as in France, the masses muddled through life beneath the dominion of royal imperialists. Bartholdi knew his audience. Rather than pressing "Enlightenment" ideals of an earlier century, he pulled his philosophical punches, enticing the khedive instead with the aura of an empire projecting power.

The khedive offered polite interest, but no guarantees of funding. Bartholdi refused to give up. Two years after his initial meeting with Pasha, he traveled again to Egypt to make a second pitch, based on the belief that an up-and-coming power constructing modern, capital projects like the Suez Canal could afford to adorn the waterway with colossal artwork. Pasha listened but ultimately turned him down. The khedive, going rapidly broke, opted for another illumination structure, a rather traditional-looking, concrete lighthouse at Port Said to help guide ships entering the canal, but Bartholdi was not included. Instead, the grant went to another French national, François Coignet. No doubt frustrated, Bartholdi returned to France and soon enlisted in the Franco-Prussian War to defend his homeland. He also took a few years to reconsider Laboulaye's original proposal for a statue gift to the United States. Even if Bartholdi and Americans were slow to realize it, Egypt's loss ended up as America's gain. In 1871, after his military service, Bartholdi undertook a trip to the United States to drum up interest in his liberty project. His visit was facilitated by republican connections going back to the American Revolution.

|||||||||||

When Marquis de Lafayette heard of the war for independence brewing across the Atlantic, he jumped at the chance to fight for liberty against the British Empire. He could have simply sent money to the American cause—he had plenty of it as one of the richest men in Paris—or leveraged his influence within the court of King Louis XVI to swing French support to the struggling colonists. Instead, Lafayette bought his own ship, the *Victoire*, and sailed to America against the wishes of King Louis to join the war. "The moment I heard of America, I loved her," Lafayette wrote, "the moment I knew she was fighting for liberty, I burnt with a desire to bleed for her."[14] On June 13, 1777, after fifty-six days at sea, Lafayette and a contingent of French volunteer soldiers landed in South Carolina and quickly made their way north to Philadelphia. By the end of July, Lafayette was enlisted as a major general in the Continental Army, and days later, he was riding alongside General George Washington.

Nineteen-year-old Lafayette, a French musketeer, did not have combat experience or much experience at anything at all. He had grown up privileged in a noble French family, receiving the best education in philosophy, literature, and military tactics. Yet Lafayette was eager to put his theoretical knowledge to the test, learning from his new mentor, General Washington, twenty-six years his senior. The two men became close, like father and adopted son, as the war progressed. They had much in common: both believed in Enlightenment values, republicanism, and the Masons society. Washington and Lafayette were also respected elites in their respective countries. Most significantly, perhaps, they spurred each other's zeal to win the war. Wounded in his first combat action at Brandywine in September 1777, Lafayette continued to serve with Washington and his troops, heading up a militia in November against three hundred hired Hessians, who were defeated by the American unit and their French officer.

The commander in chief entrusted his young comrade with important command posts and reconnaissance missions to spy on enemy forces surrounding the Army at Valley Forge. Lafayette also served American interests when he returned to France to promote an alliance at the royal court of Versailles. Throughout the war, American envoys such as Silas Deane, John Adams, and Benjamin Franklin had urged the French king to support their campaign for independence by providing funds, supplies, and, most importantly, naval power. When Lafayette came back to Boston in April 1780, he brought good news: he had helped secure the French military aid that would decide the war in America's favor.

Soon after setting foot again on American soil, Lafayette resumed his command in the Continental Army, which was engaged in land battles in Virginia, as the French fleet blockaded Lord Cornwallis at Yorktown, preventing him from receiving supplies from Britain. In October 1781, Cornwallis surrendered and accepted the British defeat that Lafayette had risked so much to achieve. For his valor and loyalty, the foreign friend of the American people was honored with statues and institutions bearing his name, such as Lafayette College in eastern Pennsylvania. Congress also declared that he was "entitled to all the rights of a citizen of the United States."[15]

The US victory and the rights available to citizens in the new nation were indeed remarkable. Common men could enjoy the "equality of condition" that Tocqueville later noted, as an entitlement unequaled anywhere else in the world. The Declaration of Independence, written in the summer of 1776, had pronounced "life, liberty, and the pursuit of happiness" as "unalienable rights" of Enlightened civilization; but the American people had to execute that theory in practice and policy in the postwar years. It was not easy or comprehensive. The revolution that Americans had achieved extended political rights and social mobility to many White men, but women and poor non-property owners were barred from voting or participating in governance. The five hundred thousand men and women enslaved by patriots and planters in the North and South were not afforded rights of any kind. George Washington expressed the conflicted interests of a slaveholding republican when he stated: "I never mean (unless some particular circumstance should compel me to it) to possess another slave by purchase: it being among my first wishes to see some plan adopted by the legislature by which slavery in the Country may be abolished by slow, sure, & imperceptible degrees."[16] However, Washington did not manumit slaves during his lifetime.

The imperfect implementation of liberties in the United States did not dampen the enthusiasm of republicans like Lafayette, who praised the freedoms unleashed by the American Revolution and anticipated their rapid dissemination. In his memoir, he wrote that "the struggle for freedom by the patriotic citizens of America, towards the close of the last century, was successful; and has proved most auspicious to human happiness. We have reason to hope, that its blessings will not be confined to this western continent. A spirit of enquiry, indeed, has gone abroad in the world."[17] The persistence of slavery, however, bothered Lafayette—so much so that he tried to convince Washington to free his slaves and take up the cause of abolition. In February 1783, he wrote his military mentor about the need to keep fighting for a revolution for all mankind: "Let us unite in purchasing a small estate where we may try the experiment to free the negroes," he proposed.[18]

While visiting the United States in 1784, Lafayette discussed plans for abolition with Washington face-to-face, and he continued to bring it up in the many letters exchanged between the two friends across the Atlantic over the remaining years of the American general's life. Washington always demurred, stating in one reply that sudden emancipation would "be productive of much inconvenience and mischief," though he granted that gradual change "by degrees . . . ought to be effected." The most celebrated war hero in the United States also happened to be the wealthiest slave owner in the country, and perhaps for reasons of self-interest, he declined to take a leadership role in this moral battle to assure liberty for all. Slavery, for Washington, was an issue tabled for the sake of protecting the Union and the continental empire. In the same letter to Lafayette, he informed his friend that the British were posted along the western frontier and stirring up the natives "for the purpose of retarding our settlements Westward."[19] The fragility of the new nation was upmost on his mind. Whatever the reasons, the Declaration of Independence and the American Revolution remained, in Lafayette's opinion, incomplete.

Hoping to sway more than one notable leader in the new nation, Lafayette broached the touchy subject with James Madison and Thomas Jefferson in letters and in person. They all expressed an admiration for Lafayette's commitment to the cause of liberty, but they told him, as Washington had, that emancipation was an untimely idea in a country with precarious social and economic structures. The issue of enslavement, which had been deferred during the American Revolution, became a point of contention again during the Constitutional Convention in 1787. Some delegates at the Convention, including Madison, recognized it as the crucial hinge of the entire sectional debate and the future of the nation. "The real difference of interests lay," he concluded, "not between the large and small [states] but between the N[orth] and Southn. [*sic*] States. The institution of slavery and its consequences formed the line of discrimination."[20]

Washington, who presided over the constitutional debates and accepted election as the first US president, agreed that American realities did not match republican rhetoric, but he hoped any unresolved wrinkles in the young democracy would iron out as northerners and southerners got used to working together on matters of national interest. He kept

Lafayette abreast of developments toward greater unity in the American government, penning a letter on the topic to his "dear Marqs" in February 1788. Assuring him that "the People of America entertain a grateful remembrance of past services as well as a favourable disposition for commercial and friendly connections with your Nation," he then turned to current events, still unfolding as ratification moved from state to state. "You appear to be, as might be expected from a real friend to this Country, anxiously concerned about its present political situation," Washington noted, referring to the Convention called to reevaluate the Articles of Confederation, which had loosely tied the American states together since the Revolution's end.

Washington made clear that the revised framework for American democracy was a delicate balance between the extremes of monarchy on one end and anarchy on the other. Compromises had been made on many issues, which he did not detail. Instead, he simply acknowledged that the proposed Constitution represented the best deal Americans from different regions and backgrounds could broker. "Should that which is now offered to the People of America, be found an experiment less perfect than it can be made," he explained, "a Constitutional door is left open for its amelioration."[21] In other words, Washington believed only time could heal the nation's open wounds, including the issue of slavery, which had divided delegates throughout the portentous summer in Philadelphia. Federalists arguing for a more centralized US government were wary of alienating southern slaveholding states that needed to vote for national unity. Consequently, the matter was left for later generations to fight over, precipitating a civil war.

|||||||||||

Nearly a century after Lafayette first landed in the Americas to help revolutionaries secure independence from Britain, Bartholdi sailed across the Atlantic to seek patrons for his statue to liberty, officially called *Liberty Enlightening the World*. He arrived in June 1871 with his assistant Marie Simon at the port of New York, a city he described as "marvelous" and bustling with "movement and animation."[22] The artist almost immediately recognized New York Harbor, particularly Bedloe's Island, as the perfect spot for his colossus, but it already operated as a fort. He also scouted Battery Park and Central Park for locations, but Bartholdi kept coming back to Bedloe's, asking the officer in charge about the possibility of using it.[23] "I was conscious when I landed at New York that I had found the idea which my friends had hoped for," he wrote in his memoir.[24]

Bartholdi's friends were French republicans associated with Laboulaye, including Oscar de Lafayette, Henri Martin, and Suez Canal creator Ferdinand de Lesseps, who founded the French-American Union to support Bartholdi's grand project. Laboulaye, in fact, had encouraged Bartholdi to visit the country, telling him: "You will study it, you will bring back to us your impressions. . . . We are convinced that it will be successful on both continents, and we will do a work that will have a far-reaching moral effect."[25] Bartholdi did not have many personal connections in the United States, but he came equipped with letters of introduction from Laboulaye, which eased his attempts to network with American notables.

Bartholdi, at first, admitted some doubts about whether his plan would gain traction, writing, "I believe that the realization of my project will be a matter of luck," given what he considered Americans' lack of imagination. "I do not intend to attach myself to the project absolutely if its realization is too difficult," he told his mother.[26] The gift monument was originally envisioned as a symbol of republican friendship, most generally, and a tribute to the American Union's survival after the Civil War; but early on, Bartholdi discovered that he piqued more interest by pitching it "from a new point of view," as a "commemorative" contribution to the nation's upcoming Centennial in 1876, the anniversary of independence. Bartholdi asked Americans to find a site and pay for the pedestal within the next five years—an ambitious but motivating deadline. "It appears to be a better way," he wrote in his journal.[27]

During his five-month visit, Bartholdi met with President Ulysses S. Grant, Generals Meade and Sheridan, Senators Sumner and Schurz, descendants of Lafayette, the landscaper Olmsted, the poet Longfellow, naturalist Louis Agassiz, Mormon leader Brigham Young, and art enthusiast Richard Butler. Bartholdi's confidence grew as he traveled, making stops at the major cities along the Eastern Seaboard before heading west to California. "I believe that good will come of it," he assured his mother in late July. "I hope that my journey will succeed from the viewpoint of art and of my career."[28]

Bartholdi recorded his impressions of American aesthetics and character (some negative) in letters and a journal. He complained that most American cities looked the same. He viewed a lot of "mediocre" art. He noted the "negroes" in Washington, DC, and Baltimore, and he poked fun at a Black church service in Philadelphia for its "ludicrous" display of animated emotion. "The orator stamped his feet and leaped from side to side like a marionette on strings." But Bartholdi's republican sensibilities overcame his dismay. "Yet it commanded respect, this demonstration by people, slaves only yesterday, who turn their minds to the ideal, who have faith, and who interest themselves so violently in moral questions."[29] As he traveled the countryside, Bartholdi saw America's natural wonders, including Niagara Falls, the Rocky Mountains, western prairies, herds of buffalo, redwood trees, Yosemite Valley, and the Pacific coastline, which he found much more awe-inspiring than "dirty" urban areas. He was impressed, if affronted, by the industrialism in Chicago, across Ohio, and in Pittsburgh, all filled with factories, smoke, and the "smells of oil everywhere."

Near Omaha, he noticed "huts of the savages" and an "Indian woman with a child on her back" not far from his train. "The railroad tracks nearly always follow the old trails of the immigrants," he wrote. Bartholdi's humanism revolted at the sight of the "astonishingly immoral" conditions of Chinese residents in San Francisco, eliciting the comment in his journal: "America should be seen in all its phases—it has some ugly ones." On the brighter side, Bartholdi's republican heart stirred upon seeing George Washington's Mount Vernon and a "copy of Lincoln's Emancipation Proclamation." Still, democracy in America was exclusive, as Bartholdi was reminded by an "old lady" on his train who lectured him about women's need to vote.[30]

The French voyager could also empathize with the Civil War veterans he encountered in the country. He, too, had been to battle during the Franco-Prussian War several months earlier, defending his home region of Alsace against a German confederate army. Getting out of France for a while was one of the reasons for his trip to America, and the statue project gave him a chance to clear his head, recover, and get back to work. It also gave him purpose. By the end of his US tour, the artist confided to his mother that the "sacred fire of his art" fueled his drive and destiny. "I believe that my work, beyond its artistic interest, will have a moral value that will be appreciated some day!"[31] Bartholdi thought the United States needed some moral refinement. "America is an adorable woman chewing tobacco," he quipped.[32]

IIIIIIIIIII

During his travels in 1871, Bartholdi witnessed a young nation expanding into an empire across the continent. The process had begun soon after British colonists arrived in the "New World" in the seventeenth century. Once independent, Americans continued to push the frontier farther west, clearing land and Indigenous peoples as they built new homes and facilities for trade. Empire-building, however, cut liberty both ways. It offered opportunities and freedom to individuals pursuing their "inalienable rights." But the illiberal means of development and protection against perceived enemies, including rival empires and native tribes, circumscribed freedom for others.

Imperial ambition made a stronger central government seem necessary in the 1780s. The new country sat open to attack from all sides, weak in comparison to the British, French, and Spanish powers with colonies already well established in the Western Hemisphere. A centralized US government could call together a coordinated defense more effectively than disparate states and quickly appropriate funds to supply it. The risk of confronting competing empires increased as Americans kept moving west. "A spirit of emigration to the western Country is very predominant," Washington informed Lafayette in 1788. "Congress have sold, in the year past, a pretty large quantity of lands on the Ohio, for public Securities, and thereby diminished the domestic debt considerably. Many of your military acquaintances . . . propose settling there. From such beginnings much may be expected."[33]

Washington welcomed the development, if kept gradual and controlled. He and his compatriots had never intended for the American republic to remain curbed along the eastern coastline. In a 1785 letter to New York City mayor James Duane, Washington referred to New York State as the "seat of the empire," even if the idea of empire existed mostly in the imaginations of Americans. New York had endured assaults from the British during the Revolution, and since the city was the center of US commercial activity, Washington recognized the importance of its survival for the fate of the republic at large. He expressed his hopes "that a well-regulated and beneficial Commerce may enrichen your Citizens. And that, your State (at present the Seat of the Empire) may set such examples of Wisdom and liberality, as shall have a tendency to strengthen and give permanency to the Union at home—and credit and respectability to it abroad."[34]

Thomas Jefferson, though wary of centralized power, also envisioned an "empire of liberty" destined to extend across the continent and around the world. In the process, however, Americans would struggle to reconcile the contradictions of empire and liberty in their fight for survival as an independent republic. As early as 1780, even before independence was fully won, Jefferson wrote:

> We shall divert through our own Country a branch of commerce which the European States have thought worthy . . . we shall form to the American union a barrier against the dangerous extension of the British Province of Canada and add to the Empire of Liberty an extensive and fertile Country thereby converting dangerous Enemies into valuable friends.[35]

Jefferson recognized the rules of the road ahead. The people of the United States would not be left alone to live out their liberties in peace.

Instead, centuries-old empires set global norms that the new country would have to abide by, compete with, and defend against, especially with so many rich resources to cultivate across the continent. If the republic hoped to endure and evade recapture, Americans had to build a semblance of empire with one foot planted in realism and the other in idealism. The balance between empire and liberty, however, wasn't an easy pose to strike. Centralized power and militance meant curtailing certain freedoms and allowing compromises that favored stability and commerce. In short, the US Constitution strengthened strongmen and their ability to contend with rivals.

The Constitutional Convention of 1787 also weighed liberties in a delicate balance between freedom and social control. Liberties in many states were taken to extremes, bordering on anarchy, and local authorities possessed limited means to maintain order. Men like Job Shattuck and Daniel Shays posed a problem. After serving as soldiers in the Revolutionary War for little to no pay, Shattuck and Shays each set out to stake a livelihood as farmers, though they struggled to meet debts in the postwar years. Resentment against merchants and tax collectors boiled into rebellion in 1786, as residents of Western Massachusetts with grievances similar to those of Shattuck and Shays harassed state officials and seized weapons to overthrow the local government.

The Massachusetts state authorities had trouble putting down the rebellion and forcing debtors to pay back taxes. They were not alone. The Articles of Confederation had purposefully made it difficult for states to exercise sovereignty over individual liberties. Such concerns about the survival of governance prompted delegates to scrap the Articles and draft an entirely new constitution to empower federal authority.

Abroad serving as ambassador in Paris in 1787, Jefferson did not attend the Constitutional Convention. He received news about the creation of a stronger central government with apprehension and insisted the new document include a Bill of Rights to preserve individual liberties. Yet he ultimately supported the Constitution, especially for reasons related to interstate commerce and defense. In 1803, President Jefferson agreed to make the Louisiana Purchase, a deal brokered with France (ruled by Napoleon Bonaparte at the time), which added nearly a million square miles to US-claimed territory west of the Mississippi River.

There were risks involved in stretching a republic too far with more people and special interests to accommodate. The vast extension of US domain only pushed the issues of slavery and Native American relocation further west, as these questions remained unresolved in the frontier regions. Poor White settlers who failed to improve their lot via social mobility could at least assume superiority to millions of Americans according to race, a condition that caused them to cling to the institution of slavery and the systemic roots of racism with a fierce self-interest. Contrary to George Washington's wishful thinking, the cracks in the American edifice grew larger, not smaller, in the 1800s.

Lafayette followed these developments from his home in France at the turn of the nineteenth century, while acting upon his own republican values, this time in Paris. The transatlantic hero documented his love of liberty when he drafted the "Declaration of the Rights of Man," the bedrock statement of the French Revolution, modeled on the Declaration of Independence that Jefferson had unveiled over a decade earlier. To Lafayette's dismay, France's chance at establishing a republic proved short lived, as the revolution's high idealism sank into mob violence and martial law before the nation eventually reinstated a monarchy.

Given these disheartening experiences, it is no wonder that Lafayette chose to celebrate a flawed American republic. It was either that or nothing at all. "We shall rejoice to trace its fruits in the gradual destruction of old despotic systems," he noted in his memoirs, though he also referred to his beloved United States as a "rising empire" and anticipated the need for further military defense along the coast and frontier. In a speech to the US Congress in 1784, he added this salute: "May this immense temple of freedom ever stand a lesson to oppressors, an example to the oppressed, a sanctuary for the rights of mankind!"[36]

Lafayette, for all his hyperbole about America, recognized the nation's shortcomings and tried to set a moral example for his compatriots. He pursued his plan to free slaves in an experiment he launched in the French colony of Cayenne, buying a plantation to demonstrate an alternative system of labor and race relations. Though his actions failed to inspire his American friends to follow suit, he did influence the thinking of a younger generation of French republicans like Édouard Laboulaye, who was in his early twenties when Lafayette died in 1834. Slavery was not abolished in the French colonies until a decade and a half later, and the practice continued in the US for nearly twenty years after that.

Lafayette would have understood the significance of Laboulaye's urge to commemorate the abolition of slavery and the endurance of the American republic after the US Civil War. Two of his descendants, the sons of Georges Washington de Lafayette, were present at the 1865 dinner party with Bartholdi when Laboulaye first suggested a gift statue of liberty. One of those grandsons, Oscar Gilbert Lafayette, later served on the French-American Union, the fundraising committee for the statue's construction. "May [my] voice at least find echoes in the country of Lafayette and prove to the United States that France has always remained faithful to America and to Liberty," Laboulaye wrote.[37]

Laboulaye was pleased to see Black Americans, including former slaves, receive the rights of citizenship and participate in governance after the ratification of the Fifteenth Amendment. Two African Americans from Mississippi, Hiram Revels and Blanche Bruce, were even elected to the US Senate. The window of equal opportunity, however, closed quickly. Once federal troops pulled out of the South in 1877 and the political climate shifted to compromise and reconciliation, state laws tightened voting requirements and reinforced discriminatory practices against Black residents.

Despite attempts to assure racial equality during and after the Civil War, racism against Blacks was so entrenched in American culture since the colonial period, national legislation could not eradicate it. As Laboulaye remarked in 1863: "the paradoxes of the eve are the truths of tomorrow."[38] He recognized that liberty in America was more complicated and precarious than rhetoric would suggest. He had learned about the complexities, in part, from his reading of *Democracy in America* by the French intellectual Alexis de Tocqueville.

IIIIIIIIIII

The French aristocrat approaching the coast of the United States for the first time didn't hide his excitement. "Yesterday evening," he addressed his mother in a letter, "the first shouts [of land] were heard, but one needed a spyglass to sight the shoreline. Today, at dawn, Long Island came into view. . . . It's a delicious spectacle."[39] The ship *Le Havre* carrying twenty-five-year-old Alexis de Tocqueville was forced by winds to land north of New York that night, May 9, 1831, at Newport. Tocqueville and his colleague Gustave de Beaumont had come to America ostensibly to report on the US prison systems for the French minister of the interior who had commissioned the trip.

However, Tocqueville ended up evaluating much more than houses of incarceration. His travel journal over the next nine and a half months became the basis for one of the most popular books of the nineteenth century: *Democracy in America*, an insightful study of the United States through foreign eyes. The stated reason for the trip, to study US prisons, amounted to a ruse. The two travelers did visit penitentiaries, but Tocqueville's burning curiosity had more to do with how free Americans interacted with each other to sustain a viable republic.

Before journeying west through the Great Lakes and as far as Green Bay, Wisconsin, the Frenchmen stayed for several weeks in New York City, which Tocqueville found disorienting because of the lack of tall landmarks that would characterize the city a hundred years later. "There is not a dome, a steeple, or a major building in sight," he complained to his mother.[40] New York was not the nation's governing capital, but by 1831, it bustled with two hundred thousand people as the most productive financial and manufacturing engine in the country. For Tocqueville and Beaumont, it also served as the first glimpse of American democracy in action. The intense passion for moneymaking on the island of Manhattan struck Tocqueville as somewhat vulgar, but he understood how and why ambitious men, given "equality of condition" in a democratic society, would tend toward commerce. "The only [passion] that deeply moves the human heart . . . is for the acquisition of wealth."[41] Trade beckoned as an open road for those unfettered from firm class ties. "In democracies there is nothing greater nor more brilliant than commerce," Tocqueville wrote, "it is what attracts the regard of the public and fills the imagination of the crowd; all energetic passions are directed toward it."[42] He stressed the importance of the Erie Canal, operational since 1825, that eased the transport of goods from the backcountry to the port of New York, making the city even more a hub of imperial activity.

The limits of liberty, however, were also evident. From the Midwest, Tocqueville and Beaumont ventured south through the more agrarian regions of the United States and then trekked up the Eastern Seaboard to Washington, DC, Philadelphia, and back to New York. Crossing the country, the young men observed how Americans submitted to the prevailing majority opinion, for better or worse. "The empire of the majority is absolute," Tocqueville observed, as it "draws a formidable circle" around free thought. Any unpopular viewpoints, in other words, were typically drowned in the waters of the mainstream. "There is no freedom of mind in America," he concluded.[43] Populism was riding the coattails of President Andrew Jackson's recent election, and the French elites could not disguise their apprehension about the dangers of a democracy directed by the most common of men.

Fortunately, Tocqueville noted, education and religion acted as a much-needed check on despotic behavior. "Liberty regards religion as its companion in all its battles and its triumphs," he stated, "as the cradle of its infancy, and the divine source of its claims."[44] Growing up Catholic in France, Tocqueville was aware of how the church could abuse its power, but he still considered religious values a crucial bedrock of human cooperation and social justice. It didn't completely cure the temptations of base instincts, but it curbed them by keeping people honest and concerned with their fellow man. While in the United States, Tocqueville marveled at how Protestant denominations fractured and flourished with their ability to extend freedom of belief to those who refused to fit the majority mold. However, he said little about the tyranny of self-righteousness other than to comment rather briefly about the possible threat of fanaticism.

Decades later, Édouard Laboulaye also equated religious values with republicanism, echoing Tocqueville when he referred to Liberty as the "daughter of the Gospel."[45] On this and most points, Laboulaye agreed with his elder counterpart's assessments of American democracy. Laboulaye cherished liberty, but as he often qualified, he favored a republican form of government with its even-keeled representation and accountability, rather than open-ended individualism. He had seen the ugly cousin of democracy—mob rule—run amok through the streets of Paris too many times, provoking violence and civil war. As ambassador John Bigelow said of his French friend: "He was one of the few conspicuous Frenchmen—perhaps beside M. de Tocqueville, it would be difficult to name a third—who knew so nearly where the sovereignty of the State properly terminated, and where the sovereignty of the People began, and he never ceased to deplore the inability of his countrymen to recognize the limitations of the powers of the State as taught by the fathers of the republic."[46]

Laboulaye said as much in his book about Tocqueville, *L'État et ses limites*, written not long after Tocqueville's death, in which Laboulaye unfavorably compared the French experience with democracy since the late 1700s with the much more stable American republic. In France, he acknowledged, leaders and revolutionaries struggled to strike the proper balance between state power and personal liberties:

> God knows, that our ignorance on this subject has cost us dear. When we look back over the long series of our revolutions since 1789 we find that parties, though divided on every thing else, are always in accord on one point. They regard power and liberty as irreconcilable enemies. With the liberals of old school to weaken power was to fortify liberty. With the partisans of order-at-any-price, to crush liberty was to fortify power; double and fatal illusions yielding only anarchy and despotism. When authority is disarmed liberty degenerates into license and perishes by its own excesses.[47]

The United States, from Laboulaye's view abroad, had successfully reconciled the age-old tension between power and liberty that France and most other nations had failed to achieve. Tocqueville, too, back in the 1830s, had identified a salient condition for the democratic phenomenon in America to flourish—the absence of a large standing army, a typical raison d'état that was considered necessary in much of the world for national or imperial defense. "The Americans have no neighbors and consequently no great wars, financial crises, ravages, or conquest to fear," he wrote. "They have almost nothing to dread from a scourge more terrible for republics than all those things put together—military glory."[48]

Conflicts along the borderlands and among encroaching empires made Tocqueville's assumptions appear erroneous. The 1823 Monroe Doctrine, for one, warned the British and French empires to respect the United States' "sphere of influence" over much of Latin America. Leaders like Monroe believed they had good reason to fear encircling foreign powers, especially since Americans had recently refought battles for independence against Great Britain during the War of 1812. Since colonial times, Americans had been creating and defending buffer zones to protect themselves against empires or Indigenous peoples challenging their land claims. The state of Georgia, for instance, was incorporated in part because it would serve as a demarcation from France and Spain. Thomas Jefferson justified the Louisiana Purchase in 1803 as practical protection for the United States and its opportunities for growth, stating that "the future destinies of this republic" depended on sealing the deal with Napoleon. Without access to lands in the west, he realized, the new nation would risk becoming hemmed in by imperial powers, holding Americans east of the Mississippi River.

Americans had valuable claims and resources to defend, and military leaders, such as Andrew Jackson, cleared land and native tribes for White settlements so that the United States could secure territories from challengers. Americans were building an empire and a stronger military right before Tocqueville's eyes. Yet the French tourist did not comment extensively or negatively on the westward creep of American territory or the subjugation of the natives already living there. Instead, he saw the frontier as a refreshing escape route for those fleeing oppressive authorities in the east and a safety valve to relieve the pressures of civil discord in dense regions.[49]

Laboulaye, like Tocqueville, gave the United States an easy pass on this issue, praising the planting of American civilization "under the empire of a free government," "root[ed]" in the soil.[50] In his reflections in *L'État et ses limites,* Laboulaye wrote that no observer of American progress could have expected less. He cited "the idealist" Irish philosopher George Berkeley, who anticipated as early as 1730 the irresistible lure of American empire-building:

> *Westward the course of empire takes its way*
> *The four first acts already past*
> *A fifth shall close the drama with the day*
> *Time's noblest offspring is the last.*[51]

In 1845, John O'Sullivan coined the phrase "Manifest Destiny" to encourage western settlement, imbued with the belief that Americans had a divine right to proliferate their superior institutions. Several years earlier, he had asked "who will set limits to our onward march?" explaining that US expansion was necessary for the "defense of humanity, of the oppressed of all nations, of the rights of conscience, the rights of personal enfranchisement." In his view, God wanted freedom and democracy to spread around the world, and Americans had a mission to make that happen. "The expansive future is our arena, and for our history," he concluded.[52] To manifest this destiny, however, settlers needed military protection, business investments to improve transportation, and a stronger central government to channel all interests into growth for the nation.

Alexander Hamilton had this notion of progress in mind when in 1790 he promoted a plan for a national bank, arguing that "such a Bank is not a mere matter of private property, but a political machine of the greatest importance to the State."[53] While Hamilton saw the potential for national power, opponents of the plan, such as Jefferson and later Andrew Jackson, expressed concern about the effects of centralized planning on democracy. Would an oligarchy of wealthy elites control the country?

Despite President Jackson's efforts to decentralize the national bank and the government in the 1830s, the central power of the US executive, the legislature, and the engines of national finance were concentrating into tighter control at the top as the American population increased. The liberties of minority groups, meanwhile, were largely marginalized. Indigenous people unwilling or unable to contribute to the momentum of national growth were displaced, even the Cherokees who had tried to assimilate. Those who challenged White settlements and ways of life were often killed.

Of course, Tocqueville knew that not every American was allowed to participate in the democratic system, a problem he criticized. During his travels along the Ohio River and into the Deep South, he witnessed racial divisions and discrimination he found disturbing. He became a vocal opponent of slavery when he returned to France. Laboulaye, an ardent abolitionist, also kept close watch on racism in his beloved republic, which he considered the greatest stain on American character. Americans' ability to reconcile state power and liberty was not as successful as the French republicans had hoped. Racism, rather than an isolated aberration from the true essence of the American republic, was an embedded thorn wedged between power and liberty that existed before, during, and after the American Revolution. The challenges of race relations, in fact, would continue to trouble the nation's democratizing efforts around the world.

IIIIIIIIIII

In October 1871, Bartholdi returned full circle to New York City before embarking for home to France. The ambitious sculptor, for the most part, liked New York. In 1871, the bustling trade center, nearing a population of one million, had transformed significantly since the Revolutionary War era, when Washington called it the "seat of the empire." A century later, it retained its reputation as the busiest hub of commerce and migration. Only Great Britain and France produced more than the US in the late 1800s, a feat that owed much to New York, which received people from around the world pursuing their happiness and augmenting their fortunes. Bartholdi perceived the city's "tiresome" obsession with "business," telling his mother that "in spite of the dominating thought of money, there is a great deal here to see and to learn."[54]

Reforms were much needed across the country, especially for women and Black Americans, denied voting rights and property rights and barred from places of power. Before the Civil War, activists Elizabeth Cady Stanton and Lucretia Mott reframed the Declaration of Independence by filling in the blanks of gender inclusion in their Declaration of Sentiments, drafted at the landmark Seneca Falls Convention in upstate New York in 1848. "We hold these truths to be self-evident; that all men and women are created equal," they corrected.[55]

During the Civil War, advocates such as Stanton and Susan B. Anthony organized for slavery's abolition and full citizenship status for Blacks. Yet the passage of the Fourteenth and Fifteenth Amendments did not extend voting guarantees to women, an incomplete victory that prompted activists to redirect their energies into demands for women's suffrage and a broader exercise of freedoms. As Anthony argued after her arrest for illegally voting, "it is downright mockery to talk to women of their enjoyment of the blessings of liberty while they are denied the use of the only means of securing them provided by this democratic-republican government: the ballot."[56] Women remained disenfranchised, except in certain states and territories, for nearly six decades after the Civil War, an injustice that caused suffragists to criticize the Statue of Liberty as a misrepresentation of American democracy when it was dedicated in 1886.

Racial tensions in the Reconstruction era also persisted. During his visit to the United States in the summer of 1871, Bartholdi may have glimpsed headlines in northern newspapers depicting Blacks as criminals deserving punishment: "Fiendish Murder By Negro—The Monster Probably Lynched," "Two Brothers Killed By Negro," "Swift Retribution—A

Georgia Negro Murders a White Planter," "Negro Outlaws."[57] Later that fall, reporters for the *New York Times* covered the trials of the Ku Klux Klan, as President Grant deployed federal troops to crack down on the hooded vigilantes terrorizing Black voters and Republicans with violence since the end of the Civil War. Federal enforcement, however, did not last long. White supremacists in southern states waited out the resolve of federal authorities, utilizing intimidation and local Jim Crow laws to deny basic civil rights to Blacks. The tactics worked. Black representation in state and national politics dropped sharply after Reconstruction effectively ended in 1877.

The constant threat of violence against Blacks who asserted their civil liberties made it nearly impossible to organize resistance among them. Over time, however, brave men and women spoke up and gained momentum as a movement. Frederick Douglass, the most visible leader of Black activists in the nineteenth century, fought for the rights of the oppressed race but also for those of women. He attended the Seneca Falls Convention in 1848 when Stanton issued the Declaration of Sentiments, and he always treated the issue of voting rights as essential for all Americans regardless of race or gender. Douglass did not shrink from criticizing the United States or the president. In 1852, he dared to ask "What, to the American slave, is your 4th of July?" His answer was sharp: "To him, your celebration is a sham."[58]

IIIIIIIIIII

Bartholdi had good reason to return to Paris with a measure of optimism about his prospects for a commission in the United States. He had received promises of support from multiple persons of clout, including President Grant, who had assured the sculptor he would have no trouble convincing Congress to approve the liberty project and appropriate Bedloe's Island for its construction.[59] At a homecoming banquet with his French republican friends, Bartholdi recounted his experiences in America and detailed the architectural achievements he had viewed across the country, especially in New York, where he saw progress on the East River

Bridge, Grand Central Station, and the Metropolitan Museum of Art. America, he believed, was a place for grand designs.

Laboulaye listened intently to these accounts of the country he loved but would never get to visit. Eager to transform his fanciful notion of a gift statue into a fixed reality, he started to raise money for the project. He sent a letter to the *New York Tribune* in October 1875 on behalf of the French-American Union, announcing plans for a copper statue dedicated to "that noble Liberty which represents the glory of the United States, and which enlightens the modern people by its example."[60] That same year, an appeal went out to the French public, requesting contributions for an "imperishable memorial" to mark the occasion of the United States' Centennial celebration, "executed in common by two peoples, associated in this fraternal work as they were of old in founding independence." The flyer explained that the French would cover the cost of the statue, while the Americans were responsible for the pedestal. "Let us each bring his mite," the committee exhorted. "The smallest subscriptions will be heartily welcomed."[61]

Donations trickled in slowly as France recovered from the war, but Bartholdi was able to use funds from side work, including a bronze statue of Marquis de Lafayette for New York's Union Square Park. He was unable to present a finished Liberty statue at the Philadelphia Centennial fair, as he had hoped. Nevertheless, the project went forward, as the French responded more generously, providing the equivalent of about $5 million in today's value for the statue and voting to gift it to America. The US Congress voted, too, on February 22, 1877 (after the Centennial in 1876), "authorizing the President to designate and set apart a site for the colossal statue of 'Liberty Enlightening the World.'"[62]

Fundraising by the American Committee to create the pedestal, unfortunately, proved a more difficult sell than in France, causing additional delays in the statue's completion. In late 1881, Bartholdi began exchanging updates with Richard Butler, secretary of the American Committee, but little headway had been made since the congressional act.[63] In 1882, a newspaper editorial acknowledged that the monumental offer from the French was "flattering" but "startling," especially since Americans were unsure of whether they lived up to the honor. "You review all the doubtful points, which make you feel anything but a model for others to imitate," the author confessed, "[and] because you have felt uncomfortable during the self-examination, you are ready to forget the courtesy of the giver."[64] The French republicans, the author suggested, were giving Americans more credit for liberty than they deserved.

The following year, a more sardonic editorial appeared, calling the expectation to raise funds for the statue "disgusting." As satire, the article got the point across regarding America's "failure" of gratitude, stating that Americans were incapable of appreciating a gift of grace and sentiment, and as such, resented the expense to erect it. "They underrated our shrewdness as a commercial people," it said of the French. "It has been established by careful computation that the pedestal will cost more than the statue would fetch were the latter to be sold as old metal."[65]

Bartholdi, in any case, was behind schedule. He needed financial support, but he also needed to figure out how to craft a sturdy-enough structure to support its gigantic proportions. His study of ancient and existing colossal art boosted his confidence that it could be done. The seventy-six-foot San Carlo Borromeo statue, on the shore of Lake Maggiore, between Switzerland and Italy, impressed him with its function, if not form. "It is an ordinary statue enlarged," he wrote dismissively. "The pedestal is deplorable." Despite its flaws, however, Bartholdi admired the statue's "material execution," utilizing hammered copper sheets supported by iron beams.

Bartholdi followed this example when he began constructing sections of his Liberty colossal at the Gaget, Gauthier & Co. studio in Paris. He and his assistants completed the head and one of the arms by pressing sheets of copper onto wooden molds, bolstered by iron braces and pylons. To hold the pieces together, Bartholdi outsourced to experts in architecture and civil engineering—first, his mentor Eugène Viollet-le-Duc, and then, a man by the name of Gustave Eiffel.[66]

Born in 1832, Eiffel, in the early 1880s, was known for building bridges and viaducts, train stations, and exhibition halls around the world. In

Construction in Paris

Liberty's face

Paris, Eiffel helped Bartholdi by designing the inner scaffolding of his statue, calculating the strength to withstand the worst hurricane winds recorded in America and in Europe. He came up with the idea of a central pylon, a forerunner to the design of a skyscraper, that would support the appendages resting upon it. After contributing to the Statue of Liberty, Eiffel moved on to other projects, most notably his masterpiece, the Eiffel Tower, which became the architectural symbol of France.

As the years passed and the concept of the statue evolved, Bartholdi's design choices changed as well. Liberty's left hand, for instance, went from originally clutching broken chains—representing emancipation from slavery in the mid-1860s—to cradling a tablet with the date of the Declaration of Independence. Both concepts reflected the interests of Laboulaye, who birthed the statue idea. But the intention to commemorate the end of the US Civil War fell by the wayside once Bartholdi began marketing it as part of the 1876 Centennial celebration of US independence. Visitors to the Philadelphia Centennial exhibits at least could glimpse a section of the statue (the arm and torch) sent by Bartholdi by ship across the Atlantic.

The French-American Union hoped the sample would whet the American public's appetite and proliferate donations to finish the pedestal as Bartholdi completed the body of the statue. In February 1884, Bartholdi wrote Richard Butler in New York to say he was finished, and that Liberty would be shipped to the United States after some public receptions in France.[67] By spring 1885, Bartholdi's "big daughter" was ready to make her way to America.[68] "At the present hour the whole work is packed up in 210 cases which in a few days are to be put on board the State vessel Isère at Rouen," Bartholdi recorded while writing his account of the project. "They will arrive in the United States toward the end of May."[69] Again, Bartholdi's estimate ended up being inaccurate. The cargo did not make it to the United States until mid-July, when it was greeted with great fanfare in New York City. Once the hoopla died down, however, the crates sat unpacked for over a year, as the fragmented French tribute awaited her American base of support. Bartholdi had to put his faith in the American people to come through for Liberty.

CHAPTER 2

BUILDING AN EMPIRE BUILDING—1929

When New York governor Al Smith ran for president of the United States in 1928, he linked himself to the image and rhetoric of liberty. One campaign button, for instance, consisted of his likeness on the right with the Statue of Liberty featured on the left against a red-white-and-blue striped background and the letters of his first name "Al" as initials for "American Liberty." Smith, a Democrat, was countering another Liberty button released by his Republican opponent, Herbert Hoover, who also invoked the word. During his speech at Madison Square Garden that October, Hoover framed his policy proposals of limited government and individualism as the "principles and ideals of the United States Government." During World War I, he acknowledged, "we necessarily turned to the Government to solve every difficult economic problem." But Hoover insisted that during peacetime, in an era of economic opportunity and growth, a "centralized despotism" and "socialistic state" "would dry up the spirit of liberty and progress."[1]

Imaged by Heritage Auctions, HA.com

Al Smith campaign button, 1928

Since 1920, Hoover's Republican Party had allowed free enterprise to flourish, he reminded his audience. "Thereby it restored confidence and hope in the American people, it freed and stimulated enterprise, it restored the Government to its position as an umpire instead of a player in the economic game."[2] The US economy in 1928 was doing relatively well, at least for business and financial investors. Hoover hoped to ride that wave of economic confidence into the White House. He did. Yet a year later, in October 1929, the most significant stock market crash in US history tumbled the nation and the world into the Great Depression.

After losing his 1928 presidential bid to Hoover, Al Smith needed a new venture. Born in New York City in 1873, Alfred Emanuel Smith was nearly thirteen years old when Lady Liberty opened to the public not far from his Irish neighborhood in Lower Manhattan. He also witnessed the building of the Brooklyn Bridge and the Tower Building, the first structure in the city to reach eleven stories. Smith, who had devoted his life to politics, wasn't in the business of architecture and engineering, but as the 1920s and his political career wound to a close, he took on a project to remake the New York skyline and his own image by raising the tallest building in the world.

John J. Raskob, the former head of finance for General Motors and the Democratic National Committee, discussed the idea of the Empire State Building with Smith soon after the 1928 campaign. According to legend, their collaboration on the project started in a men's room, as recounted by actor Eddie Dowling, who said Smith was approached at the urinals of the Lotos Club where Raskob consoled the former governor about his recent political loss by pledging: "Don't worry, Al. I'm going to build a new skyscraper—biggest in the world—and you're going to be president of the company."[3]

Whether the colorful details of this meeting are entirely true, Raskob ultimately chose to partner with Smith, offering him a salary of $50,000 a year to chair the project and bring it publicity. Marketing the building as the biggest and best was crucial for making money in rental space and tourism. It needed to compete with a crop of skyscrapers already constructed or under construction in Manhattan, including the Paramount Building, the Flatiron, the Bank of Manhattan Building, and the Chrysler Building. Plans for Rockefeller Center were also underway. The Chrysler Building, named after Walter Chrysler of the car company, was completed in 1930 at a height of 1,046 feet, including its silver spike. Raskob and Smith were late to the race to the top, but they intended to make up for lost time. Amid an economic boom in the 1920s, the men behind the Empire State Building saw their skyscraper as a vessel to reap the profits of valuable real estate, as a symbol of their superiority over competitors like Chrysler, and as a testament to American ingenuity and ambition.

IIIIIIIIIII

Raskob and Smith were incredibly ambitious. They had been so all their lives. Raised on the Lower East Side by an Irish American mother and an Italian American father, Smith lived among Catholic immigrants in a ward run by Tammany Hall. Upon the death of his father, Smith needed employment, and local political networks provided a gateway to lucrative jobs. He attended his first political meeting in 1894, just shy of twenty-one years old, and campaigned for a candidate that Tammany Hall did not support. Soon after, Smith worked for the commissioner of jurors, and he was elected to the New York State Assembly in 1904.

According to him, he won because his voice carried the loudest and farthest across the city blocks when he delivered open-air speeches. It was also because he knew New York—its every nook and cranny, its character, its people. Smith, who became a four-time governor, appealed to those people and promised to help solve their problems with Progressive Era reforms in the early 1900s. "I was determined to prove that the people of the State had made no mistake when they entrusted the highest office within their gift to a man who had risen from the lowest rung of the ladder," he recalled.[4] As a reporter noted when interviewing Smith on his sixtieth birthday, "one could not help but feel that the impelling motive behind all his efforts was a sincere desire to help the unfortunate and distressed.

To him government stands for a humanizing agency directly concerned with the man in the street."[5]

As Smith set himself as a champion of the common man, his friend John J. Raskob was a maker of American empire. Born in 1879 in Niagara County, New York, Raskob learned business acumen from his father, a cigar maker, and set out to follow in his footsteps by enrolling in a business school. But after the death of his father in 1898, Raskob returned home to support his family, eventually landing a job as the personal secretary to entrepreneur Pierre S. du Pont, of the DuPont chemical company. When du Pont became president of his family's business in 1902, Raskob went with him, serving as treasurer as well as finance manager for General Motors.

Raskob understood finance more than most Americans of his time. Driven by an opportunistic spirit, he could maneuver money for maximum returns by knowing when and how to invest it. The *New York Times* wrote of Raskob in 1928: "Here was a genius at organization with a breadth of vision and a gift for seeing into the future."[6] Business leaders looked to Raskob as a barometer of financial climate, heeding his warnings or accepting his advice, such as when he assured capitalists in 1928 that they need not fear any pushback from Democrat Al Smith. "Alfred E. Smith as President would give the country a constructive business Administration," he stated. "Business, big or little, has nothing to fear." Raskob knew that not even the president could undermine business interests. By the end of the 1920s, the American economy had become too tied to American empire to disentangle; the twin enterprises would rise or fall together. "Business has outgrown the feeling that there is something to fear in campaign years," Raskob explained. "It is on too big a scale for that."[7]

Raskob also had attained that level of power and influence. Framing his life story as a rags-to-riches "Horatio Alger" tale, the *New York Times* traced his rise from obscurity to his status as a "captain of industry," who had saved General Motors from ruin.[8] Men like Raskob, with the mind and motive to manage wealth, were encouraged by US leaders to pursue their personal fortune and channel their success into the nation's economic growth. He was celebrated for his prowess, for achieving the elusive "American Dream." People often wondered, How had he done it?

Raskob shared his recipe for success in the 1929 article "Everybody Ought to Be Rich," telling Americans that if they invested $15 per week in common stocks, they could accumulate gains and passive wealth from the dividends.[9] Such advice must have seemed naive to those making average wages of $7–$22 per week, but Raskob could only recount his experiences and the habits that had made him financially secure enough not only to weather the Depression but to pour millions into a grand development like the Empire State Building.

||||||||||

While some considered his skyscraper venture risky at a time when so many tall buildings and office rentals were already available in the city, Raskob did not abort, even after the stock market crashed in October 1929, two months after plans for the Empire State Building were officially announced. With his finger on the pulse of investment trends, his interest in large-scale properties stemmed from the real estate boom of the 1920s, including the strategic construction of skyscrapers that could reap a disproportionate amount of rental space from a relatively small land parcel. Raskob was not entirely new to real estate in 1929. He had developed some properties in Maryland and Delaware, including the nine-mile waterfront known as Pioneer Point, and as a successful financial executive, he was confident about recouping the money to cover the costs.

Adhering to the realty adage about location, location, location, Raskob and Smith believed they had found an ideal site for their skyscraper: the Waldorf-Astoria Hotel at Fifth Avenue and Thirty-Fourth Street in Midtown that the Astor family put on the market, expecting it to be demolished and redeveloped. The hotel had become dated and unfashionable, but the relative proximity to train stations in a developing downtown shopping district made it attractive to Empire State Inc.

After selling shares of General Motors, Raskob used the liquidated money to help pay for the Empire State Building, supplemented with loans from lenders such as Met Life, Smith's most recent place of employment. The board of Empire State Inc. included Pierre du Pont, Coleman du Pont, Louis G. Kaufman, Ellis P. Earle, Robert C. Brown, and, of course, its chairman, Governor Smith. As one of New York's favorite sons, Smith seemed like the perfect promoter for the new building. His New York roots (and his Catholicism) had been a liability in the 1928 election, but they were a boon for a capital project to symbolize the prominence of his home state. In its 1931 promotional materials, Empire State Inc. referred to Smith as "so well known to the public that his very presence placed the seal of integrity upon [the] undertaking."[10] He was, as one biographer called him, an "Empire Statesman."[11]

Raskob, in fact, seemed intent on merging Smith's image with the skyscraper. The financial wizard could have named the building after himself, like Chrysler and Rockefeller. Instead, he chose to call it Empire State, a clear reference to George Washington's nickname of New York as the "seat of the empire."[12] The term "Empire State," however, did not gain traction in popular parlance until the 1830s, when newspapers in Baltimore, DC, Philadelphia, and Richmond began referring to the "empire state" and "empire city." In 1836, for instance, an Illinois-based circular described New York City as "The Rome of America, the Empire city of the New World."[13] And in 1849, author R. L. Christopher wrote *Empire State Book of Practical Forms*. During construction of the Erie Canal from 1817 to 1825, newspapers in Britain and the United States predicted that the waterway, a major innovation for trade, would make New York the "London of the New World"—that is, the portal of an empire and one of "the most powerful commercial emporiums that has ever arisen."[14]

In the early 1800s, another New York governor, DeWitt Clinton, had gambled his legacy on a capital project to enhance the American empire and New York's role in its facilitation. Clinton, the "Father of the Erie Canal," helped plan and develop the route that the new waterway would take, connecting Lake Erie to the upper Hudson River and then running down into New York City, and he convinced the state legislature to fund the project as an investment in trade and transportation. Though a canal of this magnitude (over 350 miles) had been a dream of ambitious Americans for decades, many doubted its engineering practicality, calling it "Clinton's Folly," or "DeWitt's Ditch." When the canal was completed in 1825, after eight years of construction, Clinton could claim victory. Freight costs across New York dropped, profits increased, and the state recouped the $7 million it had appropriated to launch the dig. The canal aided settlements expanding west beyond the Appalachians and trade expanding east across the Atlantic from the port of New York. No one questioned which US city had achieved economic prominence. In all likelihood, references to the "empire state" and "empire city" that started popping up in newspapers across the country in the 1830s were related to the canal's opening and its positive impact on the nation's economy.

The naming origins of the Empire State *Building* are more difficult to track. It was not the first major project to carry the moniker, since New York Central Railroad's Empire State Express, a high-speed passenger train to Buffalo, already existed as early as 1891. A number of companies in New York also adopted the name to indicate their link with the state or boast their power and leverage over competitors. Raskob had been born in upstate New York, though by the 1930s he resided primarily in Delaware, the home turf of the du Ponts. But the fact that his "new building" was slated for construction in Manhattan, and that he had identified Al Smith as the best man to promote it, Raskob likely decided on the name because it simultaneously marked a location, connoted the former governor, and denoted power.

On the building's opening day on May 1, 1931, Smith clearly acknowledged the first purpose by saying "This building is named after the Empire State of our Union," as well as the last point when explaining that it was "intended to stimulate trade, commerce, and continue to make New York the imperial city of the world."[15] President Roosevelt recognized the name's link to Smith by noting that "this building is not called the Empire State Building just because it has been properly erected [for] the State of New York, but I think that its name is most highly fitting because it typifies the service that its principal backer and principal builder has rendered to the State of New York during all these years."[16] The new landmark, in other words, symbolized Smith's rise from obscurity to power over the course of the twentieth century—a course parallel to the rise of the US nation. Those multiple meanings were evident by the project's end. As the project started, Smith could only hope that the mammoth building would not appear as folly, as Clinton's canal had initially been dismissed.

IIIIIIIIIII

The leading city in population, production, and shipping, New York was still the "seat" and center of a US empire that, in the 1930s, continued to control the territories they had seized after the War of 1898, including Puerto Rico, Guam, Hawaii, and the Philippines. In the wake of World War I, some empires did expire (Germany, Austria-Hungary, and the Ottoman), and independence movements around the globe erupted to throw off colonial control and assume self-rule. Uprisings occurred in British-controlled India and Egypt, but rebels were unable to overthrow imperial forces altogether. A similar situation unfolded in French Indochina and North Africa.

President Woodrow Wilson, during the war, had raised hopes with his Fourteen Points, which asserted the right of self-determination for all nations, but the United States continued the colonial relationship in the Philippines and elsewhere. Even in sovereign countries over which the United States had no official authority, political and military officials used so-called "gunboat diplomacy," "missionary diplomacy," or "dollar diplomacy" to have their way. These practices of hard and soft power were not American inventions; the British and other empires had practiced them for centuries. But Americans realized they could flex military muscle and money to reap the benefits of empire without formally arranging colonial control.

Such strategies proved effective. President Wilson became a practitioner of missionary diplomacy, refusing to recognize the legitimacy of nondemocratic leaders in Latin America and Asia. And President William Howard Taft used dollar diplomacy to extend or withhold investments to and from nations depending on how agreeable they were to US demands. In a 1912 speech, Taft defended dollar diplomacy as crucial for maintaining access to foreign markets. "The national prosperity and power impose upon us duties which we cannot shirk if we are to be true to our ideals," he stated. "The tremendous growth of the export trade of the United States has already made that trade a very real factor in the industrial and commercial prosperity of the country."[17]

By "substituting dollars for bullets," he continued, the policy fulfilled a US commitment to peace and "humanitarian sentiments," while also advancing "legitimate commercial aims." He saw such economic partnerships as mutually beneficial and listed the many nations that had expressed gratitude for US business.[18] In rhetoric and reality, American leaders, such as Taft, Wilson, and Theodore Roosevelt, applauded their ability to reconcile empire and liberty by spreading the American Dream around the world not just for Americans but for foreigners who, they believed, needed US models of economic and political prosperity.

Americans were not new to imperialism in the 1920s and 1930s, but criticism of the practice persisted. Progressive intellectual John Dewey acknowledged in his 1927 essay "Imperialism Is Easy" that extending an empire, contrary to what he had once believed, did not develop out of some grand strategy or nefarious plot for subjugating foreign peoples; instead, as he gathered from US involvement in Mexico and other Latin American countries, it happened gradually, through incremental actions to protect business ventures abroad and secure a more stable international order conducive to US interests. "The natural movement of business enterprise," he wrote, "and the international custom which obtains as to the duty of a nation to protect the property of its nationals, suffices to bring about imperialistic undertakings." The process, when observed as a piecemeal response to threats against individual Americans, struck most people as so perfectly natural that they often failed to see it as a form of imperialism at all. It "is precisely the consciousness on the part of the public that it is innocent of imperialistic desires," Dewey stated, that makes the nation feel "aggrieved when it is accused of any such purpose."[19]

It did not help, he continued, that "the average citizen has little knowledge of the extent of American business and financial interests in Mexico" and around the world, or that the general public remains ignorant of the negative effects capitalistic ventures could have on the image of the United States abroad. "An industrially backward country with large natural resources and a government which is either inefficient or unstable . . . [may] resent being treated as infants under our tutelage." Yet widespread ignorance, Dewey argued, should not let Americans off the hook for tacitly supporting exploitative behavior. He suggested modifying the Monroe Doctrine, and by extension the Roosevelt Corollary, to make US interventions in the affairs of other nations much more difficult to undertake.[20]

Dewey, a staunch defender of democracy, believed that a moral society was one in which all were informed and included in the decisions affecting their lives. Education and engagement with local and national problems, he insisted, could redirect the United States toward the shared interests, not the special interests, of its citizens. The process of undoing imperialism around the world, he knew, would unfold as incrementally as it had developed. But he hoped as Americans realized the grand "experiment" of democracy meant considering the life, liberty, and the pursuit of happiness of everyone, whether citizen or foreigner, they would apply pressure to ensure the US government acted according to its values. "If there is one conclusion to which human experience unmistakably points," he wrote, "it is that democratic ends demand democratic methods for their realization." In other words, Americans could not achieve democracy without submitting every aspect of personal and national life through the process of democracy—that is, deciding on the best course of action "together."[21]

With a touch of American exceptionalism, Dewey saw the United States in the "New World" as potentially superior to the "Old World" of Europe and its baser cultural norms, but only if Americans had the wherewithal to stay the course of democratic action. "Resort to military force," he asserted, "is a first sure sign that we are giving up the struggle for the democratic way of life, and that the Old World has conquered morally as well as geographically—succeeding in imposing upon us its ideals and methods."[22] He believed that following the path of empires and other military powers was out of step with American ideals.

IIIIIIIIIII

As plans for the Empire State Building were coming together in the late 1920s, the actual hub of imperial activity was bustling at the New York Customs House in Lower Manhattan, not far from the Stock Exchange and the future site of the World Trade Center, where customs services were relocated in the early 1970s. A colossus in its own right, the new Customs House, completed in 1907, was designed to project classical order and civic duty. Though it did not rise to great heights, the Beaux Arts building contained multitudes in its 350,000 square feet of office space for over three thousand employees policing imports and imposing US tariffs. Over the course of the nineteenth century and into the 1910s, tariffs had been kept high to protect domestic industries from foreign competition and raise revenue for the federal government. But trade policies became increasingly controversial if they favored elites rather than average Americans.

Puck magazine cartoonist Udo Keppler, who often criticized greed, racism, and imperialism, used the image of the Statue of Liberty repeatedly to challenge political corruption. A 1911 cartoon featuring a "fat cat" enjoying the fruits of tariffs and taxes atop the Capitol building showed Lady Liberty pointing and laughing at the hypocrisy. In a 1912 piece, Keppler depicted Lady Liberty toppled from her pedestal, replaced by a golden cow representing money interests installed in her place of honor.[23] Keppler expressed the ire of many Americans in the early twentieth century who were fed up with violations of liberty and justice for the sake of personal or state wealth.

As American industry outpaced the world, tariffs were lowered, and the government relied more on income taxes for its budget. These economic developments were part of a widespread era of progressive reforms to expand liberties and enhance democracy. Changes were made to tax policy, labor laws, election processes, city sanitation, factory operations, and public health, remaking the nation in the best interests of ordinary Americans. Women finally gained the right to vote in 1920, though they were still subordinate to husbands and fathers for most life decisions. Activists fought on to secure these rights, but reform movements lost their momentum after the horrifying years of World War I and a global pandemic put a damper on popular enthusiasm for change.

Not all reformers and radicals were ready to retreat. On a warm June evening in 1919, Assistant Secretary of the Navy Franklin D. Roosevelt and his wife, Eleanor, were relaxing at their home in Washington, DC, when they heard and felt the rumblings of an explosion. The commotion had come from across the street, at the residence of Attorney General A. Mitchell Palmer. Palmer and his family survived the bombing attack, but the man who placed the device, Italian anarchist Carlo Valdinoci, did not. The blast demolished the Palmer house and triggered a coordinated response to capture the other anarchists who had been involved in mailing and detonating a series of bombs that year. In April, dozens of packages filled with dynamite had been mailed to politicians, law enforcement officers, reporters, and prominent businessmen like John D. Rockefeller—individuals whom the perpetrators considered anti-immigrant or anti-leftist. The government responded by cracking down on radical activists, including anyone critical of the United States. Emma Goldman was one woman deported to the Soviet Union for her outspokenness about the war and US imperialism. She later recalled the irony of seeing the Statue of Liberty as she looked out the porthole of the ship carrying her away from New York. Her beloved America, she lamented, was "repeating the terrible scenes of tsarist Russia" in its suppression of free speech.[24]

The chaos of 1919 became known by another name, Red Summer, a time of intense racial violence that broke out in the South and in Northern cities, like Chicago, where Blacks expected wartime service to raise the esteem of the race and break barriers to equal treatment. White supremacists dashed these hopes with blood. In Chicago, DC, and Omaha, violence made headlines that summer and into the next year. In Elaine, Arkansas, in the fall of 1919, over one hundred Blacks died during disputes over a union organized by Black sharecroppers to challenge the unfair wages of White plantation owners. Accused of fomenting an "insurrection," Blacks in the county were shot by vigilantes and federal troops on sight. Two years later, a massacre in Tulsa, Oklahoma targeted affluent Black business owners but soon extended to Blacks in general. At least three hundred were killed within twenty-four hours. These surges of pent-up racial rage helped revitalize the terrorist organization the Ku Klux Klan, threatening the physical security of Blacks who had to fight for the basic liberties that most White Americans took for granted.

As the United States remained divided over racial issues unresolved since the Civil War, the Lincoln Memorial, honoring the "Great Emancipator," opened in Washington, DC, on May 30, 1922. The ceremony, attended by 50,000, was segregated, while the remarks of the only Black speaker, Dr. Robert Russa Moton, were edited by former president Taft, who told the Tuskegee Institute educator to avoid "propaganda" that harped too much on race problems. Moton removed a few sentences from his draft, including a direct reference to Lincoln's "unfinished" work to promote racial equality. Instead, he spoke about the unfinished promises of liberty. "When the Pilgrim Fathers landed upon the shores of America in 1620, they laid the foundations of our national existence upon the bedrock of liberty," he said. "From that day to this, liberty has been the common bond of our united people. . . . Freedom is the lifeblood of the Nation. Freedom is the heritage bequeathed to all her sons. It is the underlying philosophy of our national existence."

Moton made sure to express the gratitude of the millions of Black Americans who benefited from Lincoln and his sacrifices. He spoke of Black patriotism and loyalty and reminded the audience that racism was not only a wedge between citizens but a hedge on the flourish of American exceptionalism. "Lincoln did not die for the Negro alone," Moton stated. "He freed a Nation as well as a race." The whole country and its populace, he suggested, had suffered from slavery, and they suffered still from a blinding racism that kept liberty from reaching its God-given potential to spread throughout the world.

> And now the whole world turns with anxious heart and eager eyes toward America. In the providence of God, there has been started on these shores the great experiment of the ages—an experiment in human relationships, where men and women of every nation, of every race and creed, are thrown together. Here we are engaged, consciously or unconsciously, in the great problems of determining how different races can not only live together in peace but cooperate in working out a higher and better civilization than has yet been achieved.[25]

Though Moton was there to reflect on the Lincoln Memorial, his words reinforced the message behind another monument, the Statue of Liberty.

IIIIIIIIIII

The Statue of Liberty had gone green with tarnish when it was designated a national monument in 1924 under the authority of the Antiquities Act. The nation's torchbearer, at age thirty-eight, had grown old. Since its opening day in October 1886, oxidation and sulfuric acid in the air had worn off the statue's thin copper finish, giving it a light green patina. Plans to paint the statue did not sit well with the public. Captain George C. Burnell, who worked at Bedloe's Island, told the *New York Times* in 1906, "I wish the newspapers had never mentioned [the plans]. I am in receipt of bushels of bushels of letters on the subject, and most of them protest vigorously against the proposed plan. I can't say now just what we will do, but we will have to do something."[26]

Other needed repairs seemed more pressing. Water was seeping into the pedestal. The statue had also sustained damage during World War I, when a massive explosion of ammunition and TNT on nearby Black Tom pier, caused by German saboteurs, sent a spray of shrapnel against Liberty's delicate surface. The torch, which regularly required lighting upgrades, remained closed to the public thereafter. Major improvements were completed in the late 1930s when a beautification project on the Statue was performed by the Works Progress Administration at a cost of $258,000. A ten-cent charge for riding the statue's inner elevator was implemented in 1939 to help cover the upkeep.

After Ellis Island opened in 1892 as a processing center for foreigners arriving at the port of New York, the Statue of Liberty became increasingly associated with immigration, even though French sculptor Bartholdi had not envisioned his creation for that specific purpose. He had crafted a symbol of liberty and republicanism that, he felt, transcended any particular group or interest. That broader meaning did resonate with Americans, even into the 1940s, when the *New York Times* referred to the Statue on her fifty-fourth birthday as "the most famous symbol of democracy in the United States."[27] However, a poem by Emma Lazarus, which was added to the statue's base in 1903, reinforced the notion that Liberty stood as a beacon for the "tired, huddled masses" looking to find freedom in a land of plenty.

The same year President Coolidge made Lady Liberty a national monument, US immigration policy took a significant turn. The 1924 Immigration Act, also known as the Johnson-Reed Act, set quotas that drastically reduced the number of people coming from Eastern and Southern Europe. The Act also established the US Border Patrol, and it banned Asian immigration altogether. Contradicting the spirit of Emma Lazarus's words at the base of the Statue of Liberty, Senator David A. Reed, a cosponsor of the bill, hailed the restrictions as a necessity, not choice, declaring immigration a failed experiment that threatened US empire. "America of the Melting Pot Comes to an End," he wrote.[28]

Notably, the 1924 Johnson-Reed Act garnered support from Americans left and right, Democrat and Republican. Conservative nativists against "alien blood" backed the policies, while unions like the American Federation of Labor (AFL) welcomed the measures as ways to protect wages, which were destabilized by unlimited sources of labor. Some voices, however, were raised in opposition. Brooklyn Congressman Emanuel Celler, the son of Jewish immigrants, spoke out against the policy as un-

American. Decades later, Celler cosigned the 1965 bill that repealed the 1924 restrictions.

IIIIIIIIIII

Florida businessman Mitchell Wolfson was among thousands of speculators from around the country eager to make quick money in Miami. In 1924, fifty to seventy-five Pullman railroad cars per day arrived downtown, automobiles rolled in from the Northeast and Midwest, and the sidewalks of the city-on-the-make were so crowded with tourists and investors that many people found it easier to walk in the streets. Real estate developers hired bands to fill the air with festive music. To some, it seemed more like a frenzy, as buyers clamored to make their bids. Millions of dollars changed hands daily along with the properties that were bought, sold, and resold, sometimes within minutes. Mitchell Wolfson found out how fast deals were moving in Miami firsthand. After making a deposit on a $20,000 apartment building he had purchased, he set off for a haircut. He did not get far before a man accosted him. As Wolfson recalled,

> I got half way through the Halcyon Arcade (on East Flagler Street) on my way to the barber shop when I met some fellow who said, "Mitchell, do you have anything good?" I said, "Yes, I just bought an apartment house." He said, 'What did you pay for it?' I told him and he said, 'I'll give you $10,000 profit if you'll sell it to me."

Mitchell sold him the property and went on to buy more, becoming one of the most prominent businessmen in the sun-drenched boomtown.[29]

In the early 1920s, many Americans were enjoying relative prosperity (especially compared with war-torn Europe) and making money in more ways than one. Easy credit provided loans, finance mavericks bought stocks on margin against future profits, and binder boys in Florida found loopholes in real estate laws that lined their pockets while driving property prices well above their assessed values. A lack of regulation, allowed by advocates of laissez-faire, weakened the guardrails against financial disaster. John Raskob, father of Empire State Inc., was part of the problem. He pooled and pulled investments that left smaller traders vulnerable. About 70 percent of his shares were hedged with short positions, including companies he managed. His "big short" schemes skirted the edges of legality at the time, and most of his activity would be deemed illegal after the Depression.[30]

Eventually, investors became nervous about the longevity of their good fortune. The Miami hurricane of 1926 burst the bubble in Florida real estate as owners realized the risks they had undertaken. Investors started to sell their stocks, gaining what they could before the other shoe dropped. Once the stock market crashed in October 1929 beneath the pressure of public doubt, the aftershocks were felt around the world. The United States, as an international economic powerhouse, could not isolate or contain the crisis. In the first few years of the ensuing Depression, US industrial production was cut in half, the GDP fell by about 30 percent, and at its worst, unemployment climbed close to 25 percent. When the empires of the world got together to assess the damage, most opted to protect themselves rather than work together to stabilize global markets. Steep tariffs were imposed by Great Britain and the United States, and the two countries abandoned the gold standard, devaluing currency and decimating international trade. The long arms of empire had little left to offer the world. Investments in the 1920s made a lot of people rich. In the 1930s, those risky ventures made a lot of people poor.[31]

||||||||||

On August 29, 1929, Al Smith announced plans to break ground for the Empire State Building at the Waldorf-Astoria hotel site for "one of the largest real estate undertakings in the history of the country." From that day onward, the building would always be associated with him, often described as "Smith's Building." The next day, for instance, the *New York Times* ran the announcement with the heading "Smith to Help Build Highest Skyscraper." The details were in flux, estimating overall costs at about $50 million and a final height of 1,000 feet, to be completed in a year and a half.[32] That expected elevation, however, was soon modified.

A rivalry between Raskob and Walter Chrysler over some former business deals drove the two men to compete vicariously through the size of their pinnacles. Upon hearing that Empire State was planned to reach 1,000 feet, Chrysler made the last-minute addition of a steel spire to bring the Chrysler structure to 1,046 feet. Raskob countered by sending his architects back to revise the design of Empire State and raise its height just enough to beat Chrysler. In fact, the original drawings of the building showed a flat top at the eightieth floor, but designers at Shreve, Lamb & Harmon added a peaked mast, meant to moor dirigibles, which ended up being more ornamental than functional. Certainly, the egos of two powerful men and their bragging rights were at stake. But branding was also a factor in the height contest. Envisioning the publicity that a modern marvel would attract, it made sense for Raskob to push his team to construct the tallest building in the world instead of settling for the second or third biggest. As the vice president of Empire State Inc., Robert C. Brown recalled, "The argument was advanced that the highest building would get the tourist business."[33]

The razing of the old Waldorf-Astoria started in September 1929, and the excavation for its replacement began January 22, 1930. Raskob wrote to his sister: "It is going to be a beautiful structure and, of course, the largest office building in the world. The Governor and I are having a lot of fun building it."[34] Those fun times were fleeting. Once construction on the steel frame began that spring, thousands of workers hustled to build the skyscraper, averaging 4.5 floors per week. It was finished within a year and forty-five days.

Problems of logistics and construction were plentiful. William Starrett, whose company built Empire State, compared it to conditions of war, "strife against the elements," including "water, quicksand, rock and slimy clays" obscuring the "path to bedrock." The tight urban environment also created challenges. "Traffic rumbles in the crowded highways high above us, and the subways, gas, and water mains, electric conduits and delicate telephone and signal communications demand that they not be disturbed lest the nerve system of a great city be deranged," he wrote.[35]

The materials to construct Empire State came from near and far, illustrating the access that the US empire had to resources around the globe. Chief engineer Edward Orlando McConaughey and his wife traveled to France to pick out marble samples to bring back to the architects. The limestone came from Indiana, the steel from Pittsburgh, and the lumber from the Pacific Northwest. Odds and ends were also purchased in Europe and at distant points elsewhere. It was all constructed by multiple contractors like a vertical assembly line.

Reporters described the "novel design" of the forthcoming "Smith Skyscraper," noting its series of architectural setbacks starting at the sixth floor. Even before the building opened, it received an award, in April 1931, from the Architectural League, which praised the "masterful" Art

Empire State Building under construction

Deco edifice.[36] The Empire State Building certainly showcased novelty and innovation in many of its features, but it was also a product of its time. The rise of Decorative Arts (Art Deco) in Paris before World War I made an impact on American architecture and fashion after the war, when designers coupled sleek modern elements with fine craftsmanship to add character. The rival Chrysler Building and the Golden Gate Bridge, underway in the 1930s in San Francisco, also reflected Art Deco trends. As builder Paul Starrett acknowledged, Empire State was also born of the roaring, soaring boom times of the 1920s. "The story of the Empire State Building is truly an epitome of all that has preceded. In a few pages it tells [of] all the spirit, the imaginative and technical daring, and even some of the frenzy, that animated the decade of which it was the culmination."[37] Optimism and ambition, in other words, were built into Empire State.

|||||||||||

Over the course of an evening in 1925, hundreds of guests arrived in their finest dress at the doorstep of one of the wealthiest men in America. They followed the drift of the crowd and the sound of the Old Time Orchestra through the mansion and into the ballroom. They were there to mingle and dance. Their eyes scanned the room for recognizable faces and, especially, that of their host. His name was not Jay Gatsby of West Egg, Long Island. He was Henry Ford of Dearborn, Michigan. The music was not jazz but country-folk. And the dancing did not involve doing the Charleston or the Lindy Hop. Ford had called his guests together, instead, to learn square dancing and the jigs that he recalled from his youth.

Born on a farm near Detroit in 1863, Ford made his mark on American industrialization at the turn of the century as the founder of an automobile company. He had spent years testing his skills as a machinist to perfect the technology that mass-produced the Ford Model T, debuted in 1908. Other car companies existed by then, but Ford outmaneuvered his competition by combining simplicity, affordability, and rapid production into a formula for success. Few humans in history have made money as fast as Ford. He sold millions of vehicles as a staple purchase for middle- and upper-class consumers. But Ford's influence went beyond the auto industry. His assembly-line production method (Fordism), which operated using groups of workers specializing in attaching parts of the car piecemeal and on pace rather than building the entire vehicle at once, was adopted by factory owners across the world for its efficiency. Despite his successful empire-building, however, Ford really wanted to teach the world to dance.

The automaker published a manual in 1926 entitled "Good Morning" that aimed to reintroduce "old-time" dance styles, such as line steps and polka, in music venues and public schools. He hired an instructor, Benjamin Lovett, and an orchestra to help make square dancing popular again in the Jazz Age. Speculations about why Ford felt the need to revive his preferred forms of dance reflect the hero-or-villain questions that persist about his character. For some, his moves on the dance floor appear as an innocent attempt to save a folk art from obscurity. For others, it suggests a racialized motive to challenge jazz and the Jewish composers who helped popularize it.

In the 1920s, Ford made his prejudice plain when he allowed a weekly column to appear in his own Dearborn *Independent* newspaper, called "The International Jew: The World's Problem," which propagated falsehoods about a secret oligarchy of Jews controlling the world.[38] It was compiled later into book form. Ford's antisemitism caught the eye of Adolf Hitler, who mentioned the auto mogul in his manifesto, *Mein Kampf*, as the "single great man" in America who remained independent from the Jews. Hitler reportedly hung a large portrait of his American hero in his office and kept translations of his books on hand.[39] He even awarded Ford the Grand Cross of the German Eagle in 1938 to honor Ford's seventy-fifth birthday. Some Nazis on trial in Nuremberg after World War II also credited Ford as inspiring their antisemitism as much as German fascists. Former Reich youth leader Baldur von Schirach testified at his trial that "the decisive antisemitic book which I read at that time and the book which influenced my comrades . . . was Henry Ford's book, *The International Jew*." Von Schirach went on to explain:

> In those days this book made such a deep impression on my friends and myself because we saw in Henry Ford the representative of success, also the exponent of a progressive social policy. In the poverty-stricken and wretched Germany of the time, youth looked toward America, and apart from the great benefactor, Herbert Hoover, it was Henry Ford who to us represented America.[40]

Nazis identified Ford as an American ally because of the language and tone of his publications. His opinion of Jews was not difficult to discern in the pages his newspaper devoted to the topic, including articles with titles like "Jewish Exploitation of Farmers' Organizations," "Jewish Gamblers Corrupt American Baseball," "Jewish Jazz Becomes Our National Music," and "The Jewish Associates of Benedict Arnold." After being sued for libel, Ford went to trial, and he later apologized for the crude comments, claiming he did not adequately scrutinize his newspaper for its content. His legacy, nevertheless, had been smeared along with the reputation of the Jewish men and women his paper targeted. Though Ford contributed to the rise of US empire and personified its reputation for ingenuity, he also exerted his influence by espousing illiberal rhetoric that threatened the welfare and rights of Jews around the world.

IIIIIIIIIII

Although Congress refused to join the League of Nations in 1920, fearing any entangling alliances, the country did not retreat into isolation. Business interests, for one, continued to stake claims abroad in the 1920s. A US Commerce Department survey of American foreign investments, released in 1930, indicated that at the close of 1929, Americans had made over 4,000 investments abroad, amounting to about $7.5 billion. The first of its kind, the survey had been sent to 1,750 "individuals and corporations," who acknowledged their involvement in foreign manufacturing, public utilities, and plantations. Petroleum ventures in the Middle East were increasingly popular as Americans competed with the British and French for access to the fuel sources running millions of automobiles and other engines. Notably, the report found that Canada was the foreign country with the most investments from the United States, at around $2 billion.[41]

Foreign affairs were also imperative in the minds of US policymakers. From the edges of the League of Nations, Americans remained involved in international disputes, debates, and agreements, such as the Naval Treaty in 1922, negotiated in Washington, DC, that set limits on the number of ships and naval armaments that the major powers could produce. American artists and writers also flocked to cities in Europe after the Great War to experience cosmopolitan culture and a nightlife buzzing with jazz and booze. World travel beckoned as the war years ended.

A spirit of internationalism in the 1920s especially soared with the *Spirit of St. Louis* and its daring young pilot across the Atlantic Ocean. Raised in Little Falls, Minnesota, Charles Lindbergh was an early adopter of aviation, serving in the US Army Air Service, working as a mail pilot in the Midwest, and performing barnstorming stunts. He was well aware of the Orteig Prize of $25,000 (nearly half a million dollars today) that a French-American team was offering to the pilot of the first solo transatlantic flight between New York and Paris. By 1927, when Lindbergh entered the contest, several experienced fliers had already perished in the attempt. Lindbergh tried anyway. After raising enough funds for a custom-made aircraft, constructed by the Ryan Aircraft Company of San Diego, the twenty-five-year-old Midwesterner arrived at Roosevelt Field, Long Island, for his official takeoff.

Lindbergh's vessel, the *Spirit of St. Louis*, did not inspire onlookers with confidence. "A sluggish, gray monoplane lurched its way down Roosevelt Field," *New York Times* reporter Russell Owen wrote.[42] The aircraft was small at 9 × 27 feet with a weight of 5,135 pounds, covered with thin silver-colored metal and fabric. The cabin contained a single seat behind its single engine and gas tanks. It had no front window; Lindbergh would need to rely on compass instruments alone to navigate his path to Paris. Delayed by poor weather conditions for days, Captain Lindbergh finally set off on May 20, 1927, at 7:52 in the morning. Owen, the *Times* reporter, noticed that the plane "faltered" and "staggered" before finding air beneath its wings. He heard the crowd gasp, but Lindbergh, the "unconquerable youth," was soon gone beyond the horizon. Thirty-three hours and 3,600 miles later, Lindbergh landed at Le Bourget Aerodrome just outside Paris. He had reached his destination, becoming an instant celebrity for showcasing American heroics and the freedom of the skies.

Billy Mitchell had also foreseen the possibilities of aviation and its importance for defending the US empire, which had long been facilitated by naval power. After piloting fighter planes in France during World War I, Mitchell took a special interest in airpower, arguing that it was essential for winning future wars. To demonstrate the devastating effects of aerial bombers, Mitchell convinced the US military to conduct a series of tests in the summer of 1921, targeting outdated and surplus ships. Mitchell's concerns were verified by the maneuvers, but the military was slow to heed the warning and invest in aerial technology. Mitchell was outraged. His relentless criticism resulted in his court-martial in 1927, the same year as Lindbergh's famous flight. Over time, however, his theories gained credence. Aircraft and aircraft carriers became the most valuable assets of militaries involved in World War II, including the B-25 bomber, bearing Mitchell's name.

IIIIIIIIIII

As construction on the Empire State Building progressed rapidly in 1930, spectators on the ground marveled at the so-called sky boys who walked and worked on steel beams 1,400 feet in the air. "The riveters are putting on the best open-air show in town," the *New York Times* reported of the "performers": "A man rides into the air on top of a steel beam that he maneuvers into place as a crosspiece by hanging to the cable rope with his hands and steering the beam with his feet. There is a good deal of strolling on the thin edge of nothingness."[43] For all the danger, sky boys were paid the union rate of $1.92 an hour for regular workdays, ending at 4:30 p.m., including a half-hour lunch break, during which they often ate atop the scaffolding beams. People from "every continent" stopped by to take in the

Sky boys

spectacle. As the Starrett brothers recalled in their construction notes, "this varied assortment of visitors tended to confirm our belief that New York City is the cosmopolitan hub of the world."[44]

Many of the steelworkers and riveters on the job at Fifth Avenue were New York locals, Irish and Italians, but some Mohawk high-steel experts from Montreal were also employed to do the daring work. Migrant "skywalkers" from the Kahnawake tribe in Quebec had a long history of crafting major projects like the Victoria Bridge spanning the St. Lawrence River. They had also helped raise the Chrysler Building the year before joining the Empire State Building crew. Joe Jocks was one of the men in the Mohawk riveting gang walking the beams above Midtown. As his granddaughter Lynn Beauvais recalled, he felt grateful for work during a time when millions were desperate for regular wages. "It was hard work, but they never talked about the danger. Our men have always really enjoyed their work and were proud of it," she said. Beauvais was proud of her grandfather and the important part he played in bringing the Empire State Building to record heights. But he didn't stop there. Jocks also worked as a skywalker on the World Trade Center towers when they surpassed the Empire State Building's height in the 1970s.[45]

In 1930, C. G. Poore of the *New York Times* described the sights and sounds of the skyscraper in its creation. From the street, he could hear the "stabbing rhythm of the riveting hammer" high above, as the "demonic theme song" "assault[ed] ear drums with its roar." He visualized the view from the top, anticipating the panoramic landscape that visitors to the observation deck would soon see. Manhattan was laid before the high-rising workers. They could spot the Brooklyn waterfront, as well as the rivers and bridges that seemed so distant to those on the ground. "To the man aloft they are brought startlingly near," Poore wrote. "The riveters who are putting together the last pieces of steel to crown the new hive for the buzzing activities of Wall Street see best the vast rambling extent of the port. The Statue of Liberty becomes in their eyes a park-size statue set in a small lagoon." When compared to the powerful, towering height of the newest emblem of empire, Poore suggested, the city's older monuments appeared less significant. "On the harbor side the powdery yellow haze of sunlight deepens to seaward in a filter that shows Bartholdi's torchbearer looking small and unheroic on her star pointed base."[46]

Most of the men working to build the skyscraper, however, were too busy to stop and ponder. "Yeah, it's a nice view, but we ain't got much time for that," one foreman said.[47] The laborers in the air were on a tight schedule to finish the frame so that the walls, flooring, and interior construction could keep apace. When the steelwork on the "Smith building" was finally completed in September, six months and three days after it began, workmen raised an American flag from their "slender perch on the roof beams over the eighty-fifth floor."[48] Smith was there to celebrate that banner day. It had not been easy keeping pace, especially as labor disputes threatened to break the peace. Smith, as president of Empire Inc., had to quell a disagreement about the use of all-union steelworkers, which had been the former governor's understanding when he contracted the Starrett

Brothers to oversee the general construction.[49] But in the end, the Empire State builders praised the "perfect teamwork" of all involved.[50]

Unions were on the ropes in the early 1930s after decades of attack. The overwhelming supply of laborers, desperate for employment during the Depression, did not tip the scales in their favor. Skilled workers, however, mostly associated with the AFL, maintained strong unions throughout the twentieth century, and because skilled trades were essential for constructing Empire State, they could leverage their indispensability to keep their wages (around $1.92 per hour or $15 per week) above the national average. Unionized or not, workers raised the 57,000 tons of steel used to frame the building, laid 10 million bricks, poured 62,000 cubic yards of concrete, placed 64,000 windows, and installed 67 elevators.[51] And, despite the skill of the sky boys, at least 5 of the nearly 3,500 workers died during the building's construction. One death was rumored to be a suicide. The immensity of the project also took a toll on chief builder, Paul Starrett, who admitted in his autobiography that after Empire State was completed, he "suffered a rather severe nervous breakdown."[52]

Despite the challenges, Starrett and his multiple contractors got the job done ahead of schedule. An array of ethnicities crafting the masterpiece reflected the diversity of the nation and its empire (though women, Asians, and African Americans were underrepresented or uninvolved), and the remarkable teamwork of thousands of men of different backgrounds stands as a testament to American cooperation and efficiency at a time when most of the world had crashed to a halt. Comparing skyscraper construction to a coordinated war effort, William Starrett, who oversaw Empire State with his brother Paul, described his hired help in 1928 as "soldiers of a great creative effort."[53]

The Starrett brothers knew they were crafting a structure not only for their time but, perhaps, for all time. As they explained in their *Notes on the Construction*, "The Empire State Building is constructed to stand the rigors of future centuries. . . . Perhaps it will live on to see old Empires crumble and new dynasties arise." Yet they could only leave its longevity to the circumstances of an "ever-changing world." "At the moment," they noted, "we are astounded at the marvel of its birth. . . . The massive building now stands as a majestic symbol of the enterprise and efficiency of our age . . . reflecting the glory of God, who had given such power to men."[54] While the captains of industry reaped the profits and due accolades for their achievements, it was manual laborers of all races and ethnicities who quite literally built the American empire and its most prominent architectural symbol.

IIIIIIIIIII

Although the names and voices of the men who built the Empire State Building are largely lost to history, their images are still with us, thanks to the photography of Lewis Hine, who was hired by the board of Empire State Inc. to capture the men at work for promotional purposes. Hoisted into the air with harnesses and basket lifts, he took his camera to new heights along with the sky boys to record their working-class heroics. Riveters on high beams, welders, cable climbers, and crane operators were shown dangling hundreds of feet in the air above the streets of Manhattan. Hine framed them as portraiture in action and likened them to Greek mythological figures like Icarus, the son of a craftsman who perished by flying too close to the sun.

Hine, a former schoolteacher, had used his photography for decades to educate the public about the experiences of ordinary people. In the early 1900s, he snapped thousands of photos of immigrants arriving at Ellis Island—probably some of the same people who later built New York's skyline. His 1908 photo *Climbing into the Promised Land,* for instance, depicts a group of immigrants crowded onto the stairs of the processing center at Ellis Island with their luggage. They are holding the personal records they needed to present to inspectors examining them for health and financial fitness, the determining factors for whether they would be able to pass into the country or not.

One man, in a dapper collared shirt, a tall derby hat, and fitted overcoat, glances at the camera with tired eyes. He is clutching his neat leather suitcase by its strap. His mustache is well groomed. To his left, a man appears startled, either by the photographer or the entire process of his arrival. A stocky man a little lower on the staircase also looks Hine's way. His mustache appears untrimmed, draping toward his strong jaw. It looks like he is wearing layers of clothing, probably everything he owned that could not fit into the basket of wares he carries at his left. All the men are wearing hats. A woman in the foreground has covered her head with a scarf.

By capturing the unposed moments of migrants, industrial workers, and even child laborers, Hine exposed the harsh realities of the working class and brought issues of social injustice to light. He documented images of children in factories for the National Child Labor Committee, which lobbied for federal laws prohibiting the practice. Foremen and managers did not exactly invite him in to witness the children at work. Instead, Hine wore disguises and lied about his identity, claiming on some occasions that he was an itinerant bible salesman or insurance agent. During the Depression, he worked for federal programs like the Works Progress Administration and the Tennessee Valley Authority to capture images of the time and the people who lived through it.

Photographer Dorothea Lange also documented the poverty that many Americans faced during the Depression years. Working for the government's Resettlement Administration in California, Lange did not turn a blind eye to disturbing scenes of desperate families begging for work and trying to provide for their starving children. "That the familiar world is often unsatisfactory cannot be denied, but it is not, for all that, one that we need abandon," she said.[55] Lange certainly did not ask her subjects to smile. She shot them as they were—holding their faces in their hands, on the verge of tears, dirty and despondent. She took pictures of children in rags, clinging to their weary mothers. At a pea-picking camp in Nipomo, California, in March 1936, Lange met the woman she immortalized in her most famous photo, *Migrant Mother*. "I saw and approached the hungry and desperate mother, as if drawn by a magnet," she recalled later.[56] They spoke for a few minutes. The woman, as Lange remembered, told her that they were surviving on vegetables from the fields and birds her children killed to eat. Florence Owens Thompson had grown up on Cherokee lands in Oklahoma. She was only thirty-two years old when Lange came along, but her face was lined with wrinkles, tanned by the sun, and taut with worry. When the photo of Florence appeared in the *San Francisco News* a few days later, it illustrated an editorial on the same page entitled "What Does the 'New Deal' Mean to This Mother and Her Children?"[57]

IIIIIIIIII

Two of the most prominent politicians of New York, Franklin D. Roosevelt and Al Smith had often crossed paths in the Assembly halls in Albany and at Democratic Party events. In both 1924 and 1928, Roosevelt nominated Smith as the president of the Democratic National Convention, calling him the "Happy Warrior." The lifelong New Yorkers, however, had their differences, which became more pronounced in the early 1930s as Roosevelt was chosen as the presidential nominee over Smith. Smith had climbed the political ladder from humble beginnings in the Bowery district of Manhattan. Roosevelt, on the other hand, was born into privilege, as the only son of a wealthy Dutch family residing in their sprawling rural mansion in the Hudson Valley. Roosevelt attended Harvard College and Columbia Law School and married the niece of a president in 1905, while Al Smith skipped higher education to pursue a political career.

However, Roosevelt faced a life-changing tragedy when he contracted polio in 1921 at the age of thirty-nine. He spent most of the 1920s learning how to handle the affliction, building his upper body strength, and practicing a new way of "walking" on metal braces. This meant that Roosevelt was largely out of the public eye during the decade, and therefore, he was able to escape blame for the political decisions that contributed to the onset of the Depression. By late 1928, Roosevelt was elected back to office as governor of New York, and he became a promising candidate to challenge Hoover in the election of 1932. His last national post had been during the Wilson administration, where he served as assistant secretary of the Navy. In this role, Roosevelt observed firsthand how the US Navy advanced and defended US geopolitical and economic interests around the world. The navy, in fact, acted as the primary tool of imperialism until airpower reached its ascendency in the 1940s. Roosevelt, of course, knew of Billy Mitchell's mission in favor of military aviation, and he eventually came around to Mitchell's way of thinking. As president, Roosevelt saw the import of airpower during World War II, and though Mitchell died in 1936 before he could witness the fruits of his efforts, Roosevelt posthumously promoted the former aviator to the rank of major general and asked Congress to award him with the Congressional Gold Medal, which was granted in 1946. Roosevelt always appreciated innovation.

In the early 1930s, Roosevelt began calling for innovations and federal intervention to counter the deepening Depression. He was, in part, positioning himself as the Democratic opponent to Hoover in the next election. Al Smith, who lost to Hoover in 1928, was no longer a nominee hopeful. As Smith busied himself with Empire State Inc., Roosevelt was occupying Smith's old seat as governor of New York not far from the construction site. Tensions between the two Democrats were not yet openly apparent, but Smith and his friend Raskob, as well as Hoover and the Republicans, would raise alarm bells by mid-decade about Roosevelt, his expanded executive power, and his New Deal policies, which, critics charged, were infringements upon liberty.

||||||||||||

The National Association of Manufacturers (NAM) was eager to calm labor unrest during the Great Depression and assure Americans that they lived in the best country with the best working conditions in the world. To help get their message across, they bought billboard space in cities across the country, boasting the "World's Highest Standard of Living" and declaring "There's No Way Like the American Way." For many Americans struggling during the economic crisis, that message fell flat. In Louisville, Kentucky, in 1937, African Americans lined up at a relief station to receive food after a devastating flood. Unwittingly, they highlighted the hypocrisy of the NAM's claims when photographer Margaret Bourke White took a picture of the Black relief recipients assembled in front of the NAM billboard, which featured a cheerful White family of four (and their dog) wearing elegant clothes and driving a fancy car.[58]

The contrast of privilege and poverty reflected the uncomfortable reality that the "American Way" of capitalism and imperialism did not benefit all Americans equally. Black Americans, since the Reconstruction era of the late 1800s, had been struggling against White-imposed limits to their political and economic liberties. Racial discrimination closed many doors to their employment, to housing and real estate, to home and business loans—all essential elements of social mobility. Without adequate sources of income, they were unable to make investments and accumulate savings for the future of their families. A system of structural racism, fixed to keep Blacks out, left millions living below the poverty line, working primarily as tenant farmers, housekeepers, and unskilled laborers.

During the Depression, opportunities for all Americans shrank but especially for Black Americans, who experienced the highest unemployment rates at 50 to 70 percent. New Deal programs during Roosevelt's administration offered government jobs and aid to those in need, but they were applied unevenly at the state and local level, and many Blacks fell through the gaps or were overlooked altogether. Domestic workers and tenant farmers, for example, were initially ineligible for relief. The Civilian Conservation Corps and other federal programs also enforced segregation among workers. These discriminatory conditions prompted activism. Mary McLeod Bethune organized the first National Council of Negro Women in 1935, and the National Negro Congress convened the following year. In 1937, the Southern Negro Youth Congress began fighting against Jim Crow laws that barred Blacks from voting.

One of the most dedicated Black activists in US history, Ida B. Wells-Barnett, died on March 25, 1931, at age sixty-two, not long before the Empire State Building opened. Wells had cofounded the National Association for the Advancement of Colored People (NAACP) in 1909 with W. E. B. Du Bois and Mary White Ovington, but her fight for justice and civil rights extended to all excluded Americans, such as women and their right to vote. She had witnessed some signs of progress over the decades.

Women achieved the right to vote in 1920, even as Black voting rights went unprotected throughout the South. Lynching, which Wells had challenged with her journalistic exposés, had been reduced since the 1890s but not eliminated. Education and social mobility for Black Americans still fell below national norms.

In one of her most powerful speeches of 1909, Wells had asked "why is mob murder permitted by a Christian nation?" "Thousands of American citizens have been put to death and no president has yet raised his hand in effective protest," she observed. Calling on federal law enforcement to protect all citizens, Wells-Barnett demanded anti-lynching measures "for the sake of the country's fair name."[59] Upon her passing, the *Oakland Tribune* called her "one of the greatest Negro women the world has ever produced," a "fearless" fighter against lynching. The *Chicago Defender* likewise praised her "militant" "indefatigable labors" on its front page. She had been born in 1862 in Mississippi to a family of slaves, the papers noted. But she died a hero, a champion of liberty.[60]

IIIIIIIIIII

An ad in the *New York Times* on May 1, 1981, the fiftieth anniversary of the Empire State Building's opening, projected nothing but optimism about the American economy. "America is an economic miracle of two centuries' duration," it read. "Never, in all of history, have a people enjoyed a comparable degree of freedom and prosperity."[61] The ad echoed the sentiments of the NAM billboards that had boasted the "American Way" of manufacturing in the 1930s. Back then, millions could only dream of prosperity. In 1980, Americans had hoped the new decade and the policies of Ronald Reagan would turn the recession of the 1970s around for good. Instead, the country slumped again, and interest rates and unemployment remained high. The effect on manufacturing, construction, and the auto industry was the worst since the Great Depression.

The Empire State Building by its fiftieth birthday was no longer the tallest structure in New York, and it was arguably no longer the most recognizable symbol of American empire. The World Trade Center in

Lower Manhattan, featuring the "Twin Towers" at 1,360 feet high, had surpassed it on both counts. But Americans still loved the Empire State Building, and some considered it the more elegant, perhaps innocent, representation of New York and all its glory. A week before its fiftieth-anniversary celebration, *New York Times* writer Paul Goldberger sounded nostalgic about the skyscraper. "It result[ed] from . . . its builders' desire for a great commercial symbol for New York," he explained. Raskob and Smith had won the height contest in 1931, a record that lasted forty years. But for Goldberger, the building meant so much more. "It seems to stand not only for height," he wrote, "but for every aspect of the drama that a great skyscraper can bring to the cityscape. The Empire State Building is about height, it is about commerce, it is about entertainment, it is about views, it is about the very meaning of the skyline itself."[62] That skyline had developed along with US empire and the population of its metropole. And in the 1980s, though dwarfed by the Twin Towers, the Empire State Building still stood as a masthead on the urban flagship of an empire so powerful, popular, and determined to thrive that the people of the city had set their ambitions skyward, as if that were the only way to go.

CHAPTER 3

LIBERTY LIMITED—1886

Perhaps no writer for the *New York Times* has used more syrupy prose than on October 29, 1886, the day after Lady Liberty's official unveiling. "A hundred Fourths of July broke loose yesterday," the front page announced. "The clerk of the weather had done his miserable best to make things gloomy and forbidding, but [the] American spirit rose to the occasion, bubbling with enthusiasm and frolic." The reporter's own enthusiasm burst forth as he painted the scene, describing "bands striped and feathered and zoned and trimmed and buttoned galore," and "ships of war, brilliant with bunting, pointing to the tide—the island—the waiting goddess." He remarked upon every detail: the shifting weather, the lifting music of military bands marching throughout the city, and the genial faces of spectators and honored guests such as President Grover Cleveland. People had come from all over the world to mark the international event, honor Franco-American friendship, and glimpse the "mighty figure with the lifted torch" that transatlantic teams of artists and engineers had spent decades crafting, "till all men of the thousands gathered in her honor knew that Liberty had been given and received."[1]

Women were present, too, though they could not purchase tickets to the festivities on Bedloe's Island. They accompanied their husbands to Lower Manhattan, waved handkerchiefs, and applauded the all-male panel of speakers. Two young ladies riding atop a firetruck sported costumes representing "Liberty" and "America," while one daring socialite, who had been given special permission to visit the statue earlier in the day, climbed the statue's inner scaffolding to reach the torch balcony, becoming the first female to make the "laborious" trek to the top. After descending from the torch, Elizabeth Potter Cary, the wealthy wife of a Virginian Confederate veteran turned New York City attorney, Clarence Cary, was promptly escorted off the island. Only two women had invitations to attend the ceremony at Liberty's base, and they were related to the French honorees.[2]

Not all women assembled around the island that day were filled with joy and celebration. Outrage over a statue dedicated to liberty, in the image of a woman, honoring a nation that had excluded women from equal rights, prompted the New York State Woman Suffrage Association (NYSWSA) to send a delegation of their members to protest the event and the hypocrisy embedded in it. The group rented a cattle barge, the *John Lenox*, for $100 to approach Bedloe's Island, getting close enough for spectators to hear their shouting and see their banners. In their statement, the NYSWSA called the Statue of Liberty "a gigantic lie, a travesty, and a mockery." Suffragist Lillie Devereux Blake sarcastically commented that "in erecting a statue of Liberty embodied as a woman in a land where no woman has political liberty men have shown a delightful inconsistency." A brief *New York Times* article the next day, buried on the last page, reported that the NYSWSA "were the only people who looked with disfavor upon the grand pageant."[3]

The New York branch of suffragists involved in the Liberty protest were part of the larger National Woman Suffrage Association, founded in 1869 by Susan B. Anthony and Elizabeth Cady Stanton to demand women's legal and political rights, including the vote. Protesting the 1876 Centennial a decade before the Liberty event, the organization issued a proclamation that called the entire republican edifice into question. The statement read: "In view of such degradation of one-half our people, citizens of a Republic, WE PROTEST before the assembled nations of the world against the centennial celebration, as an occasion for National rejoicing, as only through equal, impartial suffrage can a genuine republican form of government be realized."[4]

By criticizing the American republic in 1876 and 1886, women activists challenged the conceptual purpose of Liberty Enlightening the World, which Laboulaye and Bartholdi had initiated as a tribute to the shared republicanism of France and the United States. While Laboulaye was eager to express his joy and relief that republican values had survived the American Civil War, women expressed their dismay over the Fifteenth Amendment, guaranteeing voting rights to Black men but not any women. Some male abolitionists, including William Lloyd Garrison, had linked Black rights and women's rights together under the cause of universal liberties during the mid-1800s, but in the contentious battle over political gains and constitutional law, the fight for rights according to race took precedence, while women's issues were sidelined to appease a majority of men (and women) who refused to reform gender dynamics within the domestic or public realms.

As Lillie Blake, president of the NYSWSA, boarded the barge in New York City on October 28, 1886, she carried a sign reminding spectators that "American women have no freedom." She had proposed the idea of the protest earlier that month during the NYSWSA Executive Committee meeting at her apartment, and she and her co-activists had worked hard in the weeks leading up to the celebration to bring their opposition to Bedloe's Island. They covered the $100 cost of the boat rental by selling tickets to women to ride the barge, since they were unable to attend the event on Bedloe's Island. There were two exceptions: the wife of Bartholdi and the daughter of de Lesseps had been invited to join the French delegation at the main stage.[5] Otherwise excluded, many women grasped at the chance to get nearby via water vessels, which were granted access to anchor around the island. Tickets to board the *John Lenox* sold out, though not everyone among the nearly two hundred women and twenty-five male passengers intended to become part of the protest. As NYSWSA members chanted and made speeches, the spectators surrounding them strained their necks to catch a glimpse of the covered colossus through the fog and strained their ears to hear President Cleveland's speech in the late afternoon. They heard him say:

> We are not here today to bow before the representation of a fierce warlike god, filled with wrath and vengeance, but we joyously contemplate instead our own deity keeping watch and ward before the open gates of America and greater than all that have been celebrated in ancient song. Instead of grasping in her hand thunderbolts of terror and of death, she holds aloft the light which illumines the way to man's enfranchisement. We will not forget that Liberty has here made her home, nor shall her chosen altar be neglected. Willing votaries will constantly keep alive its fires and these shall gleam upon the shores of our sister Republic thence, and joined with answering rays a stream of light shall pierce the darkness of ignorance and man's oppression, until Liberty enlightens the world.[6]

Cleveland's remarks reflected his personal interpretation of the statue, which he gave public meaning. He emphasized its peaceful purpose, so different from the war-making qualities that had inspired earlier colossi. Piercing the barbarism of violence, ignorance, and oppression, Liberty's torch, he vowed, would expose mankind's malevolence and illuminate the path to loftier ideals. Though abstract and lyrical, Cleveland's words elevated the image of Liberty as a liberating figure for the world.

The audience that day built on Cleveland's imagery once they caught their first glimpse of the copper-clad statue and took in the details, all crafted with symbolism. Bartholdi stood atop the crown of his creation and dropped the French tricolor, draping her features. "Presently the veil was withdrawn from her beautiful calm face," wrote Lillie Blake, remembering the moment she witnessed from the harbor, "and the air was rent with salvos of artillery fired to hail the new goddess; the earth and the sea trembled with the mighty concussions, and steam-whistles mingled their shrill shrieks with the shouts of the multitude—all this done by men in honor of a woman."[7]

Statue of Liberty dedication day

The statue, of course, had been made by men to honor all sorts of principles and causes, none specifically intended for women. Americans familiar with antiquity recognized Bartholdi's colossus as a version of the Roman goddess Libertas, modeled on all the lady liberties that had graced coins, plaques, and pictures throughout history. As a female form, the Statue of Liberty communicated a message of purity and maternal protection, while also representing an idealized woman as dignified and silent—far less incendiary than other depictions of Liberty leading revolutionaries into battle.[8]

But Bartholdi built additional symbols into his statue to augment ancient tropes. The seven spikes extending from the diadem represented the number of continents and seas. The tablet cradled in her left arm marked July 4, 1776, American Independence Day, as the dawning of freedom, and the shackles at her feet were meant to represent emancipation, the only reference left of Laboulaye's ode to Blacks' manumission. The "beautiful calm" face that Blake described struck observers as serene but resolute, prompting many to wonder who the sculptor had used as his model. Bartholdi never said for sure, but in later years, he seemed to confirm, or at least not deny, that he had constructed an image of his mother.

Worried about his mother's health at home in France, Bartholdi had considered skipping the ceremony to remain at her side. Charlotte, however, urged him to make the journey and receive his due accolades. The French delegation arrived in New York from Le Havre, France, on October 25, three days before the scheduled unveiling. Bartholdi did not speak at the event but stood on the platform and took a bow in front of an applauding crowd. His colleagues with the French-American Union, including Count Ferdinand de Lesseps, read their speeches, reminding listeners that the statue stood as a testament to the amity and shared values of two mighty nations. Yet de Lesseps, who had built the Suez Canal, went beyond republicanism by praising the technological and industrial progress of the United States. "People will know that they have reached a land where individual initiative is developed in all its power; where progress is a religion; where great fortunes become popular by the charity they bestow." Liberty, he implied, meant liberal economics and capitalist ventures. De Lesseps wrapped up his remarks by mentioning his latest endeavor, the soon-to-be ill-fated French Panama Canal project, heralding the achievements of the "prolific alliance of the Franco-Latin and Anglo-Saxon races."[9] He referred to "free America" without irony.

A celebratory dinner at Delmonico's that evening consisted of 210 invited men, but no women. Black men were also excluded, despite Laboulaye's intention of honoring freed slaves with the statue. The *Cleveland Gazette*, a Black-owned newspaper, took notice. A month after the statue opened to the public, their front page ran an editorial titled "Postponing Bartholdi's statue until there is liberty for colored as well." "Shove the Bartholdi statue, torch and all, into the ocean," the *Gazette* suggested, "until the 'liberty' of this country is such as to make it possible for an inoffensive and industrious colored man in the South to earn a respectable living for himself and family, without being ku-kluxed, perhaps murdered, his daughter and wife outraged, and his property destroyed. The idea of the 'liberty' of this country 'enlightening the world,' or even Patagonia, is ridiculous in the extreme."[10]

Most Americans, however, accepted the statue and its lofty symbolism without question, perhaps considering it aspirational rather than representational. President Cleveland signaled as much when he spoke of Liberty's role in the continual enlightening of the populous against ignorance and forces of oppression. Allusions to one hundred years of history, since the revolutions of the late 1700s, also carried the message of liberty as a struggle throughout the ages. Speakers such as Senator William M. Evarts invoked the legacy of Lafayette and gave credit to Laboulaye, the statue's most dedicated patron, who had died in 1883 before Bartholdi finished it. American independence was celebrated anew, especially since the Liberty dedication had missed its deadline to be part of the 1876 Centennial. Unassociated with any specific event, Lady Liberty now represented abstract principles and the unfinished efforts to achieve them.

Attempts to interpret Liberty were swift and poetic. In the *Boston Globe* the following day, verses by John Boyle O'Reilly asked "What comest thou to teach? What vision hath those introverted eyes of Revolutions framed in centuries?" The poem then gives the statue a voice, as she revealed her purpose as "God's daughter" with a "truth that shall make men free." Acknowledging the slow pace of cultural and political change, she referred to "Freedom" as "growth and not creation: one man suffers, one man is free," and declared "Freedom is more than a resolution—he is not free who is free alone."[11] Liberty, the poem implied, stood for the millions of people in France, in the United States, and around the world, who were still unfree.

IIIIIIIIIII

None of the speakers that October day mentioned the challenges of Liberty's long road to completion or the fact that Americans had been reluctant to raise money for her pedestal. In 1871, while touring the United States, Bartholdi had convinced prominent New Yorkers Richard Butler, Senator Evarts, and Henry Spaulding to form the American Committee, a counterpart to the French Committee. While the French contingent raised funds to finish the statue, the Americans assumed the responsibility of financing the base to hold her. For a decade, their efforts were slow, almost nonexistent, as they faced an apathetic public recovering from war and struggling with an economic depression. It took until the mid-1880s to begin excavating the foundation on Bedloe's Island.[12]

Laboulaye's idea for a grand tribute to mark the triumph of freedom after the Civil War had missed its moment, as the contentious Reconstruction era undermined idealism about liberty. The Compromise of 1877, a corrupt backroom bargain among politicians, traded racial justice for executive power and left many of the Civil War's promises unfulfilled. Black political representation became severely limited, despite constitutional guarantees, while women and ethnic minorities were left out of national decision-making altogether. What did a monument to liberty mean to most of the American population? The American Committee failed to make that point clear. And the longer Bartholdi took to craft his statue, the more the meaning behind it shifted. What began as republican veneration for Lincoln's victory gave way to generalized sentiments about the promise of freedom, however imperfect, that the United States offered the world. The Frenchmen supporting Bartholdi admired Americans' ability to preserve the republic and maintain social order, even if such an achievement came at the expense of universal suffrage. Their country, after all, had not been so successful.

It didn't help that the Washington Monument, commemorating George Washington, competed with the Liberty promoters for attention and funding. Though the cornerstone of the Monument had been placed in the nation's capital in 1848, the project stalled until 1877 as federal funds were diverted to the Civil War and Reconstruction. Bartholdi saw part of the unfinished column when he visited DC in 1871—a tangible warning about the fate of expensive memorials in late nineteenth-century America. Critics scoffed at the price of the obelisk as well as its simple shape. Architect Henry Robinson Searle, who lost the design competition to Robert Mills, noted that "there is nothing whatever aesthetic about it, and nothing that would impress the visitor, whether native or foreign, with the grandeur of the work of Washington and his coadjutors in founding this nation." The plain, white column, eventually reaching five-hundred feet, reminded some observers, like Mark Twain, of an old factory chimney or asparagus stalk, while others have since dismissed it as a symbol of white power.[13] There were even questions about whether the initial masonry had been crafted by enslaved laborers before emancipation. The exterior structure was finally completed in 1884 and dedicated the following year, a few decades later than expected, while the American Committee struggled to fundraise for their pet project to celebrate liberty.

An initial estimate for Lady Liberty's pedestal, calculated at $125,000, was raised and quickly spent. That amount turned out to be far too little once construction bids were received. Most of the private donations came from residents in the New York area, given the makeup of the American Committee and their links to the city. Beyond Manhattan, Americans wondered why they were being asked to contribute to a New York Harbor lighthouse.[14] The US Congress hedged the issue for years and committed federal money only on the condition that the statue serve as a working lighthouse, aiding ships to port. As Bartholdi put the finishing touches on his statue in 1884, pressure on the American Committee to fulfill their promises intensified.

Part of the problem lay in geographical, not ideological, terrain, particularly the lack of proximity to the Liberty project and its creator. The French could visit Bartholdi's studio, watch him work, and feel compelled to support the notable artist making his masterpiece. Americans, in contrast, had few visuals to tug at their heart and purse strings, only vague promises and platitudes. Bartholdi had hoped to drum up interest by displaying a large portion of the statue at the 1876 Centennial exhibition in Philadelphia. Behind schedule, he was only able to send the right arm and torch, which was later displayed in Madison Square Park in New York City.

Fortunately, Joseph Pulitzer took up the cause of the American Committee, devoting more space to advertising about the statue and cajoling donations in his newspaper the *New York World*. One effective article appealed to class solidarity, encouraging workers to match their French counterparts. "The Statue cost was paid in by the masses of the French people—by the working men, the tradesmen, the shop girls, the artisans—by all, irrespective of class or condition. Let us respond in like manner," he urged.[15] Within months, Pulitzer had raised $100,000 and went on to solicit enough funds to bring the pedestal to completion.

The wealthy media mogul understood the meaning behind Lady Liberty from an amalgam of his life's experiences as an immigrant and Civil War veteran. Born into a Jewish family in Hungary, Pulitzer was recruited to fight for the Union cause, enlisting at the age of seventeen in the Lincoln Cavalry when he arrived in New York in September 1864. After the war, he briefly worked in whaling and as a waiter before becoming a reporter for the German circular the *Westliche Post* in St. Louis, Missouri. Pulitzer wanted to be a lawyer, a difficult career path for a recent immigrant who spoke broken English. But he had some role models to follow, including the German-born editor of the *Westliche Post*, Carl Schurz, who eventually became a US senator and secretary of the interior. Like Schurz, Pulitzer joined the Republican Party, voting for the Fifteenth Amendment. He also challenged corruption in St. Louis, especially after he became a state legislator. Loyal to his principles above any particular party, he switched to supporting the Democrats as they became more populist in the 1870s.

After making money and a name for himself as owner-editor of the *St. Louis Post-Dispatch*, Pulitzer set his sights on purchasing the *New York World* and taking on issues of public concern in the nation's largest city. For him, a free and critical press was crucial for preserving a free and uncorrupted country. "We are a democracy, and there is only one way to get a democracy on its feet in the matter of its individual, its social, its municipal, its State, its national conduct, and that is by keeping the public informed about what is going on," he asserted. "Our Republic and its press will rise or fall together."[16]

Pulitzer, however, did not refrain from using his news outlet to promote certain candidates, such as Grover Cleveland in the presidential election of 1884. That year, Pulitzer was elected to the House of Representatives as a Democrat from New York's Ninth District, as he led the crusade to raise Lady Liberty. His time in Congress lasted only a little over a year before he returned to journalism full time. Pulitzer had benefited from the enterprising opportunities of his adopted country, and he helped level the playing field for ordinary men and women, including immigrants like himself. From his beginnings as a poor, hired soldier, he had climbed to the highest levels of wealth and prestige. He died in 1911 while traveling along the Atlantic coastline aboard his private yacht, named *Liberty*.

IIIIIIIIIII

A tongue-in-cheek editorial at the end of 1883 acknowledged Americans' inclination toward amplitude. "The Frenchmen, when they undertook to put us to the expense of providing a pedestal, cunningly took advantage of our fondness for big things," it stated.[17] At over three-hundred-feet tall from turf to torch, the Liberty statue, had it been placed in Central or Battery Park, would have dwarfed the structures in Manhattan in the 1880s, which did not yet boast its own skyscrapers. Chicago led the way in that trend, innovating in response to urban industrialization and overcrowding. In 1885, the Home Insurance Building on West Adams Street, at 138 feet, stunned city-goers, though the earliest structures of that height were rather thick and stout-looking compared to the narrow, needle-like buildings that would later define the skyline of New York City. New York's most notable engineering achievement, the East River Bridge (renamed Brooklyn Bridge in 1915), spanned the mile across the river to connect Lower Manhattan to the opposite borough. The Gothic Revival suspension structure had taken fourteen years to build, opening to the public in 1883.

At its inauguration, the Statue of Liberty still awaited some finishing touches. Plaques and medallions meant to represent the fellowship between the United States and France were missing. The torch, crucial to its purpose as a lighthouse, wasn't working. And four large panels set to display meaningful inscriptions also appeared empty.[18] While the year of American independence was inscribed upon the tablet in Liberty's left arm, the poetry of Emma Lazarus that many would later associate with the statue had yet to be bolstered to its base. The words "Give me your tired, your poor, your huddled masses yearning to breathe free, the wretched refuse of your teeming shore, send these, the homeless, tempest-tossed to me, I lift my lamp beside the golden door!" from the sonnet "New Colossus," were not added to the monument until 1903. The poem, however, had already been written, in 1883, as part of the effort to raise money for the pedestal.[19]

Emma Lazarus was not herself an immigrant, but she sympathized with the foreigners seeking refuge in the United States, including her ancestors from Germany and Portugal. Born in 1849 into a wealthy Jewish merchant family in New York City, Lazarus began publishing poetry as a teenager during the Civil War. From the onset, her work celebrated heroism, martyrdom, and collective action. An 1871 collection featured her title poem about King "Admetus" of Greek mythology, which tells the story of how his wife Alcestis sacrificed her life for his. The voices throughout the stanzas plead with the gods to "have mercy" and remind readers that "our deeds, forever interchained and interlocked, complete each other and explain themselves."[20]

Lazarus believed that her life and deeds were connected to the fate of others. As she witnessed the arrival of Jewish refugees, escaping the pogroms of Eastern Europe and Russia and coming to New York City in the 1880s to start new lives, Lazarus increasingly found purpose in activism. She volunteered at institutions offering vocational training and language lessons to Jews who needed to find work and support their families, and she established the Society for the Improvement and Colonization of East European Jews in 1883, six years before Jane Addams cofounded Hull House in Chicago. Poems such as "New Ezekiel" told of "twenty scorching centuries of wrong" and the longing for a land of freedom for Jews in the United States or Palestine. "Let but an Ezra rise anew, To lift the *Banner of the Jew!*" she wrote.[21]

By 1883, Lazarus had cemented her legacy as an advocate for immigrants. That year, as the American Committee stepped up its fundraising for the Liberty statue's pedestal, they turned to Lazarus to pen a sonnet and donate the proceeds to their project. She gave them "The New Colossus."

A mighty woman with a torch, whose flame
Is the imprisoned lightning, and her name
Mother of Exiles. From her beacon-hand
Glows world-wide welcome.

With this greeting to incoming citizen hopefuls, Lazarus contributed significantly to how Americans and foreigners thought about the Statue of Liberty, which was not originally intended as a symbol for immigrants, in particular.[22] The speakers at the dedication ceremony in October 1886 did not focus on the topic, even as an ocean steamer carrying newcomers passed by that very day. New York politician Chauncey Depew at least made passing reference to Liberty's role as a "beacon, lighting this gateway to the continent, [to] welcome the poor and persecuted with the hope and promise of homes and citizenship."[23] The American Committee's request for Lazarus, a pro-immigrant activist, to contribute a poem also suggests that they were making the connection between the form of the liberty torch and the idea of liberty as a beacon for those arriving on American shores.

Some newspapers at the time sounded that message. The *St. Louis Globe-Democrat* on the morning of October 29, the day after Liberty's dedication ceremony, reported that "the greatest statue of the world" now stood "to welcome the coming stranger" as a "Goddess of Freedom, whom the fugitives from injustice and oppression abroad may fall down and worship."[24] In 1887, a year after the statue's dedication, an unidentified artist published an illustration "Welcome to the Land of Freedom" depicting a group of immigrants on the deck of their ship with the Statue of Liberty visible in the background.[25]

Ellis Island was not opened as a health inspection and processing center for immigrants until 1892, and its proximity to Liberty Island helped strengthen the link between the two landmarks thereafter. But in the

1880s, as the Statue of Liberty assumed her post in the harbor, New York City already served as an entry port for millions of people from all over the world. They met an ambivalent American society, balanced between nativism and cosmopolitanism. But immigrants were also filling an economic gap in the American nation. Urban industrialists who wanted cheap labor to work in factories placed ads abroad in newspapers to recruit workers, and some companies even paid for their passage. Southern states especially needed new sources of labor after slavery ended. Yet immigrants were never promised a warm welcome, free of hardship. Newcomers were crucial for industry and consumerism in an expanding capitalist economy. But they were also regarded in negative terms, as the "huddled masses" and "wretched refuse" that carried connotations of disease, poverty, and uncivilized chattel.

Dark-skinned people, whether from the Caribbean, Mexico, or the Mediterranean, were shunned. Catholic Italians and Irish, even after receiving citizenship, faced discrimination in housing and hiring from those who favored US born or European Protestants. Those from Asia, such as the Chinese people who Bartholdi had observed living in squalid conditions in San Francisco, faced rampant mistreatment. Nativists feared foreigners as a threat to liberty, believing immigrants brought with them values and customs that could divide their loyalty, undermine American institutions, or even dilute Anglo-Saxon racial superiority. Xenophobia sometimes turned to violence. Jews such as Abraham Surasky and Leo Frank were lynched, while Jewish businesses were targeted by vandals and police. And, in 1891, eleven Italians were lynched in New Orleans for an alleged murder. Pushed and pulled by circumstances, including their precarious position in US cities, nearly half of migrant Italians worked in America temporarily, before returning to their home country.

Most migrants, however, chose to stay for a variety of reasons, not least of which involved the freedom and opportunities offered by their adopted country. For all its illiberal imperfections, the United States provided a level of freedom not easily matched around the world, at least for White or White-passing men. By 1900, nearly 40 percent of New Yorkers were foreign born and many more were second-generation citizens. The late-nineteenth-century influx inspired the idea that the United States existed as a "nation of immigrants" who had passed through the "Golden Door" of New York City and ports along the Eastern Seaboard since colonial times, mostly in search of freedom. Of course, not everyone in the continental United States fit the description of "immigrant," especially those populations forcibly removed from land and brought to it over the centuries.[26]

Liberty in America was not extended to every would-be immigrant either. In 1882, the federal government passed the Chinese Exclusion Act, the first major US law that restricted immigration by race. Migrant Asians had helped build the American empire, extending railroads and infrastructure into the west. But many Americans resented their place in the workforce and their seemingly out-of-place appearance among Whites of European descent. As mayor of San Francisco James D. Phelan sought to explain "why the Chinese should be excluded," he argued, "The Chinese may be good laborers, but they are not good citizens. They may in small numbers benefit individual employers, but they breed the germs of a national disease, which spreads as they spread, and grows as they grow."[27] In the wake of the 1882 restriction and widespread racist opinions like these, some Asians saw the Statue of Liberty as an "insult," a sentiment reflected in a letter that Saum Song Bo, a Chinese American writer, sent to the *New York Sun* criticizing the fundraising of the American Committee and Joseph Pulitzer. He panned the statue as a "graven image" "holding a torch which lights the passage of those of all nations who come into this country. But are the Chinese allowed to come?" he asked. "As for the Chinese who are here, are they allowed to enjoy liberty as men of all other nationalities enjoy it?"[28]

The Chinese who had settled in the United States before the ban were largely segregated into enclaves or "Chinatowns" in New York City and San Francisco, while ethnic neighborhoods for Italians, Poles, Germans, and other minorities established turf boundaries throughout urban areas and reinforced the ward bosses who appealed to their outsider status for votes. The corruption of Tammany Hall and similar political machines did not reflect democracy in the purest sense, but they did offer immigrants a sense of empowerment and solidarity in the face of discrimination.

Despite the limits of freedom in the United States, the romanticized image of immigrants weeping with relief at the sight of the Statue of Liberty was born from personal experiences. Clara Larsen recalled coming into New York from Russia at the age of thirteen: "The people were screaming and some of them were crying and some of them were dancing. It was all kind of a joyous feeling of coming to the land of freedom and a land of love."[29] Edward Corsi remembered how the sight of it "brought silence to the decks" of his ship *Florida,* sailing in from Naples in 1907. "This symbol of America—this enormous expression of what we had all been taught was the inner meaning of this new country we were coming to—inspired awe."[30] Jews in particular embraced Lady Liberty as a symbol of their newfound freedom. Stories were told of immigrants tearing off their tefillin bindings upon reaching New York, an act of liberation to match the freedom they felt as they neared the American port. The Statue became an enduring image, sometimes even crafted into religious items like menorahs to remind families of the liberties they should not take for granted.

For some, it reminded them that liberty meant loneliness in a new country far from home. Aaron Domnitz, recounting a night of drunken revelry with fellow Russians finding fellowship in their shared struggles in America, described the profound effect that the statue could exert on their consciousness. "Through the mist, we saw the silhouette of the Statue of Liberty. Behind her, the ocean spread out far and wide, and across the ocean somewhere were the shores of the Old Country. We were silent."[31]

Many immigrants arriving throughout the late nineteenth and early twentieth century had heard about the Liberty statue in letters from relatives, and they made a point to look out for her, often shrouded in mist, as their steamers made their way through the Narrows into port. Jacob Auerbach came to the United States from Poland at the age of seventeen. He recalls his relief at "seeing that the statue was really there with its upraised arms and the light in her hand meant they really mean it, that it isn't just a fairy tale." For him and millions of other immigrants, "it was the symbol of America being an open country, open to all comers."[32]

The meaning of the Statue of Liberty often changed over time for individuals, families, and the nation as a whole. Rocco Morelli's grandfather predicted as much when they arrived from Italy in 1920. "You see that?" the older man pointed out as they sailed through the harbor. "That's a lady. That represents *liberta*, liberty. You don't know what it is today, but with the passing of the years, you will realize what the statue means to you. I am quite sure you will thank God that you are in this country."[33] The Lazarus poem and the opening of Ellis Island made the connection for immigrants clearer over time, even if speakers and spectators at Liberty's dedication missed the message. After the ceremony, the *Jewish Messenger* echoed the republican rhetoric of de Lesseps and Depew: "The words of eloquence and good cheer will serve still more powerfully to cement France and America in lasting friendship. Both republics are liberty-loving."[34] For most people emigrating from around the world, the special bond between the United States and France meant little to them. Freedom from oppression, however, meant a lot.

IIIIIIIIIII

As immigrants arrived in overcrowded cities along the Eastern Seaboard, millions moved west to claim land or pursue fortune. Alexis de Tocqueville, during his travels to the United States in the 1830s, had recognized the western frontier as a "safety valve" for discontent among dense populations. After the Civil War concluded in the mid-1860s, the promise of the West seemed more open and available than ever, aided by improvements in transportation and the triumph of free enterprise over slaveholding estates. In 1864, the *Chicago Tribune* predicted: "Europe will open her gates like a conquered city. Her people will come forth to us subdued by admiration of our glory and envy of our perfect peace. On to the Rocky Mountains and still over to the Pacific our mighty populations will spread."[35]

At the World Columbian Exposition in Chicago in 1893, which Bartholdi and his wife attended, historian Frederick Jackson Turner expounded on the significance of the western frontier as a unique feature of American development and democracy: "This perennial rebirth, this fluidity of American life, this expansion westward with its new opportunities, its continuous touch with the simplicity of primitive society, furnish the forces dominating American character." For Turner, the frontier, like no other institution or act of assimilation, aided "Americanization," a process by which settlers shed their links to their home country and the "bondage of the past."

Liberty in Turner's understanding meant individual freedom and boundless opportunity—gifts of America's claim to the continent. Echoing earlier boasts of "Manifest Destiny," the notion that Americans had a God-given right to populate and Christianize as much territory as possible, Turner argued that "America has been another name for opportunity, and the people of the United States have taken their tone from the incessant expansion which has not only been open but has even been forced upon them." He warned his listeners, however, that the invaluable asset of frontier freedom might be disappearing. In the late nineteenth century, Americans who were worried about diminishing returns across the continent began looking beyond US borders for new opportunities to build personal fortunes, a condition that connected liberty-seeking with empire-building. Meanwhile, the America west was still embroiled in imperial warfare.

In most imaginations at the time, the west seemed wild, uncivilized, and ripe for the taking. Americans and Europeans who had never ventured beyond the Mississippi heard tales of gunfights and gambling, vast herds of roaming bison, oil and gold ventures, and battles between "cowboys and Indians." Several weeks before the Liberty statue's dedication in 1886, Apache leader Geronimo surrendered to federal forces after a prolonged fight to prevent White settlers from seizing Apache lands and confining tribes to reservations. The Dawes Act, passed in February 1887, permitted the US government to control and divide nearly ninety million acres of Native American land for settlement. Describing the frontier as a "meeting point between civilization and savagery," Turner disregarded the violence of Indigenous removal, framing it instead as a rite of passage for the "colonist" appropriating the primitive ways of the natives. "Before long," Turner explained, "he has gone to planting Indian corn and plowing with a sharp stick, he shouts the war cry and takes the scalp in orthodox Indian fashion."[36] Such impressions were popularized by celebrity cowboy Buffalo Bill Cody, who performed his *Wild West* show at the 1893 Chicago Exposition where Turner spoke about frontier virtues. Featuring horse parades, stunts, and an array of Native Americans simulating border battles with costumed cowboys, the *Wild West Show* became a hit around the world, promoting an adventurous image of the American west.

Future president Theodore Roosevelt reinforced that view in his four-volume *Winning of the West*, which traced the triumph of Americans over rival empires like Spain and "uncivilized" elements along the borderlands. "It was expansion which made us a great power," he stated, countering all opponents to "national growth," including those who criticized continental conquest, the war to liberate Cuba, or the annexation of the Philippines.[37] Roosevelt often spoke of seeking peace over aggression. "Toward all other nations, large and small, our attitude must be one of cordial and sincere friendship," he insisted in 1905. His measure of American goodwill, however, came with limits. "No weak nation that acts manfully and justly should ever have cause to fear us, and no strong power should ever be able to single us out as a subject for insolent aggression," he qualified.[38] The pithy statement "speak softly and carry a big stick" defined Roosevelt's approach to foreign affairs, implying that Americans should treat others conditionally, trying diplomacy first, while brandishing arms. In 1907, for instance, he sent the Great White Fleet of naval ships around the world to demonstrate US military power and its readiness if provoked. And he chose to deploy force at times, like when he backed a revolution in Central America to secure US control of the Panama Canal Zone.

From his first days as president of the United States after the assassination of William McKinley in 1901, Roosevelt linked physical activity and strength (the "strenuous life") to the fate of a free and influential nation. "A life of ignoble ease, a life of that peace which springs merely from lack either of desire or of power to strive after great things, is as little worthy of a nation as of an individual," he wrote in 1899. "I ask only that what every self-respecting American demands from himself and from his sons shall be demanded of the American nation as a whole."[39]

In other words, Roosevelt believed the United States required strong men willing to build a nation (and empire) one homestead at a time, defending their interests against any threat, never shrinking from warfare. Otherwise, he feared the United States and the Anglo-Saxon race risked becoming weak in a world shaped by forces of power. A country committed to preserving peace at all costs, he argued, "forfeits its right to struggle for a place among the peoples that shape the destiny of mankind." The world would be wrought "if not by us, then by some stronger and more manful race," he reminded.[40] Roosevelt's approach to foreign affairs was caricatured as coercive and militant, and for some, a threat to liberty. A 1907 cartoon in *Puck* magazine drew Roosevelt's face upon the Statue of Liberty and replaced the shining torch with a menacing "big stick," which the president had suggested US leaders wield.[41]

For Roosevelt, the United States' ability to assert strength in the world depended on its use of natural resources, which he warned were rapidly depleting. In a 1908 speech entitled "Conservation as a National Duty," he stated that "the natural resources of our country are in danger of exhaustion if we permit the old wasteful methods of exploiting them longer to continue." Like Turner, Roosevelt linked national greatness to the blessings of its wilderness and the men willing to toil there. "Our position in the world has been attained by the extent and thoroughness of the control we have achieved over nature," he said.[42]

In his 1893 speech, Turner also sounded alarm bells, predicting that the "gate of escape" along the western frontier was closing. "The frontier has gone, and with its going has closed the first period of American history," he declared.[43] Referring to data collected in the 1890 census, Turner concluded that population density in the west had increased to the point that the US Census Bureau could no longer designate any "unsettled" land of fewer than two people per square mile, making the frontier line imperceptible.[44] Though greatly exaggerated, the idea that the window of America's opportunities were closing triggered anxiety about the longevity of liberty and democracy. "The frontier individualism has from the beginning promoted democracy," Turner argued.[45]

Both Turner and Roosevelt regarded liberty as individualistic and enterprising, though tempered by a respect for the rights of others. Roosevelt had built his political career, from the 1880s onward, on fighting corruption and special interests. He believed in a hierarchy of civilizations determined by strength and will, but he fell short of promoting survival of the fittest. And he deployed federal resources to protect the rights of the proverbial little guy. "We propose . . . to extend governmental power in order to secure the liberty of the wage workers, of the men and women who toil in industry, to save the liberty of the oppressed from the oppressor," he assured in his 1912 campaign.[46] Roosevelt appreciated how nature could unleash man's appetite for self-actualization, but he cautioned against a primitive view of freedom, favoring instead the Golden Rule. "The good citizen will demand liberty for himself, and as a matter of pride he will see to it that others receive liberty which he thus claims as his own," he observed in 1910. "Probably the best test of true love of liberty in any country is the way in which minorities are treated in that country."[47]

Minorities in America, however, had been regularly sidelined as collateral damage in a race for land and wealth, and those ambitions did not end when settlers reached the West Coast in the late 1800s. As the frontier pushed against the Pacific, Roosevelt and Turner were among the many Americans who looked to exert power and influence beyond the continental borders. "American energy will continually demand a wider field for its exercise," Turner stated. Roosevelt concurred: "If we are to be a really great people, we must strive in good faith to play a great part in the world." American liberties, they believed, were dependent upon extending an American empire abroad.[48]

IIIIIIIIIII

In January 1893, American sugar and fruit plantation owners in Honolulu, Hawaii, overthrew the Indigenous leader, Queen Liliuokalani, declaring a Republic of Hawaii that they hoped the US government would annex as a new territory, thereby eliminating the tariffs they had to pay to ship their products into the United States. The American diplomat to the islands, John L. Stevens, supported the coup; he deployed the US Marines to secure it and await official approval, justifying his actions as a valid response to "circumstances of disorder." Writing to Secretary of State John Foster, who also backed the plan, Stevens stated: "The Hawaiian pear is now fully ripe, and this is the golden hour for the United States to pluck it."[49] President Grover Cleveland, however, disagreed. Considering the coup an "act of war" against a sovereign people, Cleveland reminded that a democratic nation, bonded to liberty, could not act as imperialists. "While naturally sympathizing with every effort to establish a republican form of government," he said, "it has been the settled policy of the United States to concede to people of foreign countries the same freedom and independence in the management of their domestic affairs that we have always claimed for ourselves."[50]

The president acknowledged that territory had been seized or bought by Americans from Mexicans and Native Americans, but those cases, he argued, were different since they were government-approved acquisitions of lands sparsely populated. The Hawaii affair, he believed, set a dangerous precedent of meddling in parts of the world where Americans hardly had a foothold. Harking back to his speech at the Statue of Liberty's dedication during his first term as president, Cleveland told the Senate that "the United States, in aiming to maintain itself as one of the most enlightened nations, would do its citizens gross injustice if it applied to its international relations any other than a high standard of honor and morality."[51]

The question about what to do with Hawaii reflected a larger debate among Americans about the relationship between empire and liberty. American businessmen, like those in Honolulu, wanted easier access to markets and the freedom to expand their enterprise. China beckoned as a lucrative opportunity for mass consumerism and capital investments, but the United States was late in the scramble among empires to stake claims to Chinese ports, land, and infrastructure. In 1899, Secretary of State John Hay issued the first of two "Open Door Notes" to the major imperial powers, including Great Britain, France, Russia, Germany, and Japan, proposing equal access to China and its markets without set spheres of influence. Ostensibly defending China's right to sovereignty over its territory and commerce, Hay hoped to open the door to American business by convincing the empires to play fairly. In the late 1800s, China was too weak to keep unwanted foreign trade, especially British opium, at bay. When Theodore Roosevelt warned Americans of the perils of timidity, he used China as a negative example, a civilization without muscle. The United States, at the time, did not have much clout either. Instead of demanding trade access, they could only entreat the empires to agree to more democratic rules. In 1900, Chinese anti-imperialists, tired of foreign influence, fought back in the Boxer Rebellion aimed at western businesses and missionaries.

Empires into the twentieth century continued seeking wealth and power. During the 1800s, the British Empire reaped resources from all corners of the world, exerting authority over vast colonial populations in India, Burma, Malaysia, Australia, Canada, Hong Kong, and parts of Africa and the Caribbean. By 1914, on the eve of World War I, the empire ruled over four hundred million people and controlled global economies. Many Americans living in the so-called Victorian era, named after the long-standing British queen, envied the international power of Great Britain but were wary of the unethical implications of imperialism that would undermine stated values of freedom and democracy.

Debates over imperialism in the United States came to a head in the 1890s when Cuba, not far from Florida, renewed its attempt to become

1899 cartoon, US imperialism

independent from its colonial power, Spain. Americans wavered on which side to take, but most business leaders pushed the president to help Cuba and open the island to free trade. After an explosion on the USS *Maine*, anchored near Havana, was erroneously blamed on Spain, President McKinley sent the US military to aid Cuba's revolution as well as a revolt against Spanish control in the Philippines. Assistant Secretary of the Navy Theodore Roosevelt, who had longed for a war to test his mettle and American might, was eager to send US ships to the Philippines and form his own cavalry regiment to go to Cuba. He assembled the "Rough Riders" and helped defend San Juan, a feat that boosted his national prestige a few years before he became president. Once the War of 1898 ended in Spain's defeat, the United States acquired Spain's former colonies, including Puerto Rico and Guam. Filipinos resisted annexation by the United States for another three years before they, too, became a US protectorate. Cuba remained technically free, but only under conditions allowing the US government and businesses extensive power over their island. With the addition of Hawaii, which was added as a territory in 1898, America had become a global empire in the span of several months.

The consequences of colonialism were immediately apparent. How could a republic rule over foreign people, and how could the nation assimilate millions of subjects into a democracy? Such issues had emerged during the decades of US expansion across the continent, involving Indigenous peoples, but the sudden inclusion of distant lands and populations not easily displaced triggered new anxieties about national character.

Pragmatist philosopher William James did not mince words about the end of America's moral exceptionalism, which had been "scattered in five minutes by the first temptation." In his 1903 essay on the "Philippine Question," the Harvard professor despaired that the nation had succumbed to animalistic impulses. "The country has once for all regurgitated the Declaration of Independence and the Farewell Address," he wrote. "It has deliberately pushed itself into the circle of international hatreds, and joined the common pack of wolves." Rather than enlightened liberators, as the statue in New York suggested, Americans had become "objects of fear to other lands."[52]

Some critics questioned whether Filipinos and Puerto Ricans should be allowed to become citizens and vote. Others feared an influx of new workers into an already competitive labor pool, rife with radicalism and theories of revolution. All these reasons made sense to Carl Schurz, the German immigrant who rose to the ranks of US senator, in his opposition to imperialism, citing, like William James, the hypocrisy of a republic acting as an empire. Schurz voiced the disillusionment he assumed recent immigrants were feeling once they learned the United States was not the liberty-loving nation of their dreams.

> Can you imagine the feelings of a man who all his life has struggled for human liberty and popular government . . . who believed he had found what he sought in this Republic, and thus came to love this Republic even more than the land of his birth . . . [then] sees that beloved Republic in the clutches of sinister powers which seduce and betray it into an abandonment of its most sacred principles.[53]

Schurz expressed his empathy for the former Filipino "allies" who were being killed by US forces as they continued their fight for freedom, and he rejected rationales about the benefits of US expansion into foreign territories. "They pretend," he said of American imperialists, "that in extending our sway over Porto Rico and the Philippines we merely continue that sort of territorial expansion which has been practiced by this Republic from its beginning." Schurz conceded the practicalities of continental conquests toward the Pacific coast, but he discerned these new occupations as different. He saw the Filipino-American war as "a war against our own Republic . . . a war against ourselves as a free people." Reminding his audience that the whole world was watching, Schurz called upon leaders to relinquish their claims for the sake of moral "prestige." Such a magnanimous act, he promised, would "achieve the grandest triumph of the democratic idea that history knows of" and Americans would "stand infinitely mightier before the world than any number of subjugated vassals could make them."[54]

Schurz also couched his arguments in terms of civilization, expressing his fears that foreign influences could dilute the democratic system by granting the franchise to ignorant voters. Citing the "disorderly tendencies" of Indigenous peoples in Puerto Rico and the Pacific Islands, Schurz urged the United States to civilize and educate them, so "they will not with their disorders and corruptions contaminate our institutions, the integrity of which is not only to ourselves, but to liberty-loving mankind."[55] Schurz was not open minded about expanding the voting pool, even for US citizens. In 1894, he wrote an editorial for *Harper's* opposing woman's suffrage, saying, "The belief is fast gaining ground that in the democratization of our institutions by enlargements of the suffrage we have gone fully as far as the safety of the republic will warrant, and that it is much more advisable to sift the body of voters by educational requirements and the like, than to expand it by indiscriminating additions." Schurz, who had emigrated from Germany after the revolutions of 1848, seemed willing to shut the door behind him, convinced that a fragile American republic could not handle mass democratic inclusion.[56]

While Schurz referred to uncivilized peoples as a reason to resist imperialism, other American leaders saw the vulnerability of Spain's former colonies as a motive for their subjugation. President McKinley justified his decision to keep the Philippines with a measure of chagrin, claiming the territory "dropped into our laps." Ultimately, he concluded that the Filipinos, "unfit for self-government," were better off within the American empire rather than with France, Germany, or Spain. "There was nothing left for us to do but to take them all, and to educate the Filipinos, and uplift and civilize and Christianize them," he said.[57] Theodore Roosevelt concurred with McKinley. In an era of ideas about social Darwinism, based on a hierarchy of the fittest and Victorian notions of uplifting the less fortunate, Roosevelt was among the White elites who believed the superior race had a duty to help more primitive cultures assimilate into the dominant civilization. In the midst of the Filipino-American War, British writer Rudyard Kipling sent his friend Roosevelt a telling poem entitled "The White Man's Burden," celebrating the United States' rite of passage into the role of an empire. A tone of racial superiority framed the piece, as Kipling called upon Americans to:

Take up the White Man's burden—
Send forth the best ye breed—
Go bind your sons to exile
To serve your captives' need;
To wait in heavy harness
On fluttered folk and wild—
Your new-caught, sullen peoples,
Half devil and half child.

The duty of uplift, Kipling wrote, wasn't easy. It was thankless work, he warned. However, he assured Americans it was well worth the effort to reap the rewards of colonialism while gradually teaching Indigenous people the meaning of freedom.[58]

Senator Benjamin Tillman read the poem as a cautionary tale, and he used it to urge his fellow Congressman to vote against the annexation of distant islands filled with dark-skinned people. Reminding listeners of the more familiar "burden" of incorporating Black Americans into free society and the body politic, he argued that two or more races "can not [*sic*] mix or mingle without deterioration and injury to both and the ultimate destruction of the civilization of the higher." Appealing to White Americans' racist sensibilities, Tillman insisted that the "growth of commerce" abroad and the "money making of the few" amounted to sacrificing social order for profit. "Why do we as a people want to incorporate into our citizenship ten millions more of different or of differing races?" he asked. "Those peoples are not suited to our institutions. They are not ready for liberty as we understand it. They do not want it."[59] Like Schurz, Tillman factored in race and political maturity. Twelve years after Liberty Enlightening the World was unveiled in New York, US politicians were using the rhetoric of liberty to both support and forestall the United States' emergence as an empire.

||||||||||||

Returning from a two-year trip throughout Europe in 1894, Black intellectual W. E. B. Du Bois described his experience aboard a ship carrying him back to the United States.

> A new land loomed there beyond the horizon and we began searching the skies. I who was born there was also approaching something new and untried after 24 years of preparation. At last it loomed on the morning when we saw the Statue of Liberty. I know not what multitude of emotions surged in the others, but I had to recall that mischievous little French girl whose eyes twinkled as she said: 'Oh yes the Statue of Liberty! With its back toward America, and its face toward France.'[60]

Du Bois, an acute observer of the gaps between idealism and realism, noticed that Liberty's attention was turned toward arriving migrants more than the oppressed people in the nation extending behind her. By and large, Black Americans were not immigrants. They had been forcibly brought to the Western Hemisphere during the slave trade. Yet the liberties afforded to White Americans continued to elude them decades after the Civil War. The chains of bondage crushed under Liberty's left foot were barely visible, an afterthought at best. With the statue's gaze set on the wide Atlantic and her torch turned toward the rest of the world, American problems of race and class seemed to fall beyond her peripheral vision. Du Bois did not take issue with Liberty's general premise or her promise to uplift the less fortunate. But he wanted people of color to be included. While Liberty looked away, Du Bois spent much of his adult life analyzing the "Negro Problem" in America that kept Blacks from securing the means to life, liberty, and the pursuit of happiness.[61]

Born in Massachusetts in 1868, Du Bois accepted his generation's prevailing assumptions about progress and hierarchy, and he did not fault White people for their ambitions. As he explained in his autobiography, "I was not questioning the world movement in itself. What the white world was doing, its goals and ideals, I had not doubted were quite right. What was wrong was that I and people like me and thousands of others who might have my ability and aspiration, were refused permission to be a part of this world."[62] Black Americans were not the only ones left out. Du Bois identified a "color line" that "belts the world," separating the "haves" and the "have nots" on terms of color and civilization. In his writings, Du Bois often traced the rise of civilizations and talked about the need for the "talented tenth," the most educated and capable among Blacks, to set a high bar for the rest of the race to strive for. "The Negro race, like all races, is going to be saved by its exceptional men," he assured.[63] Blacks, he believed, had to help themselves. The problem was that Whites set the rules and conditions that advanced their interests at the expense of "the other."

Du Bois described his "double-consciousness," always measured in relation to superior Whites and thus always aware of his identity as "the other."[64] Blacks were not *innately* inferior, Du Bois insisted, but they absorbed the negative opinions of Whites who considered them a problem—a social problem because they were not incorporated into the dominant culture and a political problem because exclusionary practices made a lie of freedom and liberty for all. Though Du Bois realized that people of color everywhere were relegated to a lower status, he saw race issues in America as more particular and profound. "Questions of labor, caste, ignorance and race were bound to arise in America," he said, "they were simply complicated here and intensified there by the presence of the Negro."[65] While studying abroad in Germany, Du Bois had faced less discrimination than in the United States, where education for Blacks was substandard, voting rights withheld, and violence against them brutal.

Lynching, for example, threatened the lives of Blacks for any alleged infringement of racial hierarchy. In the late nineteenth century, hundreds of Blacks in the United States were taken from their homes, tortured, mutilated, and murdered by Whites who rarely faced legal consequences for their crimes. In 1892 alone, over two hundred lynchings were recorded, mostly in southern states. Du Bois spoke out against the assaults along with activists such as Ida B. Wells, the most prominent spokesperson on the issue in her time. As local White newspapers rationalized lynching as punishment for Black crimes, Wells acted as an investigative journalist, writing editorials and pamphlets that exposed the truth about White perpetrators of violence, who often attacked economically successful or "uppity" Blacks.[66] For her outspokenness, Wells became a target of threats, and her newspaper office was ransacked. Frederick Douglass wrote to Wells in 1892, commending her for her courage.

> Thank you for your faithful paper on the lynch abomination now generally practiced against colored people in the South. There has been no word equal to it in convincing power. I have spoken, but my word is feeble in comparison. . . . Brave woman![67]

Racial violence and the widespread disenfranchisement of Black Americans showed that progress since the Civil War had not been linear. Freedoms granted in the Constitution were effectively rolled back by Jim Crow laws, personal discrimination, and institutional limits on housing, business loans, employment, and education. As a Black woman, Wells experienced firsthand how minorities were mistreated in the United States. She spoke up for the millions of voiceless, voteless women and Blacks who were denied basic civil rights. "Eternal vigilance is the price of liberty," she professed.[68] Black Americans knew all too well that rights and freedoms once gained could be circumscribed or taken away. Like Du Bois noted, the most visible symbol of liberty in the United States, the statue in New

York, had her eyes turned away from the "Negro Problem," leaving people of color largely alone in bringing race problems to light.

IIIIIIIIIII

As Black Americans struggled against racial barriers, White men and women of the working class were preoccupied with their own problems of survival. The Gilded Age's gap between the poorest and the richest of Americans was wide, as businessmen such as William Vanderbilt, Andrew Carnegie, and John D. Rockefeller built corporate empires and vast mansions. Meanwhile, those employed in urban factories were crowded in tight tenement quarters that housed multiple families with many children who often earned income by taking industrial jobs along with their parents. In an era of rapid industrialization, over 90 percent of families lived below the poverty line, and periodic bouts of economic depression increased the squeeze on meager incomes.[69]

Wealth exerted a disproportionate influence on politicians and their policies. "There are two things that are important in politics. The first is money, and I can't remember what the second one is," quipped power broker Mark Hanna. Corrupt politicians reaped the financial benefits of these lobbying deals, but the nation's leaders also supported big business because they wanted to boost the economic health of the United States in a competitive global system. Enterprise expanded abroad to find export markets for the gross national product, including agriculture, and to secure raw materials for manufacturing. The fate of the republic, free marketers insisted, depended on its economic growth.

Innovations also eased life at home. Steel was used to make stronger, safer bridges and buildings, and oil fueled technologies in transportation. Corporate patrons spent a portion of their profits for the public good, establishing schools, libraries, parks, museums, and concert venues. Skyscrapers rose as symbols of corporate and national power. By the end of the nineteenth century, the US had risen from an agrarian, developing nation to the most powerful economic engine in the world. Capitalism in the United States, many argued, was doing a lot of good. As clergyman Josiah

Strong predicted in 1885, in the "final competition of the races" for limited land and resources, "the representative of the largest liberty, the purest Christianity, the highest civilization . . . will spread itself over the earth."[70]

Economic power, however, did not ease the life or the minds of every American. Poet Walt Whitman warned, "If the United States, like the countries of the Old World, are also to grow vast crops of poor, desperate, dissatisfied, nomadic, miserably-waged populations . . . then our republican experiment, notwithstanding all its surface-successes, is at heart an unhealthy failure."[71]

Joseph Pulitzer also raised concerns about the fate of republican values. "We all want prosperity, but not at the expense of liberty," he said. "Poverty is not as great a danger to liberty as is wealth, with its corrupting, demoralizing influences. . . . Let us never have a government at Washington owing its retention to the power of the millionaires rather than to the will of the millions."[72]

Millions of workers felt their freedoms violated as they were expected to spend long hours performing hard manual labor in what many considered inhumane conditions. In the 1890s, there were no safety standards, wage and hour laws, vacation days, sick days, or workers' compensation for injury. Many low-wage employees felt the need to accept the terms of their employer and avoid any infraction that could risk their jobs. Other workers decided their best bet was to join unions to protect themselves and fight for their rights. Each year, thousands of strikes erupted as laborers refused to work until employers granted their demands for wage increases, safety measures, and fewer hours.

According to union leaders such as Samuel Gompers of the AFL, freedom was at stake. "Show me the country that has no strikes and I'll show you the country in which there is no liberty," he said. Unions, he argued, were a necessary correction to cutthroat capitalism that put profits above human welfare. Calling industrial capitalism a new form of slavery, he believed that a republic could not survive without allowing workers to organize and vote in their own interests. Union action, however, was dangerous, as violence broke out between workers and the authorities hired by employers to crack down on dissent. Hundreds of men and women lost their lives, including Industrial Workers of the World (IWW) activist Joe Hill, a Swedish immigrant who was executed in 1914 for a spurious murder charge without trial in Utah. Hill had written dozens of songs advocating for workers' rights with lyrics exhorting:

> *Workers of the world awaken. Break your chains, demand your rights.*
> *All the wealth you make is taken, by exploiting parasites.*
> *Shall you kneel in deep submission from your cradle to your grave?*
> *Is the height of your ambition to be a good and willing slave?*[73]

The definition of economic freedom depended on whom one asked—the capitalist exercising their rights to free enterprise and wealth security or the laborer defending their rights to aspire to and acquire the same opportunities.

IIIIIIIIIII

On the afternoon of Saturday, December 2, 1916, President Woodrow Wilson sailed down the Hudson River on the yacht *Mayflower*, leading a procession to Bedloe's Island. He was scheduled to flip the switch to activate the new lights installed in the statue's torch, an upgrade funded by Joseph Pulitzer's paper the *New York World*, now in the hands of Pulitzer's son Ralph. The National Woman Suffrage Association announced they also would attend the ceremony, albeit in protest. They had arranged for female pilot Mrs. Richberg-Hornsby to fly over the president's procession and drop "bombs" of petitions calling for an immediate amendment to the Constitution to guarantee women's right to vote.[74] The fight for liberty, they reminded, remained woefully incomplete.

Bartholdi had died in Paris twelve years earlier, though his thoughts remained with Lady Liberty to the end of his life. His last letters to American Committee alumnus Richard Butler reflected concerns about copyrights and reproductions of his masterpiece.[75] At the 1916 ceremony, a contingent of French dignitaries were present to emphasize Bartholdi's original, republican purpose of Liberty Enlightening the World and the transatlantic friendship it sealed. The statue's meaning, however, was changing once again. During his speech that evening at the Waldorf-Astoria Hotel, Ralph Pulitzer said he looked forward to the day when people would consider the Goddess of Liberty as a Goddess of Peace, a poignant hope at a time when most of the world was at war. Wilson bolstered the theme of peace in his own remarks. "Peace is going to come to the world only with Liberty," he stated. "There is a great responsibility in having adopted Liberty as our ideal, because we must illustrate it in what we do."[76]

After World War I broke out in Europe in 1914, Wilson had committed the United States to a policy of neutrality and peace, partly to save American lives and partly to keep American commerce out of the firing line. By 1916, however, it was clear that US neutrality was no longer recognized. German submarines attacked US merchant and passenger vessels throughout the Atlantic, claiming they carried contraband to support the militaries of Great Britain and France. Sometimes they did. Over the years, public opinion in the United States had shifted to supporting the two nations with historically stronger ties to American interests.

Wilson used the image and symbolism of the Statue of Liberty effectively during his 1916 campaign for a second term and during US war mobilization the following year. A political poster showed Wilson against the backdrop of the Statue of Liberty, and "Liberty bonds" were sold to raise money for the war effort. A recruitment ad in 1917, featuring the famous statue, encouraged men to "Enlist in the Navy" "For Liberty's Sake." But Wilson, like many of his contemporaries, struggled to reconcile American principles of liberty with the American practice of imperialism. He sent the US Marines to intervene in Latin America and the Caribbean whenever disorder erupted and US interests were threatened, at one point vowing to "teach South American republics to elect good men."[77] In other areas of the world, he applied softer forms of power and aided gradual independence. The 1916 Philippine Autonomy Act allowed the US-controlled territory to form its own senate to practice self-government. Wilson believed that every nation could become democratic, but he considered stability and clean government as prerequisites. When he finally asked Congress for a declaration of war against Germany, he put the decision in these terms: "The world must be made safe for democracy," he said. "Its peace must be planted upon the tested foundations of political liberty. We have no selfish ends to serve."[78]

When Wilson went to Paris in 1918 to negotiate the postwar treaty, he hoped to reset international relations on a new footing. Like the Open Door Notes, Wilson called for equal access to foreign markets, free trade, and fair play among the major powers. The victors of the Great War, however, demanded their spoils, including added territories. Wilson in the end failed to convince imperialists in Great Britain, France, Japan, and the United States to relinquish their colonial control. However, he did help establish an American way of empire, one in which informal influence replaced formal colonial arrangements. Policymakers in the United States would continue to develop a global presence using a mix of money, diplomacy, and military deployment, all the while criticizing more traditional forms of imperialism throughout the twentieth century.

IIIIIIIIIII

On Liberty's dedication day in 1886, President Cleveland had also emphasized peace over war by highlighting the difference between the statue's pacifism and the battle memorials of antiquity. The fact that Americans were dedicating a monument to peace, he said, mattered, as it reflected the character of the nation and the course of its history. Chauncey Depew's speech that day followed Cleveland's lead: "In all ages the achievements of man and his aspirations have been represented in symbols," he told his audience. "Races have disappeared and no record remains of their rise or fall, but by their monuments we know their history. The huge monoliths of the Assyrians and the obelisks of the Egyptians tell their stories of forgotten civilizations, but the sole purpose of their erection was to glorify rulers and preserve the boasts of conquerors. They teach sad lessons of the vanity of ambition, the cruelty of arbitrary power, and the miseries of mankind."[79]

These rhetorical attempts to set the United States apart from warrior-forward civilizations was, of course, problematic. The United States had erected its own Egyptian obelisk in the nation's capital only a few years before Liberty's unveiling. The US republic, which had fought for its independence from British control in the 1770s, had annexed colonies around the world a century later. American political, military, and business leaders did make a "vanity of ambition" and boasted of their conquests. They extended the US empire out, as the fruits of empire (resources and people) came into US cities. Russian revolutionary Alexandra Kollontai noted the imbalance of imperial symbols as she sailed away from New York on her way back to join the Bolsheviks in the new Soviet Union. "Is that the Statue of Liberty?" she pondered, as her ship headed into the Atlantic. "Was this powerless, tiny figure shrinking before the all-powerful gigantic skyscrapers, those guardians of financial deals, the Statue of Liberty we had pictured to ourselves?" Kollontai was disappointed that the "kings of American capitalism" and the buildings they occupied seemed to better represent the "spirit" of America than the "pitiful, shrunken, green statue that seems to be embarrassed."[80]

Freedom remained relative and subjective. As President Wilson stated in 1916, liberty—the statue and the virtue—amounted to what Americans made of it. "We can take to ourselves the dignity of Liberty only as we illustrate the fact and the true spirit of Liberty," he said.[81] The meaning of liberty, in other words, was contingent. It did not apply to everyone equally. And, as debates about freedom and rights revealed, the symbolism of Lady Liberty was pliant enough to appeal to multiple viewpoints and cover a multitude of sins.

CHAPTER 4

EMPIRE AND LIBERTY IN CRISIS—1931

When the Empire State Building committee conducted its opening ceremonies on the morning of May 1, 1931, New York governor Franklin D. Roosevelt, former governor Al Smith, and President Herbert Hoover set aside their rivalries to celebrate the remarkable achievement. The truce was short lived. On the front page of the *New York Times* that same day, Roosevelt was quoted as deriding Hoover and his handling of the deepening economic depression. Addressing the Young Democratic Club at the Hotel Astor the previous evening, Roosevelt chastised the Republican response to the crisis as "reactionary" and "opposed to fundamental governmental reform."[1]

The occasion marked the first major speech on national issues that Roosevelt delivered since announcing his run for the 1932 presidential election. In the talk, he laid out a vision for a "broad road" forward, assuring his audience that the Democratic Party represented the best hope to lead the American people out of ruin. There was hard work to do. But from atop the tallest structure in the world, Roosevelt might have caught a glimpse of happier days ahead.

The finished Empire State Building stood as a symbol of past achievements and a brighter future, reflecting what American ingenuity, cooperation, and sheer manpower were capable of accomplishing. The cooperative spirit continued during the opening ceremonies. At 11:30 that morning, Al Smith's grandchildren cut the ribbon to clear the main entrance for visitors, and soon after, President Hoover pressed a telegraph button from his White House office to formally switch on the lights within the new 1,250-foot building. During a buffet luncheon on the eighty-sixth floor attended by 350 invited guests, Smith, who headed the events as president of Empire State Inc., read a congratulatory message from Hoover, his opponent in the 1928 election. Hoover commended everyone who took part in conceptualizing and constructing "one of the outstanding glories of a great city." Smith went further, declaring the structure an object of "universal" significance for all nations. "Probably no building in the history of the world has brought about such unusual interest in its progress," he said.[2]

Newspapers in the United States and around the globe backed Smith's claim by marking the event in their daily editions. On June 7, the *Ogden Standard-Examiner* of Utah stoked their subscribers' curiosity by offering a full-page piece comparing the Empire State Building's height to other notable structures, including the Eiffel Tower and the biblical tower of Babel.[3] Other reporters expressed pride in whatever materials their region had contributed, even years after its completion. The *Pensacola News Journal* ran an article in August 1932 reminding residents that "Tools Made Here Were Used in Construction of Empire State Building."[4]

Empire State Building

In its promotional booklet, Empire State Inc. dedicated the new structure "to the business and industry of all the world," declaring it was meant to "further the future industry, achievement and prosperity of the millions who may find aspiration in what it represents."[5] International trade had interlaced the fate of countries over the course of the early twentieth century, a circumstance that made the 1929 stock market crash in New York, the hub of US empire, a global disaster. Smith hit this point during the opening event as well, stating that his pet project was "intended to stimulate trade, commerce, and continue to make New York the imperial city of the world." "The Empire State Building," he boasted, "stands today as the greatest monument to ingenuity, to skill, to brain power, to muscle power, the tallest thing in the world today produced by the hand of man."[6] His rhetoric about the enduring power of American empire was intended for ears near and far.

The world was listening. London's *Daily Mail*, for one, had followed the Empire State Building's formation with regular updates for its Atlantic-edition readers. A full-page editorial in November 1930 by W. F. Bullock on New York's "Country Estates in the Clouds" featured an early review of the "new monster" rapidly rising in the middle of Manhattan. Bullock recounted his experience at the heights of the unfinished structure and remarked upon its magnitude and beauty. He concluded his article, however, with a backhanded compliment: "As the last real American touch, the city's lift laws have been rewritten to permit occupants to shoot up and down at the rate of 1,000 feet a minute. What more could life offer?"[7] The American pursuit of greatness, he implied, compelled an insatiable need to be the fastest, tallest, and best, as though power and size were all that mattered.

Helen Keller inferred as much when she wrote of her trip to the top of the Empire State Building and the feelings it evoked. Though blind and deaf, Keller wrote a colorful account in early 1932 of what she "saw" from the observation deck. Her "imagination," she explained, allowed her to envision "distances and horizons that reach to the end of the world." After mentioning the thrill of being "whizzed" to the heavens by the Otis elevator, Keller recalled looking down on the "jewel" of Manhattan and up to the "sun and stars" that now appeared as mere "suburbs of New York." The view, for Keller, worked like a tonic. "All sense of depression and hard times vanished [and] I felt like being frivolous with the stars." Keller ventured to guess that foreigners would scoff at such sentiments. "A Frenchman," she presumed, might find fault with American proclivity for playing "god," with the "highest, the largest, the most costly . . . vanity." But whereas the world decried American hubris, Keller defended her nation's "passionate skill, arduous and fearless idealism." "Let cynics and supersensitive souls say what they will about American materialism," she told critics. "Beneath the surface are poetry, mysticism and inspiration that the Empire Building somehow symbolizes."[8]

The buoyancy of American optimism may have seemed misplaced from the viewpoint of foreign observers struggling with a recession made worse by US protectionist policies. Contrary to Roosevelt's criticisms of the Republican administration, Hoover had made some efforts to intervene in the market to boost the domestic economy, at the expense of international stability. The Smoot-Hawley Tariff, passed in June 1930, initiated the highest tariffs on imports in US history, spurring retaliatory policies worldwide. In 1931, Great Britain abandoned the gold standard, which had anchored exchange rates and international finance, and the US followed suit two years later, during Roosevelt's first term. Given this context, British belittling of American engineering triumphs like Empire State likely had more to do with resentments over US self-aggrandizement during hard times.

Reports on the Empire State Building's official dedication in newspapers abroad were otherwise brief. The *London Times* noted the event hosted by Smith with a 230-word summary among columns of minor news items. There were bigger stories to report, particularly as May Day riots erupted around Europe. Protests were quelled by police in London's Hyde Park, while the Socialist Party filled public spaces in Berlin, and communists took to the streets in Johannesburg. In Japan, one thousand labor activists were arrested during demonstrations that month. Meanwhile, unrest in Spain, transitioning to a precarious republic, made headlines daily. So did imperial expansion. As ordinary people struggled to find work and make ends meet, leaders in Italy, Germany, and Japan exploited the chaos to make plays for power and forge inroads further afield. Japan moved on mainland China in the fall of 1931, occupying much of Manchuria after the staged Mukden incident that military leaders used as a pretext for retaliation. Less than two years later, in March 1933, the island empire made its ambitions official by withdrawing from the League of Nations, which had attempted to forestall international conflict since World War I. Signs of another world war became more apparent by the mid-to-late 1930s, but in 1931, Americans were mostly concerned about receiving their next paycheck.

IIIIIIIIIII

During the opening ceremonies, Al Smith did not fail to thank the thousands of workers who labored to finish the Empire State Building nearly two weeks ahead of schedule. But he referred to them only in the abstract, using the fictionalized figure of little "Tony" and his mother, who had been featured in a recent issue of the *Evening Post*, to illustrate his praise. The *Post* depicted a young mother, gazing from the roof of their tenement quarters to the new skyscraper, telling her son to take pride: "Tony, your old man is building that."[9] Smith did not go on to mention what had happened to that working-class family now that the building was completed or whether Tony's old man was out of a job.

While teams of unionized laborers moved on to the next major project, the end of the Empire State construction left many workers high and dry. About eight million people in the United States were unemployed in 1931, approaching 15 percent by the spring, and the end was nowhere in sight. Unemployment rates broke records in 1933 when they reached nearly 25 percent, despite the best efforts of federal intervention. In an attempt to reduce the pool of job seekers and relieve the strains on public welfare, Hoover issued an executive decision in the fall of 1930 to refuse almost all new visas. The policy halted immigration by nearly 90 percent, while eighteen thousand deportations reversed the flow of noncitizen travelers. More people were leaving the country than coming in.

Aniello Conte, an undocumented Italian migrant who helped construct the colossus on Fifth Avenue, was among those forced to go home.

Home, for Conte, was the fishing island of Ponza, off the west coast of Italy, where his wife and children waited for him and the wages he made while working odd jobs in New York. In the early 1930s, Conte picked up day-laborer slots as a brick-and-cement layer on Empire State, commuting to the construction site from his 150th Street tenement dwelling in the Bronx. After the project ended, Conte traveled home to see his family and the fruits of his labor, including a new house he could afford to build because of his employment in the United States. He lived the rest of his life as a fisherman and farmer on Ponza, passing away in 1983, just short of his one-hundredth birthday. His journeys to America, however, remained poignant, inspiring at least one of his descendants to follow in his footsteps. In the 1970s, four decades after Conte's adventures in New York City, his daughter Florinda and her husband immigrated to the United States, settling in the Melrose Park area of the Bronx where her father had lived to make ends meet during the Depression.[10]

As bad as the economic woes were in the United States in the 1930s, unemployment rates abroad were often much worse. Italians, under fascist control throughout the 1920s, had not fully recovered from the effects of the Great War, and they relied heavily on trade. When the United States cut back on their investments and trade agreements in foreign countries, economies were devastated. In Germany, the Weimar Republic could no longer pay its World War I reparations to France and Great Britain, causing a vicious cycle of decreased cash flow. Vienna Kreditanstalt, Austria's major bank, collapsed in May of 1931, and a panic soon spread throughout Europe. World unemployment peaked in 1932 at about 30 percent, a situation that made the masses desperate for a leader who could promise not only relief but a return to glory. The Empire State Building had provided some relief for wage earners, but it also stood as a source of pride and a promise of American greatness. In 1933, Adolf Hitler assumed power in Germany with a similar message, pledging to restore the strength and dignity of the Vaterland. He did not fulfill that promise by building a modernized monument. Instead, he built a modernized army.

IIIIIIIIIII

About a month after the first visitors entered the Empire State Building and marveled at its height, the *Ogden Standard-Examiner* speculated about what made New York City's modern miracle possible when countless other attempts at constructing a tower to the heavens had failed. Reminding readers of "the first skyscraper" assembled but ultimately unfinished on the plains of ancient Babylon, the *Ogden* article posed a bold claim of revisionist history. The biblical story of the Tower of Babel is typically told as a cautionary tale about human hubris. In the traditional telling, the team of artisans constructing the tower were working together well—so well, in fact, that their ambitions offended God. To thwart their progress, God put a curse upon their project by jumbling their communication. Suddenly, the workmen began speaking in a variety of languages, unintelligible to each other. The tower, after that, could go no higher.

The *Ogden Standard-Examiner*, however, had a different take on the reason why the Babel project was abandoned. It wasn't the confusion of languages, they argued, but the lack of mechanized devices to transport heavy materials. In short, the success of the Empire State Building came down to one apparatus: the elevator. The article's headline put it succinctly, stating that "elevators made possible the 1,248-foot tower and the lack of them doomed the Biblical skyscraper." Diversity, the Ogden editorial made clear, was not the problem, especially since New York City's population and workforce was composed of multiple ethnicities and languages. "Among the seven million people who live within the boundaries of the five counties which make up New York City, there are represented more races and nationalities than in any other metropolis. And they all do business." Differences, the essay suggested, did not impose limits on what a workforce could do when united in purpose. But the elevator made up for the gaps in human weakness, providing mechanics where muscle fell short. Contrary to *Daily Mail* journalist W. F. Bullock and his derogatory comment about the American demand for efficiency, the Utah journalists, in agreement with Helen Keller, celebrated the need for speed. "Imagine traveling straight up, inside a man-made structure, at a speed greater than twenty miles an hour!" they exclaimed.[11]

In a second piece posted in late May entitled "Taking the Lift to the Sun," *Daily Mail* correspondent Bullock gauged reactions from visitors at the top of the skyscraper, "where they look down on the rest of the world." Bullock's snide remark was in keeping with his earlier criticisms of American hustle, but he captured in words what the thrill was all about. "At night, millions of lights" dazzle "as a kaleidoscope of flickering colour," he wrote. "Awed by the solemnity, a visitor stood breathless." One woman fretted: "Is it my imagination or do you think the building is moving?"[12]

The British reporter was not the only critic with mixed reviews of the new structure or doubts about its justification in the midst of the Depression. American author Edmund Wilson, writing for the *New Republic* in 1931, also commented on its handsome design but ultimate uselessness. In the most vivid prose, Wilson described the "towering plinth" as exuding an "effect of lightness," despite its mass, with its "silver cap" "as bright and brittle as a Christmas-tree globe." On cold winter mornings, he went on, "it seems semi-translucent like a cake of ice." "Only rarely," he admitted, "in glaring midday does it look metallic, functional and hard like a machine-part." Yet Wilson still appraised the building as containing little value. If need nudged the mothers of invention, the Empire State Inc. investors, Wilson argued, had it backward. The abundant office space, he predicted, would remain largely unoccupied, at best siphoning business from nearby buildings. At worst, it would cause more traffic jams in an already congested part of the city. For Wilson, the building's beauty did not supersede the sum of its parts, especially when juxtaposed with the squalid circumstances of many New Yorkers struggling with the effects of failed capitalism in 1931.

> And here is the pile of stone, brick, nickel and steel, the shell of offices, shafts, windows and steps, that outmultiplies and outstacks them all—that, more purposeless and superfluous than any, is being advertised as a triumph in the hour when the planless competitive society, the

> dehumanized urban community, of which it represents the culmination, is bankrupt.

For all of Wilson's vitriol, however, his flamboyant depictions of every detail of the building, both inside and out, must have piqued the interest of readers inspired to see it for themselves. His editorial tour of the interior included the grand entrance hall "made of gray German marble with an effect of crushed strawberries," and the elevator doors resembling "Egyptian tombs." Wilson even illustrated the awesome views from the top that left most observers speechless:

> To the west, the steamboats and barges moving slowly along the Hudson; to the south, the narrowing wedge of the island studded and pronged at the lower end with its own planting of enormous buildings; to the east, the iron blue-gray East River, strung across with black skeleton bridges, a gray airplane above it; to the north, the dwindled Chrysler tower, a tinny; scaled armadillo-tail ending in a stiff stinglike drill.[13]

Al Smith couldn't have promoted it better himself.

After only a few weeks open, the Empire State Building appeared to be a hit, as thousands arrived to pay the dollar ticket to make the trip to the top. Most were tourists from out of state or out of the country, not local New Yorkers. City residents, nevertheless, also registered their opinions about living or working in or near the new building. "We get plenty of sunlight and that aids work," one unnamed office employee told W. F. Bullock. "We see lots of airplanes, dirigibles, and occasionally a Zeppelin." Supervisors disliked the constant distractions, taking workers' attention from their tasks. And, by most accounts, life in Midtown Manhattan was no longer routine. "Sometimes we see a dreadful tragedy," the employee acknowledged. "The other day we saw a girl jump from the twenty-fifth floor. We didn't like that."[14]

Suicides and suicide attempts started even before the building became publicly accessible. During construction, one laid-off worker allegedly utilized the elevator shaft to hurl himself to his death. Then, in November 1932, an unidentified German man leaped from the 102nd floor in front of twenty-or-so stunned tourists. Some attempts were nonfatal, with visitors landing on a nearby ledge or girders, or getting swept by the wind into a lower window. Others intending to jump lost their nerve once they reached the summit. By 1934, the observatory manager, Joe Bolton, was training employees to spot possible despondents as they lined up to purchase tickets. The sheer height of the building lent drama to the act of self-demise. So did the lack of safety barriers at the edge of the eighty-sixth-floor balcony. In the first sixteen years of its existence, the building's open-air deck did not include the protective metal caging that was installed in 1947, after five jumps occurred within a three-week period, including that of twenty-three-year-old Evelyn McHale, a bookkeeper who landed on a parked limousine "so calmly" and without apparent injury that a photograph of her taken within minutes of her death was dubbed "the most beautiful suicide."[15]

The Empire State Building attracted attention for its grandeur from most visitors and passersby. However, it could also trigger bouts of anxiety in those intimidated by its looming size. In the Valentine's Day 1931 edition of the New York *Daily News*, a fictionalized woman named Nancy becomes increasingly frightened by the skyscraper as it grows "taller and taller" during the final weeks of construction. "Nancy rode down 5th Ave. atop a bus," the short story began, "watching over her shoulder the Empire State building falling down upon her." The height of the building, which dwarfed the structures surrounding it, seemed "impossible" to Nancy. "The whole unearthly beauty of it was almost impossible to bear." As she goes about her errands, Nancy can't escape the feeling that the skyscraper is watching her and she becomes wary of turning her back on it, like committing "a sacrilege." But being near the structure also had its perks. Though Nancy lived in "bleak" conditions, the ambitious project on Fifth Avenue could make her forget her more mundane troubles. "Five months in New York had taught Nancy that one didn't mind going to bed hungry if there was a building so tall that it lived with the stars and sun to look at in the morning."[16] Despite the economic Depression, the Empire State Building gave New Yorkers at least something to think about, and talk about, even if its modern advancements caused them some anxiety, as though it were a relentless beast bent on pursuing them wherever they went.

IIIIIIIIIII

The petite blonde standing on the Empire State Building's observatory level did not look entirely comfortable. Behind a shy smile, she appeared as if she had forced herself to visit the open-air deck, marshaling a determination to be part of it or make her peace with it, nerves notwithstanding. Observers gathered as much as she gamely answered their questions, admitting to a fear of heights. She could have pretended to be brave. She was an actress, after all. Her name was Fay Wray.

While promoting the new film, *King Kong*, in which she had a starring role, Wray took time to stop in New York City to check out the landmark that her movie helped make famous and more profitable. In the closing scenes, Kong scales the Empire State Building's highest point, clutching a screaming Wray in his hand. Released in 1933, the movie begins in New York with eccentric director Carl Denham scouring Times Square for a woman brave enough or desperate enough to venture with him to parts unknown and star as his leading lady. He finds Ann Darrow, played by Wray, who is reduced to stealing food to feed herself during the Depression.

In the absence of other prospects, she takes the job, sailing with an all-male crew to a remote island populated by dark-skinned natives, armed with spears and covered in tribal paint. The islanders are afraid, the crew discovers, but not of the White newcomers. Their fear, instead, is stoked by the presence of a giant black gorilla, called Kong, who occasionally raids their village for human bounty. When Kong becomes enamored of Ann Darrow, the film crew fights to save her, which they eventually do, before capturing Kong to take back to New York for public display. However, their moneymaking scheme goes quickly awry, as Kong breaks loose from his chains, finds Darrow, and carries her to the top of the Empire State

Building, where the gorilla-creature is eventually killed by fighter planes. That moment marked the skyscraper as well as Wray for the rest of her life. As the actress remarked in the late 1960s, "I no longer make an effort to escape. When I'm in New York, I look at the Empire State Building and feel as though it belongs to me . . . or is it vice versa?"[17]

In its time, *King Kong* was received enthusiastically as a cutting-edge action film, dazzling audiences with its special effects. Since then, critics have unpacked the film's patronizing depiction of foreign cultures and the persistence of racial stereotypes. Carl Denham and his film crew initially judge the natives of Skull Island as primitive, superstitious, and thus ignorant—that is, until they, too, encounter Kong, the black beast. The monster-like figure of Kong, in the form of a gorilla, is also racially charged. Blacks in the United States were often ridiculed by White supremacists and eugenicists for their African ancestry, dark skin color, and so-called "ape-like" facial features.

The fact that Kong becomes obsessed with the beautiful blonde, Ann Darrow, sets up another trope of American race culture that had served as the basis for "good vs. evil" film narratives dating back to the release of D. W. Griffith's racist epic *Birth of a Nation* in 1915. Like the lazy, lustful, black-faced characters featured in Griffith's film, Kong must be put in his place by White superiors. Denham voices the problem and its solution in the dialogue of *King Kong*, vowing that he'll use "more than chains" to subdue the beast. "He's always been king of his world, but we'll teach him fear." Once Kong escapes the New York theater and climbs the Empire State Building with a terrified Darrow in hand, city officials deploy all means to save her. The black beast, the movie insinuates, cannot be allowed to ascend the heights of empire, especially in the company of a captive White woman. The imagery, again, harked back to the film *Birth of a Nation*, which depicted the Ku Klux Klan (KKK) as protectors of White women against alleged Black male aggression.

Despite its flaws, *King Kong* put the Empire State Building on the map for moviegoers around the world. The publicity boosted the building's ticket sales and real estate values, which had muddled through the early

Depression years as unprofitable, after the initial excitement of opening day died down. Al Smith, for one, was grateful for the film. Since May 1931, he had hustled to attract attention to the skyscraper and raise its prestige for the sake of selling office and retail space within its 102 stories. Edmund Wilson's predictions were vindicated as the building stood 75 percent vacant a year after its completion, engendering gibes such as "Smith's Folly" and "Empty State Building." There were *some* renters, including jeweler Irven (Jack) Brod, who moved in a month after it opened and kept his company there into the twenty-first century. He recalled how the building remained largely unoccupied until after World War II. Undoubtedly, though, Empire State became an instant landmark. "You don't have to say 350 Fifth Avenue," Brod explained. "Everyone knows it."[18]

Yet stakeholder debts went upward of $1 million higher each year until the end of the decade, while a steady but low rate of tourism failed to make up the difference. In its first year, the landmark's observation deck brought in about $2 million in revenue, an impressive figure for the time. Visitors came to see the building, but also to experience the dizzying heights of its eighty-sixth floor. Empire State Inc. promoters tried to describe the feeling: "Up there, among the clouds, the drum-beat of New York is stilled, the nervous staccato of the city's life is left behind. In the superb heights of Empire State, the mind is free."[19]

IIIIIIIIIII

Tourism profits were down everywhere during the Depression, including at the Statue of Liberty, which was under the management of the National Park Service in 1933. As late as December 29, however, Secretary of the Interior Harold Ickes was demanding that the War Department grant National Park jurisdiction over the entire island, the bulk of which had been retained for military defense. "The use of any part of the island for utilitarian purposes is contrary to the conception and message of the monument," Ickes argued.[20] In other words, a military presence did not dovetail easily with the peace-loving message of liberty. An empire, built upon military power, was also seemingly incompatible. Yet the shiny new symbol of empire in Midtown Manhattan stood as a symbol of American greatness, even as it stole some of Lady Liberty's thunder and the island's visiting crowds. Ickes, for one, wanted to make sure that Liberty was not completely eclipsed. The Department of the Interior announced plans to pour money into the upkeep and beautification of the monument and its surroundings once it became a National Park.

Two years earlier, on November 15, 1931, a *New York Times* editorial about the Statue of Liberty made the case that Americans should not neglect the "harbor goddess" that had long watched over them and the best of their values. The author, Walter B. Hayward, reminded readers of Lady Liberty's history and the peaceful meaning assigned to her since arriving at Bedloe's Island in the late 1800s. "Thus America adopted [the] Statue of Liberty," he wrote, "and gave it symbolic character. There it stands . . . unchanging in a world of change . . . a source of wonder in a city of wonders." Unlike the new Empire State Building, the Liberty monument had witnessed a constant stream of changes in population, technology, and commerce over the course of a century. "Who remembers the passenger ships of forty-five years ago," Hayward asked rhetorically. "Well, they are in the memory book of the Goddess." Longing for a simpler time, Hayward lamented that "America had now become a world power, and New York had become a metropolis." "Here, indeed, was bewildering progress: a city in transformation, destroying, building and destroying again; restless, unsatisfied, and often achieving the seemingly impossible."

Hayward was referring to the impossible feat of the tallest building constructed over the previous year, an achievement met with a measure of unease. "The skyscraper," he continued, "had definitely taken its place as the building of the future, symbolizing the might and enterprise of the metropolis in its skyline" while "the Goddess, secure in her altar, surveyed it all." The dichotomy, for Hayward, was set: the Empire State Building represented New York's commercial and industrial empire (oppressive measures and all), while Lady Liberty stood quietly to the south as a shrine to freedom. They both, however, offered Americans hope of opportunities for a better tomorrow. Though Liberty's veneer may have faded, for Hayward the veneration toward her never would. She remained pure. "The hands that remade the city could, and would not, touch her. She was inviolate. It is something to be a Goddess, to be of the passing world and yet to stand aloof." Aloof, perhaps, but Hayward clearly worried that his favorite American monument would become surpassed. As Al Smith pushed his modern marvel upon the public, Hayward did his best to boost tourism to Bedloe's Island. "One should journey . . . to see the Goddess at close range," he encouraged. "In a city of superlative heights, she remains majestic and impressive." She also, according to Hayward, rose above the fray of cutthroat competition raging across the rest of New York, the nation, and the world. Claiming the still waters of the harbor as the "empire" of the Goddess, Hayward concluded with a dismissal toward the likes of Smith and his self-serving enterprise. "We can leave the flourish of pride to them. The Goddess is far removed from the pomp and vanity of man."[21]

Yet Smith kept making headway and headlines by hosting celebrities and foreign dignitaries at the top of the Empire State Building for photos and soundbites. British politician and future prime minister Winston Churchill visited in February 1932, declaring between puffs of cigar smoke that it was a "marvelous sight."[22] Smith's dance card filled with the likes of Mary Pickford, Fay Wray, and the King of Thailand as he continued to welcome visitors to the tallest structure in the world. The media coverage, unfortunately, didn't pay the bills, and Smith resorted to soliciting leases from friends and colleagues. At the opening day luncheon, Smith had joked with Governor Roosevelt about bringing state offices to the building, and he lobbied hard for federal renting when Roosevelt became president. These requests, almost demands, ran the risk of affronting Roosevelt, especially since Smith had not done much to hide his disdain when Roosevelt won the Democratic Party's favor. As the decade unfolded, the relationship between the two rivals deteriorated further as Smith increasingly criticized Roosevelt's policies and accused him of straying too far toward socialism. The New Deal, Smith claimed, posed a threat to free enterprise and individual initiative.

IIIIIIIIIII

President Franklin D. Roosevelt made a lot of controversial decisions in his first term: appointing the first female cabinet secretary, abandoning the gold standard, expanding executive power, and opening diplomacy and trade with the Soviet Union. The United States had refused to recognize the USSR as a legitimate state ever since the Bolshevik revolution of 1917. If a socialist revolution against the tsarist regime could occur in Russia, Americans feared that a similar upheaval could overthrow capitalism and shake the social order in the United States. Any form of socialism became suspect along with its advocates, like Eugene Debs, who was jailed for sedition in 1918 for speaking out against the war and encouraging strikes, or radical journalist John Reed, who had witnessed the Bolshevik revolution and wrote positively of it in *Ten Days That Shook the World*.

Reed had been born into a family of wealthy capitalists in Portland, Oregon, and he attended Harvard College where he became radicalized by Walter Lippmann and fellow socialists at the school. As a writer for *The Masses*, he supported unions and workers' rights. He also blasted American imperialism in Mexico and in Europe during World War I. "We must not be duped by this editorial buncombe about Liberalism going forth to Holy War against Tyranny," he wrote.[23] Reed became persona non grata in the United States after he lionized the Bolsheviks and cofounded the Communist Labor Party of America. But he continued his radical activism and his visits to the Soviet Union, even volunteering to serve as their official representative in New York. When Reed died of typhus during a trip to Moscow in 1920, the Soviets honored him with a funeral and buried him in a grave at the Kremlin, the resting place of three other Americans whom the Soviets recognized as friends of their regime.

By the 1930s, the brutal suppression of freedoms for millions of people under the rule of Joseph Stalin seemed to confirm American fears of communism as a threat to liberty. Roosevelt distrusted Stalin, and he knew of his ironfisted approach to domestic and foreign affairs. However, the president was desperate for export markets during the Depression, and he hoped that by opening talks with the Soviet dictatorship he could seal a deal for selling American products, such as farming implements, to the large empire. Partnering with the Soviets soon proved problematic, as the "Great Purge" murders of Stalin's rivals appalled the first US ambassador to Moscow, William C. Bullitt. Roosevelt's overtures to a totalitarian state, meanwhile, added fuel to the fire of his critics, who claimed the New Dealer harbored socialist sympathies. But, as the president would later quip once the United States and Great Britain allied with the Soviet Union to fight the German Wehrmacht, it was sometimes necessary to walk with the devil, temporarily, to cross a dangerous bridge.

IIIIIIIIIII

Social welfare programs, whether federal or nonprofit, were also accused of creeping toward socialism. Hull House in Chicago, which Jane Addams and Ellen Gates Starr cofounded as a cultural and social outreach center in 1889, weathered its share of vitriol over the decades, especially since Addams criticized capitalism as a cause of, not an antidote for, social unrest. When Eugene Debs spoke at Hull House in 1903, the *Nebraska Daily News-Press* was among the media outlets that questioned "is Hull house [*sic*] a school of socialism?" or wondered whether Jane Addams was "a socialist."[24] She wasn't, at least not in the typical understanding of the term. But as an activist for peace and justice, Addams gained international notoriety. On December 10, 1931, she became the second-ever woman recipient of the Nobel Peace Prize, though she had to share it with a man, Nicholas Murray Butler, president of Columbia University, who later spoke at the fiftieth anniversary of the Statue of Liberty.

Unfortunately, an illness resulting in hospitalization prevented Addams from making the trip to Oslo to accept the award in person. She was seventy years old. Over her entire life, Addams had put her values into practice, helping immigrants adjust to their environs in Chicago, advocating for children's and women's rights everywhere, and promoting peace in all matters. As the Nobel Committee put it when announcing their decision, Addams and Butler were chosen that year "for their assiduous effort to revive the ideal of peace."[25] Butler's association with the Carnegie Endowment for International Peace likely garnered him the accolade. With Addams, her absolute pacifism, particularly during the war-glory years of 1914–1918, made the honor seem long overdue.

Addams's 1922 publication *Peace and Bread in Time of War* offered an autobiographical account of her mission to defend peace. She had traveled the country during World War I on a lecture circuit to speak out against the militant mentality that threatened the gains of goodwill. "We revolted not only against the cruelty and barbarity of war," she wrote, "but even more against the reversal of human relationships which war implied."[26] In other words, the outbreak of open combat broke the bonds of amity between neighbors, between immigrant groups in the United States, and between nations, which progressives had worked so hard to forge in the early twentieth century. In the 1920s, as leaders implemented a new world order, Addams dared to hope that international organizations such as the League of Nations and food-relief programs would pave the way to recovery. In the 1930s, she lamented the conditions of the Great Depression that once again put global cooperation on hold. Addams pressed her old food-relief ally, Herbert Hoover, to provide federal aid, maintain international agreements, and create long-term programs such as Social Security for elderly Americans' survival.

Fittingly, Addams was awarded the Nobel Peace Prize at the same time Harold Ickes fought to secure the whole of Bedloe's Island to revitalize the grounds of Liberty. Ickes referred to Addams as "the truest American" he had ever known, a woman who carried a torch for the poor and oppressed in Chicago and around the world.[27] For Addams, peace and liberty sealed a packaged deal, as communities during peacetime could flourish without the incitement of fear that provoked hostilities. War, in contrast, trampled upon the fruits of cooperation and narrowed freedom of speech, assembly, and belief. "We believed that war, seeking its end through coercion, not only interrupted but fatally reversed this process of cooperating good will which, if it had a chance, would eventually include the human family itself," she explained in *Peace and Bread*.[28] The same held true for capitalism, with its cutthroat competition and wealth accumulation, that left the masses reeling from its highs and lows, unable to trust good times in good faith.

The effects of capitalism, however, continued to make waves over the course of the 1930s, and the men behind the Empire State Building did not damper their rhetoric about the glory of industry. The US imperial city and its "business activity," they boasted, was now "crowned with an imposing structure of commerce."[29] As Al Smith and company struggled to make money on their new skyscraper, Manhattan businesses wasted no time capitalizing on the landmark's proximity in their marketing ads. The Hotel New Yorker and Hotel McAlpin welcomed the newcomer to the neighborhood in the opening day's edition of the *New York Times*, while Weber and Heilbroner showed an image of their shirts stacked next to a rendering of the tallest building. Fox Furs went further by creating a giant sign, visible from Empire State's observatory, to remind those at the top that they should shop at their store when they returned to the ground. Granted, the average wage earner and out-of-workers could not afford such luxury items or stay in expensive hotels, but the ads appealed to those with disposable income.

If icons are built, over time, not born anew, then the advertising campaigns contributed to the process, burning the image of the Empire State Building into the minds of millions. The recipe for icon making, however, also calls for emotional connections, even quality time, just like any relationship. On that front, the commercial content reaching the public may not have done the trick.

The magic of movies, like *King Kong*, offered a stronger dose of emotional punch, as audiences identified with either the lovestruck creature or Darrow, the object of his affections. They felt their hearts race as Kong scaled the skyscraper, pursued by authorities, generating a thrill that could be recreated later by visiting the pinnacle in real life. The film, unlike paper ads, took them on an exciting ride that peaked at the top of the Empire State Building. However, the claim that the hit film translated immediately into dollars for Empire Inc. investors isn't quite accurate. It wasn't until the 1940s that tenancy reached near capacity, and the building started breaking even only in the 1950s. So much for the high hopes the tallest building had raised on its opening day.

On February 14, 1931, as artisans were putting the final touches on the Empire State Building and the character "Nancy" roamed nervously in the shadow of the skyscraper, New York theaters premiered another would-be classic film, the adaptation of *Dracula* starring Bela Lugosi. The themes of the vampire story, originally written in 1897, resonated with Depression-era audiences on multiple levels: fear of immigrants, financial drain, and lust for power. There were real-life monsters let loose upon the world. That winter in Germany, for instance, the National Socialist Party was swelling its ranks and engendering violence at the behest of its charismatic leader, Adolf Hitler, whose racial and imperial ambitions would soon suck the life out of much of Europe.

IIIIIIIIIII

On March 4, 1933, the new leader of the nation addressed the legislative assembly with his inaugural speech. Alluding to the "dark days" of the Depression, which had deepened over three years, he called for reform and redistribution on a "national scale," including "national planning for and supervision of all forms of transportation and of communications." To "act quickly," the leader demanded an unprecedent allowance of executive power, "as great as the power that would be given to me if we were in fact invaded by a foreign foe." Franklin D. Roosevelt had just become the thirty-second president of the United States. And he needed the American people to stay united to meet the domestic crisis, not for the sake of wealth, per se, but to preserve democracy and national pride. "Happiness lies not in the mere possession of money; it lies in the joy of achievement, in the thrill of creative effort," he reminded.[30]

On the overcast afternoon of May 1, 1931, while attending the Sky High Luncheon to mark the skyscraper's opening day, Roosevelt had stood on the Empire State Building's eighty-sixth floor, supported by steel braces around his legs. The temperature was gradually warming to near sixty degrees, but Lady Liberty at the southern tip of Manhattan remained obscured by mist. Speaking to the lunch guests later, the then governor of New York admitted to being "awestruck" by the vistas he could see from the tower. The content of his speech, indeed, stressed vision and visionaries, like Al Smith, with "their grasp of the needs of the future . . . and the possibilities of modern science." The building is "needed by the whole nation," Roosevelt stated, perceiving the positive example the project had set for future cooperation and achievement, as a "mark of vision and faith that will hold good for many, many years to come."[31] Roosevelt would return to the theme of vision ("without vision the people perish") in his first speech to Congress less than two years later, as the newly elected president. Perhaps he thought of the fast and unified action that built the Empire State Building when he crafted his rhetoric during his first term and during the war. Perhaps he appreciated the lights that were turned on at the top of the building on election night in November 1932, to celebrate his victory over Herbert Hoover.

It is impossible, of course, to know what Roosevelt was thinking as he looked down upon New York on that May Day in 1931. By accepting the Democratic nomination for the next presidency, he had volunteered to take the helm of a nation sinking in economic despair. He didn't have a solid plan, even as he assumed office on inauguration day. But Roosevelt projected and kept faith in the American ability to meet the challenge with innovation and hard work. After all, he had relied upon those traits to build himself back from the crippling effects of polio.

The New Deal he implemented during his first term as president represented Roosevelt's greatest experiment of vision, faith, and hard work. The programs provided temporary relief and government-funded employment during the worst years of the Great Depression, but the New Deal didn't act as a cure-all. It would take massive federal spending and expedited war production in the 1940s to finally turn the tide of the US economy. However, the New Deal, in Roosevelt's mind, was about universal principles as much as domestic policy change. During his first two terms in office, Roosevelt alluded to his worldview in speeches and fireside chats, including his first presidential address to Congress when he exhorted Americans to do their duty as good neighbors in "a world of neighbors," maintaining that the "interdependence" of nations demanded a concern with more than one's own backyard. The concepts crystallized more fully in his wartime promises for global self-determination, a dismantling of empires, and universal freedoms from want and fear that were outlined in the Four Freedoms speech and the Atlantic Charter.

At first glance, Roosevelt's aims for a new world order seem altruistic and out of sync with his practical political style. But when considered in the longer history of American "imperialism by idealism," it becomes clear that Roosevelt wasn't expecting the United States to relinquish its influence and power around the world, but rather to wield it more ethically and effectively, thereby preventing another outbreak of major warfare in the future.

That was all ahead of him in 1931 as he ascended the Empire State Building as New York's governor and gazed across the expanse. Still, the signs of conflicts to come were discernible on the horizon. Roosevelt was familiar enough with US empire and well aware of the threat that Italian, German, and especially Japanese expansion posed to US-held territories. In his younger years, he had idolized his distant relative, Teddy Roosevelt, for his exploits in Cuba during the War of 1898 and in Panama to build a canal. He followed in TR's footsteps to become assistant secretary of the Navy from 1913 to 1920, a post that gave him an insider's perspective on war and international relations, and then into the gubernatorial office of New York. The vulnerability of the Philippines and Guam in the early 1930s certainly would have been on FDR's mind.

The plight of Jews in Germany and elsewhere also posed a challenge for international relations, especially as US leaders had stemmed the tide of immigration during the 1920s and 1930s. Foreign visas during the Depression years fell dramatically. The bans from entry, however, did not apply evenly, as Jewish intellectuals, mostly scientists, were offered asylum, university posts, and citizenship paths above other applicants. Physicist Albert Einstein was one of those who immigrated to the United States after Hitler came to power. Already celebrated as the brightest mind of his time, Einstein received a warm welcome when he toured the country from 1930 to 1931, serving as a research fellow at the California Institute of Technology on the West Coast and accepting the keys to New York City in the Northeast. In the mid-1930s, the famed theorist was teaching at Princeton University, which bent the Ivy League's quotas limiting Jewish faculty to hire Einstein. Einstein's contacts within the scientific community in Europe would benefit the US war effort when he alerted President Roosevelt to the Nazi's stockpiling of uranium and their experiments with nuclear weapons, a tip that led to the launch of the Manhattan Project. While many Jewish refuge seekers were denied liberty in the United States and other havens around the world, the "brain drain" of Germany, where Nazi antisemitism purged universities of unwanted academics, enhanced the United States' intellectual prestige and output.

Einstein appreciated his sanctuary on US soil, but it quickly became clear that he had not escaped the racism he had fled in Germany. The treatment of Black Americans, in particular, compelled him to speak out against the double standards in his adopted country. Einstein was outraged by the scandal in Scottsboro, Alabama, that began when nine Black teenagers were falsely accused of raping two White women on a train in March 1931. Later that year, after the Scottsboro boys were convicted of the crime, he wrote to the editors of *The Crisis* magazine to congratulate them on the twenty-first anniversary of the publication and to comment upon its continued relevance. Einstein was troubled, he noted, by White supremacy in the United States and the effects it exerted on the psyches of Blacks, who could not help but feel the inferior status assigned to them. Addressing W. E. B. Du Bois and *The Crisis*, he said he hoped that "emancipation of the soul of the minority can be attained," through a closer sense of unity among Blacks across the nation and a "conscious educational enlightenment among the minority" race.[32]

Jane Addams joined Einstein and a chorus of voices calling upon Americans to rid the nation of its most glaring hypocrisy. In her last memoir, *The*

Second Twenty Years at Hull House, she highlighted the "problem of race relations" and feared that most Whites, since the abolitionists, had become "indifferent to the gravest situation in our American life." The issue, she reminded, affected not only personal dignity but also national dignity and the image of democracy. "To continually suspect, suppress or fear any large group in a community must finally result in a loss of enthusiasm for that type of government which gives free play to . . . a majority of its citizens."[33] Besides Hull House, integrated communities providing Depression-era relief to supplement the race-based gaps of the New Deal included Catholic Worker in New York, Highlander Folk School in Tennessee, and the Delta Cooperative Farms that missionary Sherwood Eddy founded in Mississippi. They all faced severe backlash, often vandalism, and at least threats of violence, from locals opposed to interracial comingling.

||||||||||

In the spring of 1935, John Dewey mourned the passing of his friend Jane Addams, who had succumbed to cancer at a hospital in Chicago. Addams's friends and family held services at Hull House, where over four thousand people of all ethnicities and social classes attended to pay their respects. Dewey, at home in New York, where he was thinking and writing a lot about the concept of liberty, didn't make it to Chicago until a few days after the funeral. The two social theorists had always been close, but they became philosophically closer after World War I, when Dewey realized that the crusade to make the world "safe for democracy" with militance was a mistake, just as Addams had warned.

Dewey, who had retired from teaching in the mid-1930s, continued to fight the global rise of fascism and militarism the best way he knew how, not by demanding an adherence to peace or religion, per se, but by appealing to America's democratic and religious sensibilities. These values, he argued, when tested and practiced, made "liberty and justice for all" unconditional. Dewey believed that the notion of liberty had to evolve with the times, revised from its traditional association with economic individualism to a social understanding of freedom as mutually beneficial. Especially in an age of industrial capitalism and economic integration, it was imperative, Dewey reasoned, to regard liberty as a communal asset, available to all in equal measure. The value of one's own freedom was tied to and dependent upon the freedom of others.

Religious commitments could help. By this, Dewey did not mean institutional religion in churches alone but the fellowship of community members striving toward a better society, choosing together the best option to benefit everyone. In his short 1934 treatise, *A Common Faith*, the philosopher encouraged his readers to look beyond the dogma of Scripture or the dividing lines of denomination and, instead, elevate religious values to their civic purpose: the realization of ideal ends. "Any activity pursued in [*sic*] behalf of an ideal end against obstacles and in spite of threats of personal loss because of conviction," he explained, "is religious in quality."

For Dewey, God did not exist as an abstract, supernatural figure in the sky. Rather, God operated as a spirit binding and inspiring people in fellowship with one another. "It is the *active* relation between ideal and actual to which I would give the name 'God,'" he stated. In the "distracted age" of the 1930s, Dewey believed that this functioning of "God" was urgently needed, as a "light shining into the murky places of social existence." "What would be the consequence . . . [for] values . . . if [they were] clearly held to and cultivated with the ardor and the devotion that have at times marked historic religions?"[34]

Dewey felt an urgency to root civic ideals in religious devotion, particularly during times of crisis, when they were most at risk. The concept of liberty became an intense topic of debate when conservative critics of Roosevelt's New Deal claimed that welfare programs and economic regulations imperiled the individualism at the center of capitalism. In "Liberty and Social Control," Dewey took to the debate, deconstructing the abstract idea of liberty to its practical purpose. "Today there is no word more bandied about than liberty," he began before providing a basic definition: "Liberty is a demand for power, either for possession of powers of action not already possessed or for retention and expansion of powers already possessed." While Dewey acknowledged the social movements earlier in the nation's history to expand liberty to more people, he decried the more recent tendency to leverage liberty to protect the privileges of elites.[35]

While industrialists such as Henry Ford held that "individualism is what makes cooperation worth living,"[36] Dewey turned the argument on its head, depicting capitalism as an impediment to personal freedom because the system favored a few prosperous entrepreneurs at the expense of the many. This arrangement, he avowed, undermined democracy to the extent that it limited the options for wageworkers and the unemployed. As Dewey reasoned, democracy demanded full participation in the process, from setting the rules of the game to reaping its benefits, but capitalism failed to support inclusion. The "every man for himself" system favored competition, not cooperation, and relied upon coercive means to maintain the power of those at the top. Liberty, Dewey concluded, was a casualty of capitalism, not its mainstay.

Dewey regarded capitalism as akin to war, especially since both enterprises incited antagonism and imposed conformity to fulfill their objectives. The social control exerted to maintain both systems, he argued, led inevitably to social disorder and the loss of democratic values. Dewey had seen it before, during World War I, and he hoped for an alternative ending in the mid-1930s, even as he heard rumblings of military mobilization in the distance. Into the 1940s, he continued to wage intellectual battle against theologians like Reinhold Niebuhr and other "just war" theorists who rationalized a militant defense of liberty and America's exceptional qualities against fascism and communism. To be truly exceptional, Dewey insisted, Americans needed to refuse the bait of violence by standing above the fray and allowing the nation's values to prove worthy apart from force. The ends of peace and freedom, as Addams had long argued, had to match the means to get there.

Along with the triumph of the Empire State Building in May 1931, the trappings of US pride and exceptionalism remained firm in 1931, despite the Depression, Dust Bowls, and subsequent turmoil abroad. On March 3 of that year, "The Star-Spangled Banner" officially became the US national anthem by an act of Congress and Hoover's presidential stamp. The lyrics, originally written as a poem by Francis Scott Key during the War of 1812, expressed the outlook of an underdog destined for glory. Key, a lawyer held captive aboard an enemy ship near Baltimore, did not expect the US troops at Fort McHenry to withstand the British bombardment overnight. They did, however, and when Key spotted his nation's flag still flying above the fort the next morning, he was inspired to document the proud moment for posterity. Americans know the first verse of Key's poem well. The "broad stripes and bright stars" survived "the perilous fight" to continue "gallantly streaming." The Maryland native then voiced his relief upon seeing "proof" "that our flag was still there," yet waving "o'er the land of the free and the home of the brave."

The final verse of Key's poem strikes a far less humble tone. In those lines, Key rallies his fellow patriots to stand firm in the conviction that they must always defend their God-given liberties and land from any incursion:

O thus be it ever when freemen shall stand
Between their lov'd home and the war's desolation!
Blest with vict'ry and peace may the heav'n rescued land
Praise the power that hath made and preserv'd us a nation!
Then conquer we must, when our cause it is just,
And this be our motto—"In God is our trust,"
And the star-spangled banner in triumph shall wave
O'er the land of the free and the home of the brave.[37]

Empire and liberty, Key suggested, were tied together on a warpath as the nation conquered perceived threats. The young country, in 1814, was still developing politically, socially, economically, and imperially across the continent, clearing lands, containing native peoples, and building infrastructure to prosper along the frontier. Resources were rich, but their cultivation was still rough. And it was all open to attack. The precarious situation made a defense of liberty a never-ending battle.

In 1814, Key's poem was set to the tune of the popular song "Anacreon in Heaven," and it vied for national anthem status for over a century against classics like "God Bless America" before achieving the honor in 1931. The timing proved apt. Throughout his presidency, Franklin Roosevelt would borrow Key's bullhorn, echoing the call for bravery in defense of both liberty and territory in times of crisis.

IIIIIIIIIII

Wiley Post and Harold Gatty knew they could beat the twenty-one-day record for a round-the-world flight that a German Graf Zeppelin had set in 1930. In June of 1931, they embarked on a single-engine Lockheed Vega aircraft named the *Winnie Mae,* taking off from Roosevelt Field on Long Island to test their mettle. Their trip took a little over eight days, with stops at Berlin, Moscow, and Nome, Alaska. When they returned safely to Roosevelt Field, they were hailed as heroes. During the 1920s, many records had been set for transatlantic flights by Charles Lindbergh and other daring men. Amelia Earhart, in the 1930s, also stepped forward to make her mark for women. Such feats helped advance aviation technology, making planes faster and safer. Aircraft without wings, such as dirigibles or zeppelins, were also in vogue. Fueled by hydrogen gas, they were huge, stunning, and dangerous. An incident in the spring of 1937 made their risks most evident.

The skies above Manhattan on May 6 portended rain, but the storms held off long enough that late afternoon for New Yorkers to catch a clear view of an extraordinary sight. The German Zeppelin airship, named the *Hindenburg* after the nation's war hero and former president, sailed past the city's skyscrapers on its way to New Jersey. The Zeppelin had flown across New York before, making appearances in 1936 not long after it was built. The flight in 1937 followed a similar route, taking sixty hours to cross the Atlantic from Europe to North America, carrying ninety-seven passengers and crew on board.

Those viewing the spectacle from the city pavements couldn't see the small but telling insignia, but onlookers at the uppermost floors of the Empire State Building were close enough to notice the Nazi swastika painted on the airship's tail. Before his death in 1934, German president Paul von Hindenburg had helped the Nazis solidify their power by appointing Adolf Hitler to the chancellorship. When Hindenburg died, Hitler declared himself führer and assumed absolute power in Germany. He immediately dismantled civil liberties by suspending freedom of speech, persecuting political opponents, replacing judges with loyal enablers, deploying paramilitary forces against Jews and other perceived undesirables, and controlling all forms of media. Germany's short-lived Weimar Republic was over, demonstrating how quickly democracies could crumble to a dictator. Hitler, who reveled in symbols of his power, displayed military might with tanks, planes, and zeppelins like the *Hindenburg*.

The *Hindenburg* airship was already behind schedule as it slowly made its way to Lakehurst, New Jersey, where it planned to land and transfer passengers. Ticket holders for its return voyage to Germany waited impatiently in the rain to board. They never got the chance. At around 7:25 p.m., Captain Max Pruss struggled to control the massive flying machine on its approach to Lakehurst Naval Air Station. As the ground crew worked to secure the mooring lines, eyewitnesses glimpsed the first signs of trouble. Dim blue flames appeared, soon erupting into a fire at the port-side fin. Screams from the aircraft were audible. Spectators and cameramen watched in horror as the Zeppelin began to fall and the hull exploded into a blaze. In less than a minute, the *Hindenburg* disaster took the lives of thirty-five passengers.

The event would be remembered as one of the worst human tragedies of the modern era. The next day, the *New York Times* recounted the "hysterical scene" that "ended in a holocaust."[38] President Roosevelt sent a note of condolence to Adolf Hitler, expressing grief over the "tragic loss of life."[39] The accident sparked a public relations problem for the German aeronautics industry, bringing the airship era to an abrupt end. Yet German engineering marched on, put to work building the Luftwaffe and Wehrmacht machinery used to invade Poland in September 1939, thus triggering a world war that would pit American and German unity, ingenuity, and idealism against each other.

CHAPTER 5

EMPIRE AND LIBERTY AT WAR—1941

Franklin Roosevelt's inaugural speech in 1933 inspired Americans to hope that relief from the Great Depression was on its way. "This great Nation will endure as it has endured, will revive and will prosper," he promised. "So, first of all, let me assert my firm belief that the only thing we have to fear is fear itself." His demands for unprecedented power to meet the crisis, however, made some people nervous. Roosevelt referred to the US Constitution and rule of law but asserted that "action may call for temporary departure from that normal balance of public procedure." Hoover's mishandling of the economic disaster had turned Congress over to the Democrats in the election of 1932, giving the new president broad latitude to push legislation and implement his agenda. But Roosevelt vowed to overstep any congressional inefficiencies by assuming "broad Executive power to wage a war against the emergency."[1]

In an era of dictators using the economic crisis to justify their increased power, Roosevelt's speech was alarming to his Republican opponents and a number of former allies, like Al Smith. Hoover and Smith expressed their discontent by forming the American Liberty League in 1934, a platform denouncing Roosevelt and the New Deal as un-American. Smith appeared at the Mayflower Hotel in Washington, DC, in 1936 to highlight the "dangers" the president's radical departure from national norms posed to the balance of power. "We don't want autocrats, either in or out of office; we wouldn't even take a good one," he stated. For Smith, there was plenty to fear from the Roosevelt administration, which had expanded bureaucracy and centralized control. As he reminded, "This country belongs to the people, and it doesn't belong to any Administration." But Smith dug in deeper, stoking fears of communism to warn Americans away from unbridled support of Roosevelt and the current Congress. "There can be only one Capitol—Washington or Moscow. There can be only one atmosphere of government, the clear, pure, fresh air of free America, or the foul breath of Communistic Russia," he said.

Smith may have harbored some resentment against the man who had outmaneuvered him to gain the presidency. He even alluded to it at the top of his speech by assuring that he had "no axe to grind."[2] But Smith's critique made sense as part of his overriding concerns about fascism and communism—twin terrors that he feared would spread totalitarianism around the world and into the United States. In 1933, at Madison Square Garden, Smith had delivered a scathing renunciation of Adolf Hitler, who assumed power in Germany a few weeks before Roosevelt's inauguration. Hitler, Smith reminded, was anything but democratic.

The Nazi leader in Germany had proved as much by his suppression of basic civil rights and his cruelty toward Jews. But Smith laid much of the blame on the German people who had allowed it to happen, a turn of events that served as a cautionary tale about democratic caprice. The nascent German Republic, after World War I, had established democratic institutions, but republican values had not rooted in the hearts of the public. Facing hard times in the 1920s and 1930s, Germans fell in for a leader promising economic and political renewal. "It is clear that the world has not yet been made safe for democracy," Smith concluded in a nod to Woodrow Wilson.[3] He hoped Americans would remain true to their love of liberty and freedom by rejecting a concentration of power in the nation's highest office.

The rhetoric and intentions of Franklin Roosevelt and the Führer were quite different. Roosevelt spoke often of liberty, including his celebration of the Statue of Liberty's fiftieth anniversary in 1936. "Liberty and peace are living things," Roosevelt told his audience at the monument. "In each generation—if they are to be maintained—they must be guarded and vitalized anew." Like Smith, the president put the onus on the will of the people, exhorting them to remember the past and the purpose of the statue in New York Harbor but also extend its promise forward and outward: "The richness of the promise has not run out. If we keep the faith for our day as those who came before us kept the faith for theirs, then you and I can smile with confidence into the future."[4]

Challenges to liberty were at play domestically and abroad, and the statue during this time became a symbol for "world freedom."[5] As the 1930s unfolded amid a global Depression, imperialists seized the opportunity to extend not liberty but dominion over territories they had long coveted. The Japanese military moved on Manchuria and Korea; Mussolini sought to claim a sphere of influence in the Balkans, Greece, and Ethiopia for his revitalized Roman empire; and the dictator in Germany enlarged his rule over regions in Central and Eastern Europe. But as Roosevelt reminded in his 1936 speech, imperial aims could have unintended consequences. The American colonies, he explained, had been established by a greedy British Empire seeking resources in the New World, never knowing that they had planted the seeds of a liberty-loving people. As exceptional stewards of freedom, Americans, he said, had to seize their own opportunities to defend and protect liberty whenever threatened.

Ironically, that meant aiding another empire, the British Empire, which stood as the last bulwark against fascism in Europe. Roosevelt clearly identified Britain, a constitutional monarchy, as the lesser of evils among empires vying for the world. He had a hard time, however, convincing Americans that Britain deserved special favor, especially since he himself had used "America first" rhetoric to focus on national economic recovery in the 1930s. The Depression had not abated, making foreign aid a tough sell to those in need of financial help. What's more, Americans recalled with disdain how support for Great Britain had led the United States slowly but surely into the Great War in 1917, a slippery slope that they wanted to avoid repeating. Roosevelt used back channels to offer Britain and its prime minister, Winston Churchill, whatever he could. Yet the

US president was unwilling to run too far ahead of public opinion—an indication, if the Liberty League needed one, that Roosevelt was acting more like a democrat than a dictator.

Al Smith also made his choice for the lesser of evils by swinging his support back to Roosevelt on the issue of aid to Britain. Though troubled by the president's wielding of power domestically, Smith's fear of fascism made fighting the Führer imperative. In October 1939, Smith broadcasted a nationwide radio address assuring Americans that Roosevelt was "so clearly right, so obviously on the side of common sense and sound judgment," regarding the war in Europe, that he urged the country to "stand solidly" behind him by amending the Neutrality Acts, 1930s legislation that restricted US intervention in foreign wars. In this case, Smith took "no stock in quibbling over constitutional questions" to expediate a quick fix to help Britain. "In a crisis there is no time for legalistic hair-splitting," he said.[6]

Neither Smith nor Roosevelt wanted war. In his previous post as assistant secretary of the Navy, Roosevelt had witnessed the devastation that armed conflict caused. "I have seen war," he lamented. "I have seen war on land and sea. . . . I have seen cities destroyed. . . . I have seen children starving. . . . I hate war." He believed that circumstances in the late 1930s and early 1940s, however, demanded a response from the United States as an "arsenal of democracy" and defender of freedoms.[7]

The freedoms of Jews in fascist Germany were nearly nonexistent, and as news of oppression and pogroms filtered across the Atlantic, notable public figures in the United States tried to rouse Americans' sympathies for the Jewish plight. Henry Morgenthau Jr., Roosevelt's secretary of the treasury, pleaded with the president and State Department to open more channels for Jewish immigration, which had been severely limited by policies in 1924. The State Department refused to budge on the quotas, an impasse that prompted officials working under Morgenthau in the Treasury Department to prepare a report accusing the United States of betraying its values. "Unless remedial steps of a drastic nature are taken," they stated, "we may as well take down that plaque from the Statue of Liberty and black out the 'lamp beside the golden door.'"[8]

Evidence of German atrocities had existed at least since Kristallnacht on November 9, 1938, when Nazis launched a coordinated attack on Jews in Germany and Austria. Hitler's writings and speeches also made his intentions against Jews very clear. Prominent Jews in the United States government, such as Morgenthau and Emanuel Celler, worked hard to convince US officials to take in more refugees. Time and again, Roosevelt and the State Department caved to the weight of public opinion against bending the rules to help them. Appeals to liberty did not persuade a majority of Americans that the United States should offer asylum or intervene against Germany or Japan. An attack on US empire, however, changed their minds.

IIIIIIIIIII

The US national flag hoisted during World War II had altered since the American Revolution, and it would soon alter again. The star-spangled banner in the 1940s still featured thirteen stripes (one for each of the original colonies) with colors reflecting the paradox of US identity. Red stripes represented valor and war readiness along with white for purity and blue for justice. Those oft-competing values had brought forth a nation of forty-eight states by World War II, denoted by forty-eight stars in the upper-left corner. The flag at that time did not include the "territories" that the United States had acquired in the late 1800s. Puerto Rico, the Philippines, and Guam were unrepresented in the design, as were Hawaii and Alaska, which would not become states until 1959. Though the flag did not fully indicate it, the United States was an empire in the 1940s, and its colonial holdings were incredibly vulnerable.

After the War of 1898 and the subsequent Filipino-American War, policymakers in the United States considered the Philippines a valuable keepsake for managing and protecting US interests in the Pacific. The cluster of islands and archipelagoes composing the Philippines were well situated to the southeast of the Chinese mainland, where Americans made trade and investment deals, and it buffered Japanese access to the South Pacific. The US Asiatic Fleet commanded the naval base at Manila and could be deployed to restore order in the region. In the mid-1930s, those forces were on high alert to protect American nationals in China and prevent Japanese moves upon the Philippines.

The Japanese had aims of expansion throughout the twentieth century, especially after their 1905 victory over Russian forces signaled to the world that they had the military power to back imperial ambitions. During the Depression, their isolated, island geography underscored their dependence on imports. Even before leaving the League of Nations, Japan invaded Korea and Manchuria, an area in northeastern China rich with resources. The French and British territories throughout Southeast Asia as well as the Philippine Islands were also attractive. Over twenty thousand Japanese laborers had emigrated to the Philippines to take part in the lumber and fishing industries as well as hemp production. Rubber

World War II war bonds poster

and petroleum reserves, needed to fuel an empire, dangled as prizes if the Japanese military could wrest control of them. In the 1920s, aviator Billy Mitchell had warned that the Japanese were poised to strike against the Philippines and Hawaii. By the 1940s, tensions between the United States and Japan had escalated to the point that Roosevelt imposed restrictive trade sanctions, a measure short of war, to contain Japanese aggression. Those policies were ultimately ineffective.

After the attack on Pearl Harbor, Roosevelt was careful to convince Americans that Hawaii counted as US land, and that the Japanese bombings amounted to an assault on American liberty. For the rest of the war, he would craft an image of the United States as a defender of freedoms and not of empire, even as he used the concept of empire to justify the fight. Americans, he insisted, had to liberate the world from imperial takeovers. He did not mention that at least eighteen million of those people had been under US rule.

|||||||||||

When *The Wizard of Oz* premiered in Wisconsin in August 1939, it immediately captured moviegoers' imaginations. Nobody had seen anything quite like it on screen. The film followed the unintended journey of young Dorothy from Kansas, transported to the strange but vibrant land of Oz, vividly portrayed in the ruby-red, emerald-green, and yellow-gold hues of Technicolor. There were witches, Munchkins, and flying monkeys. Dorothy found friends to help guide her home, and she eventually followed her heart back to Kansas. Cinema would never be the same. A month later, when the German army invaded Poland, both France and Britain declared war on Hitler's expansion. The world would never be the same either.

The Wizard of Oz was adapted from a series of children's stories written by L. Frank Baum, a journalist living in South Dakota and later Chicago with his wife and four children. He published his first best-selling children's book, *The Wonderful Wizard of Oz*, in 1900 and developed it into a multibook series thereafter. It inspired fantasy novels such as *The Wonderful Mother of Oz* by Sally Roesch Wagner and *Herland* by

Charlotte Perkins Gilman, both feminist tales by women's rights advocates that were clearly indebted to the land of Oz. Baum didn't mind. He kept company, in fact, with some of the leading suffragists of his day, including Matilda Gage (his mother-in-law) and Susan B. Anthony, who stayed with the Baums when she visited Aberdeen, South Dakota. Baum supported women's rights. Yet he was not so open minded about the rights of Native Americans.

While residing in South Dakota in the 1890s, not long after federal troops killed Sitting Bull and over 150 Sioux for challenging White settlers, Baum wrote two editorials in his Aberdeen paper addressing the incidents. Baum described Sitting Bull as a "proud" hero, whose "shrewdness and daring" matched a "white man's spirit of hatred and revenge." "What wonder that his wild nature, untamed by years of subjection, should still revolt?" he wrote. In the wake of Sitting Bull's death at Standing Rock, however, Baum wondered how his tribesman could find the strength to go on:

> With his fall the nobility of the Redskin is extinguished, and what few are left are a pack of whining curs who lick the hand that smites them. The Whites, by law of conquest, by justice of civilization, are masters of the American continent, and the best safety of the frontier settlements will be secured by the total annihilation of the few remaining Indians. . . . Better that they die than live the miserable wretches that they are.[9]

In a follow-up piece weeks later, Baum reiterated his proposal to extinguish "these untamed and untamable creatures from the face of the earth." He tempered his harsh language with a sense of fait accompli, acknowledging that White settlers had "wronged them for centuries" so that their annihilation would amount to a massive mercy kill. Yet Baum could not cover his base motives to protect the "future safety" of "our settlers and soldiers." Unless the natives were completely removed, he predicted, "we may expect future years to be as full of trouble with the redskins as those have been in the past."[10] Baum was not worried about Native Americans outnumbering or overcoming Whites, not at the end of the nineteenth century when Indigenous populations had been relegated to reservations. But he did consider them a pestilence.

Racialized fears in the United States were largely focused elsewhere in the late 1800s. The influx of Asians from China and Japan terrified many Americans, as did Japan's rise in power in the early twentieth century. Journalists and policymakers often mentioned the "yellow peril" of Asian migration, and rumors circulated about a possible Sino-Japanese invasion of the United States. Twenty Chinese workers were lynched in the massacre of 1871 in Los Angeles, and Congress passed the Chinese Exclusion Act of 1882, which wasn't repealed until 1943, after China joined the Allies to fight Japan.

In 1906, the San Francisco earthquake disaster prompted Californians to call for strict segregation of Japanese children in their own schools and an informal agreement was negotiated to narrow the path of Japanese immigration, two developments that Japan resented. Politicians such as Albert Johnson and David Reed pushed for further restrictions upon Asians in anti-immigration laws in the 1920s, which provoked Japan's outrage. The English-language *Japan Times and Mail* in Tokyo called it "The Senate's Declaration of War," denouncing it as "an amendment which they know is a most humiliating one to the Japanese race" one that "cuts the Japanese minds deep, a wound that will hurt and rankle for generations and generations."[11]

The US government did not take Japanese threats lightly. In fact, Americans were afraid of the Japanese, either as economic or military competition, well before Pearl Harbor. Japan's inclusion in the Washington Naval Conference of 1921–22 smacked of a backhanded compliment, since the Japanese naval limit was capped much lower than Great Britain or the United States, but their seat at the negotiating table marked their status as a major power. Fears of Japanese imperialism were confirmed when the island nation invaded Korea and Manchuria during the Great Depression. Americans had long considered China a weak and vulnerable (though venerable) nation, bullied by multiple empires. The Open Door

Notes of the late 1800s had defended their sovereignty. In the 1930s, Japan violated that sovereignty again, and the League of Nations was unable to stop it. The United States also failed to prevent the surprise invasion that Japan unleashed on two US territories in late 1941: Hawaii and, ten hours later, the Philippines. Roosevelt rightly called December 7 a "date which will live in infamy." Americans would never feel safe from foreign attack again.

The Empire State Building was affected by the new sense of insecurity, as dimout and blackout policies were implemented in New York City and other major cities to make it more difficult for foreign enemies to target landmark buildings. The tower lights of Empire State were kept off for most of the war, except for an hour in February 1944 to honor the birthday of inventor Thomas Edison. One Long Island resident informed the *New York Times* that additional safety precautions were warranted, given that he could sometimes see sunlight reflected off the metal spires atop Empire State and the Chrysler Building. Since "these two buildings," he wrote, "would be the first visible from the sea . . . and possibly from the air," he wondered "whether it would not be advantageous to entirely dull these surfaces and investigate all such reflections from building tops."[12]

The skyscraper provided office space for several wartime agencies including the War Production Board, the Office of War Information, and the Office of Scientific Research and Development. It also remained a popular attraction for servicemembers passing through the city, especially those returning home in 1945. For a few, the visit ended tragically. One discharged naval gunner used Empire State's eighty-sixth floor to end his life before the end of the war. A week before Christmas 1943, William Lloyd Rambo dove from a parapet nearly a quarter mile to the sidewalk below.[13] These incidents helped convince the building's owners to add protective caging to the observation deck in 1947.

Even a change of management at Empire State had military significance. Retired lieutenant general Hugh A. Drum took over Al Smith's former command as president of the building in late 1944, telling reporters that his time in the Army had prepared him to run the real estate of Empire State most efficiently. Socialist writer Upton Sinclair argued that such military efficiency, particularly the industrial empire built by Adolf Hitler, should be preserved by the Allies in peacetime, transitioning the remarkable war-making capabilities of Germany to benefit the whole of Europe. "It will become a producers' and consumers' co-operative, self-sustaining and conducted on strict business lines; a corporation not for profit but for public service," he proposed.[14] Hitler's infrastructure for evil, Sinclair suggested, could be repurposed for good.

IIIIIIIIIII

From his Bavarian prison in the mid-1920s, Adolf Hitler wrote his manifesto *Mein Kampf*, detailing his plans for racial purity and state power in Germany. He included some positive remarks on the United States. He admired Henry Ford, he said, as an alternative to the Jewish moneymakers, and he appreciated the dominant "Teutonic" population in America for keeping so-called inferior races at bay through anti-immigration laws, eugenics, and imperial conquest.

> There is today one state in which at least weak beginnings toward a better conception are noticeable. Of course, it is not our model German Republic, but the American Union, in which an effort is made to consult reason at least partially. By refusing immigration on principle to elements in poor health, by simply excluding certain races from naturalization, it professes in slow beginnings a view which is peculiar to the folkish state concept.[15]

The Immigration Act of 1924 had come to Hitler's attention, and he approved of its basis in eugenics, a popular pseudoscience that unpacked an individual's character and intelligence through an analysis of racial attributes. It was used to evaluate all kinds of people, including Whites of European ancestry, but became especially exploited to denigrate people of color. In the 1928 *New York Times* profile of financial wizard John J. Raskob, who would soon bankroll the Empire State Building, the author wrote that "Raskob is partly Alsatian, partly Irish. The Alsatian blood is probably Teutonic, for there is something of the intensity and thoroughness of the German in him, while a twinkle in the narrow brown eyes betrays the Irish heritage of humor."[16] His German genes, the article implied, accounted for the CEO's work ethic and success. Eugenicists were far less kind in their conclusions about people of African or Asian descent, arguing that they had smaller brains and more primitive tendencies.

Eugenicists also singled out Jews. Hitler acknowledged Jews were "cunning" but denied they had any culture or intellect of their own that they had not supposedly absorbed, like "parasites," from the nations and cultures of their diaspora. He warned the major powers not to be deceived. "In every mingling of Aryan blood with that of lower peoples the result was the end of the cultured people."[17] There were plenty of people in the United States who agreed with him. In his critique of Hitler, Al Smith had pointed to the KKK as the American equivalent of fascists because of their hatred toward foreigners, Blacks, Jews, and Catholics (like Smith). But there were many others unaffiliated with the KKK who were quick to deny Jewish refugees even temporary asylum in the United States, justifying the bans as crucial for national security.

President Roosevelt also made racial decisions based on perceived threats to national security. The decisions were, for him, temporary measures, not fundamental or personal, a distinction that may have assuaged his conscience even if it didn't alleviate the suffering the policies caused. During World War II, Dorothea Lange, the Depression-era photographer, documented conditions at internment camps holding Japanese Americans who were relocated in the United States and Canada because of concerns that they would serve as saboteurs or spies for enemy Japan. Mostly from the West Coast, over 100,000 Japanese and US citizens were detained in the sparsely furnished camps; and many lost their properties and businesses while they were gone.[18]

Roosevelt did not expel Jewish refugees already living in the United States by 1939, but he did little to override US policies of exclusion toward Jews seeking asylum thereafter. One of the ships of would-be immigrants, the SS *St. Louis*, carrying about nine hundred refugees, was turned away at ports in Cuba and Florida. The vessel continued up to Canada, where they were also denied entry. A *New York Times* article reported on the fate of the "saddest ship afloat today," which was forced to return to Germany with its "cargo of despair." The article noted sardonically that "Germany, with all the hospitality of its concentration camps, will welcome these unfortunate home."[19] As many as a third of those on the *St. Louis* were later killed while in Nazi detention.

Unlike Hitler and the KKK, Roosevelt did not believe that foreigners, generally, constituted a threat to America. Instead, he spoke of immigrants as empowering America. When he called upon Congress in 1943 to repeal the Chinese Exclusion Act, Roosevelt said it had been a national "mistake."[20] Years earlier, at the fiftieth-anniversary celebration of the Statue of Liberty, he portrayed the freedom-seeking immigrants who made their way to America not as strangers but as fellow agents of liberty, all speaking "the universal language of human aspiration." The new arrivals, he argued, "made the New World's freedom safer, richer, more far-reaching, more capable of growth" because they valued the liberty they had been denied in their homelands. "The realization that we are all bound together by hope of a common future rather than by reverence for a common past has helped us to build upon this continent a unity unapproached in any similar area or population in the whole world."[21] Roosevelt, as president of the United States, considered it his duty to inspire Americans to embrace liberty, and in so doing, choose unity and peace over enmity and violence. Exercising liberty for oneself entailed extending it to others.

Across the Atlantic, Hitler set a far different tone, drawing on fears and exhorting his followers to preserve their privileges and their past by erecting barriers against liberties. According to Hitler, empires fell as their racial superiority became diluted, creating an existential threat so dire that niceties were, for him, detrimental. As he asserted, the powerful must fight and kill to survive. He had seen the British do it. He had seen Americans do it. Determined to build a Reich of his own, Hitler looked to the United States as an empire worth emulating, as long as he could expunge what he considered an unnatural, impractical regard for liberty.

IIIIIIIIIII

Well before Congress declared war on Japan and Germany, Roosevelt was already preparing Americans for their mission to liberate the world. To do so, he told them, they would need to find a unity of purpose as if their lives and those of millions depended on it. Elevating the threat of German and Japanese imperialism to that of a "great emergency" in his 1941 annual address, Roosevelt presaged that the free peoples of the world would remain free or perish together. He buttressed his argument by simultaneously appealing to Americans' higher ideals and their self-interest, asking them to "visualize what the downfall of democratic nations might mean to our own democracy." "No realistic American," he said, "can expect from a dictator's peace international generosity, or return of true independence, or world disarmament, or freedom of expression, or freedom of religion—or even good business."[22]

By citing specifics, the president put the stakes into terms the average person could understand. He hit the same theme later, in his "fireside chat" about Lend-Lease, comparing aid to Great Britain to a simple scenario: lending one's neighbor a garden hose if the house caught fire, not only to help someone in need, but to protect one's own property.[23] He warned that the metaphorical fire that had engulfed much of the world by 1941 could make its way to US shores. Self-interest, he made clear, was embedded in the greater good.

Once Roosevelt laid out the problem, he identified the crux of the solution: people working together. "We must all prepare to make the sacrifices that the emergency . . . demands. Whatever stands in the way of speed and efficiency in defense preparations must give way to the national need." He had witnessed Americans approach past challenges with effective cooperation, from the Empire State Building project to the New Deal programs needed to alleviate the Depression. He exhorted his country to unite again, while calling out the "slackers" and "trouble makers" who might resist the common cause. Those unwilling to contribute to the effort to defend liberty, he stated bluntly, didn't "deserve" it.[24]

The president, however, had carrots as well as sticks to offer. Meeting the short-term challenge with maximum effort, he told his audience, would produce long-term benefits, namely a new world order that would dissolve imperialism in favor of liberty once and for all. He listed the "four freedoms" that he wanted to guarantee once the war was over: freedom of speech, freedom to worship, freedom from want, and freedom from fear "everywhere in the world."[25]

Roosevelt's plan was born of idealism but also pragmatism—empires weren't working, and the wars they generated caused destruction and disrupted commerce. It was far better, he believed, to cooperate than compete. "The world order which we seek is the cooperation of free countries, working together in a friendly, civilized society."[26] Roosevelt's vision was projected more formally in the Atlantic Charter he and Churchill released in August 1941. Framing it as a statement of "common principles," the two leaders acknowledged "the right of all peoples to choose the form of government under which they will live." They also proposed fairer trade, economic security, and territorial integrity for the world.[27]

Though ambitious and seemingly altruistic, dismantling the trappings of imperialism, for both men, did not mean abandoning the economic opportunities that empires reaped. Roosevelt's diplomatic Good Neighbor campaign in Latin America reflected his plan regionally. It aimed to soften the exploitive and invasive approach that the United States had pursued in the past, essentially angling for an *invitation* into Latin American affairs from the region's leaders and people once they realized the mutual benefits of a US partnership. The United States, in short, had to shed its imperialist image. Roosevelt pressured Great Britain, which had long set the rules of international relations, to do the same. Both nations needed to set a better example if they were to have any chance of undermining the legitimacy of dictators, like Joseph Stalin, who wanted to compete with the major powers—all empires. American empire had painted the US republic into a corner bounded by hypocrisy. Roosevelt in the 1940s was trying to forge an honorable path out. At the peace conference after World War I, President Wilson had also tried but ultimately failed to convince the victors to forgo their spoils and set the world on a more peaceful course. Roosevelt hoped to salvage a second chance.

Military campaigns in World War II required cooperation; war production did as well. Before long, Roosevelt and the rest of the nation found out how costly dissent could be for the war effort, when Black labor organizer A. Philip Randolph called for a March on Washington to protest segregation in defense industries. Using the president's own rhetoric, Randolph exposed the missing racial component of Roosevelt's celebration of American democracy and freedom. "If American democracy will not insure equality of opportunity, freedom and justice to its citizens, black and white, it is a hollow mockery and belies the principles for which it is supposed to stand," he said.

Though Randolph risked appearing like one of the unpatriotic "trouble makers" the president had criticized, he felt he had no choice. Blacks, denied voting rights, had little recourse for making their voices heard through political channels. And Jim Crow customs were not confined to southern states and cities; they were replicated in workplaces across the nation, even those contracted by the federal government. Randolph applied the only leverage Black workers had—the threat to protest and strike—to get the president and Congress to correct their racial blind spots. Addressing "Negro America" in 1941, he announced, "We call upon you to demonstrate for the abolition of Jim-Crowism in all Government departments and defense employment."[28]

Roosevelt met Randolph's demands (and prevented the protest) by passing Executive Order 8802 to enforce equity in federal hiring practices. His response was telling. While Hitler suppressed unwanted groups and coerced unruly elements into line for his agenda, Roosevelt had learned valuable lessons about the relationship between liberty and national power during his years in office. People would not tolerate oppressive regimes for long. Inevitably, riots and revolutions would upend the system. It was far more practical and efficient, he believed, to channel aspirations into an unfiltered stream of progress.

Randolph wanted Blacks to be included in that progress, and he outlined his own vision of a postwar order extending democracy and freedom to everyone:

> Unless this war sounds the death knell to the old Anglo-American empire systems, the hapless story of which is one of exploitation for the profit and power of a monopoly-capitalist economy, it will have been fought in vain. Our aim then must not only be to defeat Nazism, fascism, and militarism on the battlefield but to win the peace, for democracy, for freedom and the Brotherhood of man without regard to his pigmentation, land of his birth or the God of his fathers.[29]

Randolph reminded Roosevelt and the entire popular front against fascism that liberty-loving Americans had to defeat forces of tyranny on the home front as well as abroad.

The Statue of Liberty remained a poignant symbol of freedom during the war, and plans to build replicas of the icon floated in the press. Jersey City residents unveiled a thirteen-foot miniature to help sell war bonds in 1943. A year later, New York City reproduced another copy for bond drives in Times Square. Ideas for new statues of liberty circulated internationally as well. In March 1945, the *New York Times* relayed information from unnamed sources that Hitler intended to erect a "Goddess of Liberty" in the harbor at Hamburg, Germany. Meanwhile, British Labour Party minister Arthur Greenwood encouraged Americans to craft a new version made of the nation's gold reserves "in order to tell the world that we no longer worship the golden calf."[30] Greenwood, like A. Philip Randolph, believed that money lust in America and around the world undermined the freedoms the statue was supposed to represent.

|||||||||||

Franklin Roosevelt's distant kinsman Theodore Roosevelt had craved power since his youth, and by age forty-two, he reached his apex by becoming the youngest president in US history in 1901, after the assassination of William McKinley. Yet Teddy Roosevelt still had competition for the title of most powerful man in the nation. The "king of Wall Street," J. P. Morgan, made millions in corporate takeovers, targeting struggling but promising companies that he bought cheap and revitalized for profit. He created the massive corporation US Steel, and he was building the biggest railroad company in history before Roosevelt got in his way.

In 1902, the president brought Morgan down to size by directing his attorney general to break up Morgan's railroad company, Northern Securities, which he argued violated the Sherman Anti-Trust Act. The Supreme Court agreed in a 5–4 decision, a major victory for a president who had long prided himself on fighting corruption. Morgan was furious; he was used to having his way in the world, including with most politicians. But Roosevelt's popularity among voters soared along with his reputation as a man of integrity, the rare politician who couldn't be bought. As a favorite son of one of the wealthiest merchant families in the country, Roosevelt's actions seemed opposed to the interests of his class. He had multiple motivations, however, for reining in capitalism: morals, pride, a belief in democratic fairness, and a pronounced fear of socialist revolution that could have erupted in the absence of reforms.

Thirty years later, Teddy's younger relative Franklin Roosevelt followed his example by setting limits on financial aspirations. For FDR, as well as TR, economic liberty cut both ways. Capitalism favored the financially fittest, those with the will to seize opportunities and amass fortunes. The capitalist system by its design, however, created collateral damage, not only institutions or the environment but also people—laborers who didn't have the mind, time, or start-up funds to make deals for their benefit. The odds were also stacked against small business owners who couldn't compete with much larger companies.

Income disparities across class sectors in the 1920s destabilized the economy while decades of underregulated business practices had raised profit indicators that were bound to fall. They crashed harder than most expected. By 1932, Americans who went down with the ship run ashore by captains of industry had had enough. "Practices of the unscrupulous money changers stand indicted in the court of public opinion, rejected by the hearts and minds of men," Franklin Roosevelt said.[31] The president could have been talking directly to financier John Raskob, who joined his Empire State colleague Al Smith in the Liberty League to criticize Roosevelt and the New Deal. Though Roosevelt's administration set its sights on providing relief and recovery with New Deal programs, they also promised sweeping reforms to prevent another major recession. That's what got Raskob's attention, as well as Republicans like Herbert Hoover.

In 1936, Hoover voiced his opposition to Roosevelt and Congress in his "Challenge to Liberty" speech, which framed centralized government and public spending as violations of liberty. "Freedom does not die from frontal attack," Hoover said. "It dies because men in power no longer believe in a system based upon Liberty." The prime offender, he identified, was President Roosevelt, who had proposed policies that undermined free enterprise and individualism. Referring to Roosevelt's rededication of the Statue of Liberty two days prior, Hoover called the statue "the forgotten woman" in an era of New Deal illiberalism. Republicans, he reminded, had never lost faith in the free and competitive market that would correct itself without "coercion." "We propose to turn the whole direction of this country toward liberty, not away from it," he vowed. Government intervention, he believed, was a problem, not a solution. As he stated, "We propose to amend the tax laws so as not to defeat free men and free enterprise."[32]

Though capitalism could exert a negative impact from time to time, Hoover and laissez-faire advocates argued that big business created collateral benefits by making the entire "pie" bigger, in the form of a robust economy, offering more jobs and gross national product. They thought regulations made as much sense as putting brakes on a rocket. Far better to let it fly. Earlier in 1936, Al Smith had compared the New Deal to a "vast octopus set up by government, that wound its arms around all the business of the country, paralyzed big business, and choked little business to death."[33] For Smith, Hoover, and Raskob, too much government control of the economy violated liberties by creating an unfair environment that encumbered capitalists from pursuing their fullest potential.

For Roosevelt and other reformers, that was exactly the point. The National Industrial Recovery Act, Agricultural Adjustment Act, National Labor Relations Board (Wagner Act), the Glass-Steagall Act, and the Banking Act established parameters on what businesses and banks could do to make money, setting fair rules to level the playing field for more citizens to secure financial well-being. Laissez-faire capitalists, meanwhile, called foul. Opposed to what he regarded as unnecessary restrictions on private enterprise, Hoover warned that New Deal programs were clever ruses to dupe the public into allowing powerful men to amass wealth at the expense of individual freedom. "It is through taking vast sums of the people's money and then manipulating its spending to build up personal power," Hoover charged, that lead to a concentration of wealth at the top. He expressed alarm that public funds were being used to "subsidize special groups of our citizens and special regions of the country."[34]

New Dealers, on the other hand, pointed to the special interests of capitalists who had been subsidized by the government and granted tax breaks for decades. The free market, to New Deal liberals, amounted to a myth propagated by the rich to convince the public that their practices were perfectly natural and innocent. All the while, venture capitalists gamed the system for their own benefit, gambling with the economic security of all citizens. Though the masses rarely chased high rewards, they still suffered the risks to no fault of their own when the economy took a turn for the worse. Bust times might appear as a temporary, insignificant setback to wealthy men like Raskob or Hoover, but they had far deeper repercussions for those without safety nets to cushion the blow.

While Raskob, Smith, and Hoover talked in terms of economic liberty, Roosevelt had economic empires in mind when he spoke of reforming an oppressive system. Empires, he knew, were not built by following the rules or being polite. They were more often ruthless and indifferent to the welfare of those they exploited for wealth. The president's domestic policies, in terms of empire and liberty, also matched his approach to foreign affairs. He wanted to reset conditions for a fair, cooperative spirit among various interest groups or nations, with a governing body acting as a referee.

IIIIIIIIIII

Roosevelt didn't trust many power-hungry men, and he certainly didn't trust ruthless dictators. But he had to keep Joseph Stalin on his side. The Russian army, since late 1941 when they had joined the Allies, was crucial for fighting the Germans in eastern Europe, while the British and Americans made their way through North Africa and Italy and island-hopped around the Pacific to push back the Japanese. Churchill and Roosevelt needed Stalin to hold the line, but they didn't expect him to act in good faith once his imperial interests were at stake. The Soviet dictator had already shown his tendency to make antidemocratic decisions earlier in the war when he signed the Molotov-Ribbentrop Pact with Hitler to divide Poland, an agreement that became null and void when Hitler sent his army to invade Russia. Stalin switched his allegiance to the Allies after that, though his territorial greed simmered below the surface, and Roosevelt knew he would have a hard time preventing the Russians from claiming land after the war.

Stalin, for his part, distrusted Churchill and Roosevelt, believing the two leaders were conspiring against him and keeping secrets. Though often paranoid about challenges to his power, Stalin found evidence to reinforce his sense of betrayal. His requests for a cross-Channel offensive to divide Germany's attention and take the pressure off the eastern front were rebuffed until the summer of 1944. Meanwhile, his spies reported on a top-secret program in the United States to weaponize nuclear power. Rather than confront Roosevelt about the lack of disclosure, the Soviet leader took notes on the Manhattan Project, began developing his own nuclear weapons program, and pocketed his resentments for later.

As the US president grappled with ways to maintain the support of a wary ally, he also worked to bolster the morale of US soldiers around the world. In the "Four Freedoms" speech, he had deconstructed democracy down to basic values to appeal to Americans' sense of personal liberty, simplifying the mission for millions deployed. But servicemembers enlisted or fought as draftees for a variety of reasons. Many dedicated themselves to preserving the freedoms that their families and neighbors enjoyed at home, but some motivations stemmed from lofty idealism about liberty for all.

Over one million Black Americans served in the armed forces during World War II, where they faced segregation, discrimination, and the indignity of menial jobs. Like World War I veterans, many Black soldiers and sailors channeled their service toward achieving victory against oppression abroad and stateside. The editors of the *Pittsburgh Courier* especially promoted the double "V" theme in the pages of their paper, exposing the hypocrisy of a nation that expected Blacks to help liberate foreign lands while they were denied basic liberties, like voting rights and equal employment, at home. The slogan exploded in popularity, and the paper regularly updated its readers about the deluge of endorsements for an expanded democracy for all US citizens. Calling it "Freedom's Crusade," the *Courier* framed the concept as significant "for all Americans, white and black, because it provides a suitable slogan for all God-fearing, liberty-loving men and women to rally around." Readers such as Lonie V. Johnson of Florence, Texas, wrote the paper to express appreciation for the drive for double "V," noting that it "is important because many Americans are more dangerous to us than some of our enemies abroad."[35]

The double "V" public relations campaign had been sparked by an aircraft manufacturing worker named James G. Thompson, who wrote a letter to the *Pittsburgh Courier*, asking "Should I Sacrifice to Live 'Half American'?" Blacks risking their lives during wartime often asked the same question. Across the country, VV clubs sprang up to demand an end to Jim Crow laws, federal discrimination, and racial violence. Membership in organizations such as the NAACP increased substantially, and activism for civil rights carried the war momentum into local politics, as Black veterans inspired their friends, family, and neighbors to organize. One of the most motivated among these veterans, Medgar Evers, who had served in the US Army in Europe, became active in the push for voting rights in his home state of Mississippi. Despite receiving GI Bill benefits, he was denied the opportunity to study law at the University of Mississippi because of his race. He fought the law instead at the grassroots level, traveling throughout Mississippi to raise awareness about the shortcomings of democracy for Black citizens. In a radio broadcast in May 1963, Evers declared, "The Negro has been here in America since 1619, a total of 344 years. He is not going anywhere else; this country is his home." Blacks, as bona fide Americans, he insisted, had to be included in the American political system. "Let me appeal to the consciences of many silent, responsible citizens of the white community who know that a victory for democracy in Jackson will be a victory for democracy everywhere."[36]

Evers continued to challenge Jim Crow customs despite death threats from White supremacists, until June 12, 1963, when he was shot by a sniper outside his home. Evers died about an hour later, age thirty-seven, and was buried at Arlington National Cemetery. The rifle used to kill him was found abandoned, bearing the fingerprints of Marine Corps veteran Byron De La Beckwith. An all-White male jury found Beckwith not guilty of the crime. Yet Bob Dylan accused the entire nation of the murder in the lyrics of his folk song dedicated to Evers, "Only a Pawn in Their Game," which blamed the killing not on any individual but on the larger culture of racism that enabled racist thoughts to become actions.

Hispanic and Asian Americans also served in the war, though in smaller percentages than Black Americans. So did Native Americans. Ira Hayes, of Arizona, became one of the most iconic heroes of World War II, immortalized in photographs, films, and monuments before his tragic death. At the age of nineteen, Hayes enlisted in the US Marine Corps Reserve and volunteered for paratrooper training before deploying to the Pacific to fight in battles from Guadalcanal to the Japanese islands. Part of the Fifth Marine Battalion that drove the enemy from Iwo Jima, Hayes helped hoist an American flag on Mount Suribachi along with five other Marines, as a photojournalist snapped the indelible image of American heroism. The composition of six servicemembers raising the national colors during a perilous battle harked back to the words that Francis Scott Key had expressed upon seeing that the "flag was still there" after the attack upon Fort McHenry. Whether or not Americans registered the comparison consciously, the photo became incredibly popular as a memorial to the American bravery and teamwork that ultimately prevailed to defend the republic.

That experience took its toll on Ira Hayes in the postwar years. Though he participated in dedication ceremonies and even portrayed himself in the John Wayne movie *Sands of Iwo Jima,* the veteran suffered from post-traumatic stress disorder and struggled with alcoholism. He was found dead alongside a road twelve days after his thirty-second birthday, after a night of card playing in Bapchule, Arizona.

Hayes, like Evers, had a folk song written for him, "The Ballad of Ira Hayes," by Peter La Farge, which was later covered by Johnny Cash. La Farge's ode to the war hero went light on patriotism, heavy on criticism toward a nation that had confined Native Americans to substandard reservations. The songwriter, assuming the perspective of Hayes as resentful of racial inequalities, tells the story of "the White man's greed," and the paratrooper's postwar fate as "just a Pima Indian" with "no money, no crops, no chance." La Farge dismissed reenactments of the Iwo Jima flag raising as empty gestures, "as you'd throw a dog a bone." Hayes, he implied, died like a dog in a ditch, never receiving his due, especially since so many minorities who fought for freedom abroad had to continue the fight for freedom and security at home. War was hell for them. So was racism.

IIIIIIIIIII

Woody Guthrie, one of the most prolific and recognizable folk singers of the Depression years, recorded what was bound to be his most famous song in 1944. "This Land Is Your Land," sung by millions of schoolchildren as a simple, patriotic tune, originated as a critique of American privatization. Guthrie began jotting down the lyrics several years earlier than its release, as a pointed response to Irving Berlin's civil hymn "God Bless America." To Guthrie, the lyrical emphasis on "my home sweet home" in "God Bless America" sounded too self-serving. Instead, he claimed that the American nation was "made for you and me." An early version of Guthrie's song included verses drawing attention to a host of social inequities. He made caustic references to private property and food-relief lines that, for him, gave lie to the idea that America provided for everyone. The United States, he insisted, had to find the means to do better by elevating liberty for all.

Though Guthrie was among the musicians blacklisted in the 1950s for alleged communist activity, he balked at labels designed to divide people. "Jesus don't care if you call it socialism or communism, or just me and you," he wrote in his memoir. "We all just mortally got to work together . . . own everything together."[37] More than Marxist doctrine, Guthrie, who penned a song imagining Christ as president to help the poor, promoted basic Christian ethics: help one another and do unto others as you would want others to do to you.

Guthrie's philosophical stance on the meaning of America dovetailed with that of Vice President Henry Wallace, who spoke of "the century of the common man" as an alternative to notions of American empire. "Some have spoken of the 'American Century,'" Wallace stated, referring to the rather imperialist *Life* magazine editorial by Henry Luce, but "I say that the century on which we are entering . . . can and must be the century of the common man." According to Wallace, freedom-loving people in foreign lands would not accept an American system imposed on them from above. Instead, they were likely to resent and reject such impertinence as another form of oppression. The United States, he urged, had to preserve its moral standing and practice its republican values to earn a reputation of benevolence throughout the world.[38]

Not everyone discerned the differences between the worldviews of Wallace and Luce. Leftist critic Dwight Macdonald, remarking upon the dueling essays in 1948, concluded that both men condoned US imperialism, though he acknowledged that Luce did so more "bluntly" and "without the doubletalk to which liberals are accustomed." Wallace's "passionate rhetoric" may have masked the particulars of his imperialist intentions, Macdonald explained, but his call for democratic reconstruction made him "the Woodrow Wilson of World War II."[39] An April 1941 editorial in *Christian Century* also detected a paternalistic strain in the vice president's triumphal language, even before his "Common Man" speech became public. Noting Wallace's rigid religious interpretation of the war as a battle between good and evil, the author dubbed Wallace "the high priest of a new religion of nationalism" "primarily concerned with the survival of the State." Wallace's seemingly virtuous verbiage about peace and democracy, according to the article, concealed a coercive edge, designed to shape the world into America's image. In the breach between idealism and realism, *Christian Century* concluded, Wallace's "messianism becomes imperialism."[40]

Wallace, however, believed he was echoing the anti-imperialist intentions of President Roosevelt, who wanted to see basic freedoms normalized throughout the world. Wallace and Roosevelt spoke in terms of a worldwide expansion of the New Deal, bringing relief and recovery through cooperative work and public projects. Yet as Hoover had argued in his diatribes against the New Deal in the 1930s, centralized, top-down programs were inherently coercive. During the Cold War that emerged in the late 1940s and continued for four decades, US policymakers would not always recognize the fine line separating international aid from international control nor appreciate the mixed consequences of American actions in the world.

Henry Wallace may have muddled his rhetoric about American influence around the globe, but he believed that the US nation and its people had to cultivate a *spiritual* sense of democracy and liberty in themselves and others. Federal judge Learned Hand eloquently expressed this sentiment in a 1944 address delivered in Central Park. Attempting to unpack the essence of liberty, Hand rejected a self-centered definition of liberty that meant "freedom to do as one likes." He also dismissed the misconception that liberty was tied to or safeguarded by political documents or institutions. Unfettered from these "false hopes," Hand asserted that "liberty lies in the hearts of men and women." Striving to capture it, Hand described true liberty as akin to humility, "the spirit which is not too sure that it is right," and "the spirit which seeks to understand the minds of other[s]" and "weighs their interests alongside its own without bias."

Warning against American pride in "winning" or any assumed God-given right to prescribe the freedom of others, Hand acknowledged that the United States was aspiring to ideals that Americans proclaimed to possess but never fully practiced. It is a "spirit of America that has never existed," he said. On a more positive note, Hand affirmed his belief that the "spirit of liberty," though often dormant, remained latent in the collective conscience of Americans, many of whom had come to the continent for the sake of freedom.[41]

Like President Roosevelt and philosopher John Dewey, Hand called upon Americans to construct liberty and democracy via cooperation. The intangible nature of the terms, however, left Americans without a clear plan for balancing personal freedom with the general welfare. Dewey, as a philosopher, tried to dissolve the apparent dualism between the two, but he had a hard time communicating the methods for liquidating liberty as a personal asset into binding social currency. Education, he believed, was highly important in the process, giving citizens the tools to decide on the best course of action in local, national, and global affairs.

Back in the 1760s, John Adams expressed a similar concern. "Liberty," he wrote, "cannot be preserved without a general knowledge among the people." Foremost, Adams believed that the poor and otherwise ignorant needed to know about those in power to keep them accountable, and he identified a free press as essential to bringing news to the masses. However, he also exhorted Americans to learn everything related to liberty, as though it were an object to be studied. By the 1930s and 1940s, Roosevelt, Wallace, Hand, and Dewey all spoke of liberty as an ongoing, creative project.[42]

IIIIIIIIIII

The *New York Times* on October 4, 1944, pronounced the death of former New York governor and Empire State enthusiast Al Smith. The remarkable success that the seventy-year-old politician had achieved in his life, the obituary stated, "had no exact parallel in American history." "No other city urchin, earning a precarious living in the streets in his early days, ever rose so superior to his lack of youthful advantages and had so distinguished a public career." Though Smith had exerted a positive influence on national and foreign affairs, including his "untiring" efforts to support the war against fascism, the *Times* described Smith as "distinctly a product of New York City," "born in the shadow of the Brooklyn Bridge." The article noted his involvement with the Empire State Building, "his principal business activity for many years," as well as some of his public squabbles, namely a "personal hatred" of William Randolph Hearst and his strained relationship with President Roosevelt. It listed his late wife and their five children.[43]

Smith's old rival, Franklin Roosevelt, did not outlive him for long. The president, serving an unprecedented fourth term in the executive office, died of a brain hemorrhage on April 12, 1945, in Georgia, before he could witness the end of the world war that had consumed so much of his energy. Germany surrendered less than a month later, on May 7, after the suicide of Hitler, who realized his military could no longer withstand the Allied assault. But as people around the world celebrated V-E (Victory in Europe) Day, they had to await a victory over Japan. After Harry S. Truman was sworn in as the next president, he received reports for the first time about the unfinished Manhattan Project and weighed the implications of atomic power. The bomb did not pass its test in Los Alamos until mid-July. Meanwhile, the US Marine Corps struggled to secure Okinawa and prepare for an amphibious landing on the home island of Japan. No one could predict how long the war in the Pacific would drag on.

Thousands of servicemembers had already returned to the United States. The Statue of Liberty was there to welcome them. After V-E Day, special lighting arrangements were made to greet and celebrate the troops, guaranteeing that Lady Liberty would be illuminated each evening as veterans entered New York Harbor. "The returning American soldier always looks for the 'Old Lady' with her flaming torch aloft," the papers noted.[44] The Statue of Liberty had taken on multiple meanings for a diversity of causes and demographics by 1945. The landmark still stirred the hearts of recent immigrants, but during the war, she symbolized democracy and "world freedom" like never before. Referred to in countless political speeches and campaigns, Lady Liberty was also exploited by politicians from Al Smith to Franklin Roosevelt to Herbert Hoover as a benchmark for their platforms.

The variety of groups adopting the statue as their symbol, however, offended some Americans. Carl Beck of New York wrote a letter to the editor of the *New York Times* in May 1944 to voice his concern about the proliferation, and thus cheapening, of the statue's true meaning. "Miss Liberty is not only a symbol for all America but bids fair to be the symbol of all democracy the world over, having already appeared on United Nations posters," he wrote. But Beck took issue with the "factional or partisan" use of Lady Liberty that, he argued, violated "good taste." He asked, "Who in Congress will introduce a bill to protect Miss Liberty, owned by all the people of the United States . . . as is our American flag, from being used as a trade-mark or special group symbol?" Beck expressed his fear that the propagation of the statue for branding purposes would dilute its "great meaning and significance."[45] Visitations to Bedloe's Island skyrocketed during and after the war, according to officials, who estimated that a fifth of those making the trip to the statue were soldiers and sailors. The superintendent of the island noted a mood shift among the visitors as well. "They approach the statue much more seriously than before," he said.[46]

Lieutenant Colonel William Franklin Smith Jr. of Alabama, a West Point graduate and US pilot with the Eighth Air Force, likely saw the statue as he approached New York in the spring of 1945, returning to his wife and child living in Watertown, Massachusetts. Despite his homecoming, Smith still served as a military transport pilot, and on July 27, 1945, he prepared to conduct a routine personnel transfer on a B-25 Mitchell the following morning from Bedford Air Field to LaGuardia Airport. As his wife Martha Molloy Smith recalled, "He bounced the baby on his lap after dinner" the evening before his flight, and happily commented that his son, Billy, seemed to recognize him for the first time. Smith's wife, an Army Corps nurse, had a bad feeling the next morning just before the

Lieutenant Colonel's takeoff. "He was so dubious about the weather and said flying conditions would be poor." Flustered, he accidentally grabbed the car keys before boarding the plane.[47]

Smith had flown plenty of missions in Europe before his return stateside that spring, but his aviation skills failed him on that fateful July morning when he became lost in the fog surrounding New York City. After deciding to forgo a landing at LaGuardia, he radioed for permission to land at Newark Airport instead. He never made it to the airstrip. With zero visibility, Smith crashed the B-25 directly into the Empire State Building around 9:40 a.m., shattering the skyscraper's north side between the 78th and 80th floors. A total of fourteen people died instantly or in the aftermath, including Smith, his passengers, and several civilians within the building, some of whom perished trying to escape the flames.

About fifty to sixty visitors on the 86th observation level stood atop the chaos. Tour guide Louis Petley remembered that he was apologizing for the fog blocking the skyline view when he heard the crash and saw fire. He managed to shepherd his group down the stairway and into an elevator.[48] The famed Otis elevators of the Empire State Building were still partly operational but severely compromised. First aid workers found out just how unreliable they were when they tried to evacuate Betty Lou Oliver, an elevator operator who had been badly burned, by attempting to lower her from the eightieth floor to ground level using an intact lift. But the cables came loose, and the woman plummeted seventy-five stories to the basement. Astonishingly, she survived, though sustaining multiple fractures, and set the record for the longest survived elevator fall. Because the crash occurred on a Saturday, there were only about 1,500 of the typical 5,500 workers present. The incident nevertheless shocked all those who experienced it. Phillip Kerby saw a young woman engulfed in flames screaming that she was going to jump from the window of the 79th story. She was eventually rescued by firemen who arrived at the top floors within forty minutes after the crash. Some survivors remembered seeing a "little man in a T-shirt" shouting for people to leave. "I always knew these skyscrapers weren't safe," he told them.[49]

Observers on the ground also witnessed the tragedy unfold as they saw the plane just before impact. "I heard the roar of the plane's engines," Stan Lomax, a sports announcer, recalled. "I knew it would crash." An off-duty air force officer, Lieutenant Aubrey B. Condit, spotted the B-25 from a nearby skyscraper and noticed the pilot's last-ditch effort to swerve away. "I knew what was going to happen when I saw the B-25 come down out of the clouds and the fog." But Condit could do nothing but pray. "Then the plane hit and I saw it silhouetted against the flames," he said. "For a second the plane was outlined then the whole thing burst into a livid pillar of flame. Then there was an explosion which shook me like nothing has before."[50] The B-25's pilot, Smith, and his two passengers were recorded as noncombat casualties of World War II. One of them was navy aviator Albert Perna. The second, air force sergeant Christopher S. Domitrovich of Illinois, had survived the invasions of Normandy and Holland the year prior.

When Mayor Fiorello La Guardia reached the scene two hours after the crash, he immediately noticed the heat. "It was just an oven," he said. Journalist Oscar Fraley rushed to the seventy-ninth floor where the offices of the National Catholic Welfare Conference were located. The twenty workers on that level bore the brunt of the crash. Fraley saw eleven "charred bodies" lying upon desks. A man stumbled into the room, carrying a bag filled with body parts he had found on a parapet below. "Strangely, everyone talked in whispers," Fraley wrote. The reporter made his way to the area where the plane had demolished an outer wall. "Standing on the edge of nothing I looked down into the street jammed with crowds," he recalled. "I could see a body lying on a parapet . . . [and] steel girders hung loosely like spaghetti."[51] Archbishop Francis J. Spellman might have been among the dead or injured had his 10 a.m. appointment in the building not been canceled.[52]

The crash took a human toll and caused an estimated $1 million in damage to the Empire State Building, mostly from fire, not structural issues. The lower-floor offices were largely unaffected and able to reopen within forty-eight hours. But the loss of life and property had to be accounted for, and military officials quickly wrote reports that pinned the incident on pilot, not mechanical, error. Smith, navigating by sight in poor conditions, had violated the city's regulation against flying below five thousand feet in Manhattan. As Army authorities explained, the Empire State Building was such an obvious landmark for pilots on clearer days that they often "feared it would serve as a guide to incoming enemy bombers should New York ever be bombed."[53] Smith could not see it through the fog until the very end.

Longtime tenant of the building Jack Brod was not in his office on the morning of the crash, but he heard about it from a "hysterical" telephone operator at the site, who misinterpreted the noise as a Japanese attack. "They're bombing the building," she cried.[54] The woman's reaction revealed an unease among Americans as the war raged on in the Pacific. Even on the East Coast, people sensed their vulnerability to submarine and aerial warfare. Pilot Smith's wife expressed her disbelief that her husband had survived so many dangerous missions abroad only to be killed in an accident in New York. But she consoled herself with her son Billy and the words her husband often repeated about the possible outcomes of military service. "He told me to be a real soldier should his number ever come up," she relayed.[55]

The war in July of 1945 was nearing its end. President Truman dropped a nuclear bomb on Hiroshima on August 6, and when that failed to elicit a response, the military dropped a second bomb on Nagasaki. The next day, Japanese leadership announced its intention to surrender, which was officially signed in early September, six years after the war began. The presence of nuclear weapons, however, did not make the world any safer. Even as they ended one major war, they indirectly proliferated dozens of smaller wars in the coming decades.

Some empires had been defeated or nearly spent by war's end. Japan, Italy, and Germany were occupied by the Allied powers, their military capabilities dismantled, and their governments reformed. The Netherlands and Denmark were recovered. France lay in physical and financial ruins, as it struggled to recover from the Vichy regime and restore its hold on colonies in Asia and North Africa. But one empire in particular seized the opportunity to expand. Stalin refused to demobilize his army from the territories it now controlled across Eastern Europe, including parts of Germany and long-coveted Poland, despite demands to open free elections. Those living under Soviet rule wouldn't regain their freedom for nearly fifty years.

Elsewhere in the world, revolutionary movements took advantage of the power gap to fight for liberty from their colonizers. Over thirty new states in Africa and Asia emerged between 1945 and 1960. India, Pakistan, Egypt, Indonesia, and Israel were established. The Philippines achieved independence from the United States. China's civil war resumed and then ended in 1949 when Mao Zedong declared a communist state, officially the People's Republic, while the former US ally Chiang Kai-shek and his followers were forced to evacuate to Taiwan. Dozens of communist movements gained momentum throughout the 1940s and 1950s, often supported by China and Russia. Some leaders, like Ho Chi Minh in Vietnam, adopted the language of the US Declaration of Independence. Others, like those in North Korea, thumbed their noses at US attempts to thwart them. The world once again became lost in the fog between empire and liberty in the Cold War era.

CHAPTER 6

FREEDOM LIGHTS IN THE COLD WAR ERA—1973

When the World Trade Center (WTC) opened on April 4, 1973, the complex of seven buildings in Lower Manhattan instantly broke building-height records and became a target of criticism. The idea for the complex had originated in the early 1960s with multimillionaire David Rockefeller, who pitched it as an economic stimulus for New York's Financial District. Critics were vocal from the start.

The *New York Times*, on August 6, 1966, devoted its major headlines to President Lyndon Johnson and the Vietnam War, but the WTC's groundbreaking received brief mention as a disruption of the city's peace. "The early morning quiet along the Hudson River waterfront was shattered" by "chattering jackhammers" preparing the first stage of construction on the $525-million complex, the paper noted. The article estimated that "some 8,000 workers" would build the Trade Center over the next four years, including "twin" 110-story towers.[1]

Seven years later, coverage of the WTC's opening day made front-page news, announcing that the two 1,350-foot towers were now "the largest buildings in the world." In an era of economic recession, the giant landmarks in Lower Manhattan projected a similar sense of confidence in US economic prowess that the builders of the Empire State Building had projected during the Great Depression. President Richard Nixon welcomed the WTC in his keynote message as "a major factor for the expansion of the nation's international trade," while Governor Nelson Rockefeller, who had approved the project in cooperation with his brother, noted the benefits of streamlining operations of the State of New York, the primary tenant of the South Tower. "The World Trade Center is our address . . . and we're proud of it," he said, echoing the pride that former governor Al Smith had expressed when opening the Empire State Building as a symbol of New York's lofty status four decades earlier.[2]

The new complex put the Empire State Building figuratively and almost literally in its shadow, rising one hundred feet higher than the iconic skyscraper in Midtown. Governor Rockefeller alluded to the passing of the torch, noting that the World Trade Center was now the emblem of the "Empire State" and its economy, enabling "the Port of New York to retain its accustomed place as the major capital of world commerce." But the new buildings were also a boon to neighboring states and the entire nation, as New Jersey governor Cahill reminded the audience, calling the WTC "an industrial and trade United Nations."[3] The United States, not just New York, was tied to the newest, highest helm of world trade.

Economic power, everyone agreed, defined the buildings' purpose. The seven structures of the WTC contained nine million square feet of office space, but economists dismissed real estate as window dressing and pinpointed the heart of the complex as the World Trade Institute, an educational site dedicated to global commerce. As institute director Jack Zwick, a former Columbia University finance professor, told journalists during a tour, the Institute's mission to provide accurate trade information and language courses for international business executives gave the WTC its substance and driving force. "It's all intended to make trading easier and make people better able to plan trading strategies," he explained.[4]

The WTC's blunt business function, however, left little to character, according to multiple observers. "The towers are pure technology, the lobbies are pure schmaltz," reviewer Ada Louise Huxtable wrote. The plain block columns designed by Japanese American architect Minoru Yamasaki, Huxtable opined, contained no aesthetic value comparable to classic skyscrapers in Chicago and New York, which were "bone-beautiful," with bold exteriors combining "the strength and subtlety of great art." The World Trade Center, in Huxtable's opinion, did nothing to elevate trends in great architecture. Instead, the buildings amounted to hollow spectacle, "the ultimate Disney-land fairytale blockbuster," or "General Motors Gothic," that assumed the old American adage: the bigger, the better. The Twin Towers, for all their height, failed to offer better views of the city or a more effective use of its surrounding environment. "It is being looked on more as a monster than as marvel," she concluded, implying that the Trade Center's visual impact remained on a "smaller scale" than predecessors like Empire State.[5]

Nearly all reporters on opening day noted the "controversial" context of the buildings, especially the decision to finance them through a public entity, the New York Port Authority, rather than private enterprise. But design flaws were most apparent to critics who thought the monoliths appeared misplaced, looming "incongruously over Lower Manhattan like dandelions on a well-mowed lawn." Comparing the structures to anything organic amounted to generosity, as most writers described them as cold and impersonal "examples of institutional arrogance."[6] Even the achievement of tallest buildings seemed unexceptional since the Sears Tower in Chicago was scheduled to open the following year and break the height record once again.

The World Trade Center may have received more favorable reviews had it opened in the early 1960s or the 1990s when American confidence was more robust. In the early 1970s, events related to the Vietnam War, domestic turmoil, political corruption, and economic decline had darkened the mood of the nation. As architectural historian Justin Beal observed, "between 1962 and 1973, the politics and culture changed so drastically in the city. You can see the shift in the reception [of the buildings as] big symbols of government and bureaucracy, authoritarian power." That shift, he said, affected the public's reaction to the Twin Towers. "There are all these metaphors to violence [so] they took on a sinister feeling."[7] In other words, Americans had been severely humbled by the nation's recent past, and they were reluctant to embrace garish symbols of hubris in the early 1970s. A lot had happened since the victory parades in 1945.

IIIIIIIIIII

The Empire State Building was first illuminated to celebrate the election of Franklin D. Roosevelt in 1932, but the installation of the so-called Freedom Lights in 1956 marked a new phase in the building's image. The Freedom Lights, consisting of four revolving beacons atop the tower, reinforced the message of welcome and freedom that had long been associated with the Statue of Liberty. Americans in the 1950s were eager to emphasize freedom as an American value anywhere they could, setting the United States apart from authoritarian regimes such as the Soviet Union and China.

With the addition of the new lighting feature, the Empire State Building was effectively pressed into service for the Cold War, an intense, global competition between Americans and communists to project power and ideology, fought primarily through proxies and propaganda. The symbolic tie between empire and liberty that the Freedom Lights represented was replicated by policymakers abroad in an ongoing effort to enlighten the world about the superiority of democracy and the American way of life. But when influence alone seemed ineffective, Americans, like their communist adversaries, resorted to force.

At the end of World War II, the Soviet Union refused to withdraw its armies from Eastern Europe or hold open elections in their occupied territories, essentially subjugating millions of people under communist rule. But the Cold War was about more than geographic conquest. It quickly became a contest for the "hearts and minds" of populations struggling for independence during a massive wave of decolonization in the wake of World War II. The United States, as the most powerful and stable nation in the postwar period, sought to lead the world away from communist influence by multiple means, using ideas to promote democracy, offering money and programs to support developing nations, and deploying the military to contain the spread of communism.

The United States had never taken such an active leadership role in international affairs, but most Americans did not consider these interventions as imperialist acts. They saw them as gifts to a chaotic and vulnerable world in need of freedom, especially freedom from communist rule. But the power the United States leveraged often amounted to illiberal means of shaping the world in its image, demonstrating a lack of faith in democracy's survival. The most powerful nation in the world was not always so sure of its stated values in the postwar era.

Instead of expressing confidence in the inherent, organic appeal of democracy, American policymakers used coercive measures of money and militance to turn their idealism into realism. This approach to solving perceived problems in the world was not exactly new. American leaders had used a combination of carrots and sticks throughout US history to bolster control of countries short of actual conquest. The Bretton Woods Conference in 1944 extended "dollar diplomacy" by establishing gold and the US dollar as the standard for international currency, assuming American economic leadership, a role that Great Britain once performed. The Cold War, however, amplified the urgency to gain traction in all areas of the world before communists could take them over.

President Harry Truman set the tone at the top of his administration. In 1947, he addressed Congress on the need to support countries threatened by communist aggression. At first applied specifically to Greece and Turkey, two countries struggling against communist control, the "Truman Doctrine" was later extended globally, setting a new level of vigilance that required a much bigger military than Americans had ever maintained long term before. Truman's plan to offer foreign aid and keep a standing army ready to intervene in global crises faced the challenge of convincing the American public that such expenditures and involvement were necessary. To make the case, Truman and his fellow interventionists appealed to Americans' love of liberty.

In a 1948 speech to Congress, Truman detailed the plight of war-weary and thus weakened European nations vulnerable to Soviet threats and called upon Americans to dutifully help Europeans defend their freedoms. "The time has come when the free men and women of the world must face the threat to their liberty squarely and courageously," he said. Like Roosevelt, Truman put foreign affairs in terms of national security, arguing that measures to "give support to the free and democratic nations of Europe" would also "improve the solid foundation of our own national strength."

Unlike Roosevelt, Truman did not have much trouble bridging the gap between national and international well-being. Whereas Roosevelt had carefully connected the fate of the world to Americans' self-interest, Truman, in the postwar era, could assume that most Americans accepted globalism, the notion that the entire world falls within US national interest. The experience of World War II had made those interconnections clear. "The United States," he stated, "has a tremendous responsibility to act according to the measure of our power for good in the world. We have learned that we must earn the peace we seek just as we earned victory in the war, not by wishful thinking but by realistic effort." The victory of World War II, in other words, was not yet secure. The president could count on recent events to illustrate the stakes, as memories of Hitler and Pearl Harbor helped him push for preventive military measures in lieu of diplomacy, reminding Americans that appeasement would never stop dictators bent on hegemony.[8] Flexing all forms of their apparent power, Americans framed their role in the Cold War as an alpha among underdogs continuing the fight for the greater good.

||||||||||

President Truman was not living in the White House when assassins attempted to end his life. While renovations were underway on the official residence in the fall of 1950, Truman, his wife, and their immediate staff moved to nearby Blair House, a smaller building typically used as overflow quarters for the president's guests. Situated along the curb of Pennsylvania Avenue without a large lawn surrounding it, Blair House did not provide much of a buffer between the president and the public, a source of tension for security officers on guard.

The attack happened suddenly around 2:20 p.m. on the first day of November. Truman had returned to Blair House an hour earlier and ascended the stairs to take a nap. As staffer J. B. West wrote in his memoir, "the house was so quiet, the day so close, it was a struggle to stay awake." An eruption of gunfire just outside the house broke the calm, and West rushed to the window to see what was going on. "I saw the White House policeman Davidson and Secret Service agent Boring, their pistols drawn and shooting." West hurried to secure the entrance, which had been left wide open by a gaping doorman, frozen in disbelief as the scene unfolded. "Close the door," West shouted. First Lady Bess Truman emerged from upstairs to assess the danger. "Eyes wide, she turned quickly and walked back upstairs," West recalled. She likely did not see Officer Birdzell fall to the ground bleeding or witness the deaths of Officer Coffelt and one of the assailants, whom West could only describe at the time as "a man in a darked striped suit."[9]

There were two assailants, Oscar Collazo and Griselio Torresola, both Puerto Rican nationalists who wanted independence from the United States. They mortally wounded Officer Leslie Coffelt, who returned fire to kill Torresola. Truman was unharmed. The would-be assassins were part of a burgeoning independence movement, which had tried to overthrow the Puerto Rican government two days before the attack on Blair House. The uprisings and the assassination attempt certainly got the attention of the US government, which retaliated by bombing the most active regions of rebellion. But independence from the United States was still a possibility. In 1952, Truman supported a plebiscite giving Puerto Rico an opportunity to decide on a new constitution under the quasi-colonial relationship that had existed since 1898. Puerto Ricans did not vote themselves out of the empire, and calls for full independence have since remained controversial.

Formal political ties had to be weighed against the economic ties that bound Puerto Rico to US interests. The island nation, reliant on US trade and investments, was unlikely to buck American influence. Such were the advantages of the United States' informal empire. However, the same could not be assumed of other nations around the world, particularly communist regimes. The Soviets had rejected US offers to include them in economic institutions such as the World Trade Organization and International Monetary Fund. Chinese Communists under Mao Zedong and Cuban Communists surrounding Fidel Castro also refused to cooperate. As more areas of the world became exposed to communism, US policymakers feared that long-standing methods of dollar diplomacy to coerce favorable terms would be stymied, an unprecedented situation that added to the pressure to build stronger military capabilities as a hard-power backstop. The first test of the United States' response to this new world order occurred in Korea.

Since World War II, the Allies had tried to keep the Soviets from occupying the Korean peninsula, but in the north, pro-communist forces were difficult to dislodge as civil war in the country ensued. The North Koreans spurned demands to hold open elections to unite the peninsula, and most nations, including the United States, refused to recognize the communist-led Democratic People's Republic of Korea (DPRK), which had no democratic governance. Without diplomatic or economic means to pressure North Korea, Truman, in 1950, committed US troops to a United Nations coalition to defend the fledgling democracy in South Korea from a communist invasion. General Douglas MacArthur returned to command UN forces, comprising mostly US personnel, and achieved some early success in pushing the communists back across the midpoint line before facing the new challenge of added opponents from China. The North Koreans had garnered the support of both major communist powers, the Soviets and the Chinese, to secure their dominance on the peninsula.

After the triumphs of World War II on multiple fronts, Americans had reason to believe they could clinch victory in a relatively small region. But the ways of war had changed since 1945, and total-war strategies were no longer practical. Nuclear weapons now forced restraint. By 1950, the Soviets had stockpiles of nuclear weapons, which made escalation of any conflict an existential threat. J. B. West remembered the president's dilemma during the Korean War. "General MacArthur was pressing for retaliation, but the President felt that would draw the Russians into a Third World War," he wrote."[10] In the end, the United States had to settle for a stalemate along the thirty-eighth parallel and a tentative peace in a divided Korea. The war, however, never officially ended, as US troops remained to protect the South. In the first major armed action after World War II, Americans learned a hard lesson: neither economic nor military power could guarantee victory.

IIIIIIIIII

When Ho Chi Minh declared the independence of Vietnam after World War II, he made direct reference to the two republics responsible for creating the Statue of Liberty: America and France. Quoting from the Declaration of Independence, he proclaimed, "All men are created equal. They are endowed by their Creator with certain inalienable rights, among them are Life, Liberty, and the pursuit of Happiness." He also harked back to the "Rights of Man," which had inspired the 1789 revolution of Vietnam's French oppressors. "All men are born free and with equal rights, and must always remain free and have equal rights," Ho wrote, reaffirming that "those are undeniable truths."[11]

Ho had appealed to the French and American love of liberty before, back when he was a much younger man living in Paris after World War I. President Woodrow Wilson was also in Paris that summer, negotiating the postwar peace terms with Britain, Italy, and France. Wilson's plan for loosening if not eliminating colonial control, ideas which were outlined in his Fourteen Points, did not make much headway at the Versailles Conference. The victors wanted their spoils in the form of new territories or old colonial holdings. The Fourteen Points, however, had caught the attention of independence movements throughout the world, and leaders like Ho Chi Minh hoped the United States would live up to their rhetoric of liberty and help deliver a new world order.

Ho wanted to speak with Wilson about the situation in Vietnam, a nation under French control since the late 1800s. He moved to Paris and worked odd jobs for a chance to get close to Wilson and French prime minister Georges Clemenceau, a former republican activist. Ho never got close enough. Unable to directly address the US president or the prime minister, Ho sent a letter to Secretary of State Robert Lansing, referring to the United States and France as republics. The letter, written in French on behalf of the Annamite (Vietnamese) people, proposed a plan for gradual independence. The Vietnamese nationalist did not denounce the French, but humbly asked that France, as "a republic," and in the interest of "worldwide justice," honor their values of "liberty" and "universal brotherhood."[12]

Whether Wilson ever received the missive remains unknown. Ho, though disappointed, stayed in Paris for a few more years, supporting French socialists and absorbing Vladimir Lenin's communist theories. Wilson knew that Lenin voiced a more radical version of decolonization than he was ready to endorse, and he feared that Lenin's message might unleash the chaos of global revolutions. Lenin certainly won over Ho, who was convinced after the Treaty of Versailles that the capitalist powers would never relinquish imperialism unless forced. Ho remembered sitting alone in a room in Paris, reading Lenin for the first time, and becoming "overjoyed with tears." "I shouted out aloud as if addressing large crowds," he wrote of the moment, "Dear martyr compatriots! This is what we need, this is the path to our liberation!"[13]

Ho met Lenin in the early 1920s in Moscow, where he developed a more radical ideology. Writing a heartfelt obituary for his revolutionary hero in 1924, Ho expressed gratitude on the part of all people of color for Lenin's unbiased, unconditional support for their right to live freely. He called Lenin a "father, teacher, comrade and adviser," for setting the course of history as a "bright star showing us the way to the socialist revolution."[14] By emphasizing Lenin's surprising and refreshing role as a *White* anti-colonialist, Ho named the problem of imperialism as inherently racist, a point that Asians, Latin Americans, Africans, and Black Americans could all relate to.

Ho, however, did not give up on the United States as a potential ally in his cause. Despite his commitment to communism, he was willing to work with anyone who could help the Vietnamese achieve freedom. He struggled alongside Allied liberators to oust the Japanese during World War II, and he once again appealed to Americans in his Declaration of Independence for Vietnam in 1945. Though some US officials saw Ho as a nationalist rather than a communist, most regarded Ho as a wolf in sheep's clothing, covering his despotic communism in the guise of republican language. President Truman, who received a letter from the Vietnamese leader that echoed his entreaties of 1919, was among those who distrusted Ho's intentions. Ho asked Truman and "the American people to interfere urgently in support of our independence . . . in keeping with the principles of the Atlantic and San Francisco Charters" that undergirded the United Nations.[15] Yet the United States did nothing to counter French colonialism in Southeast Asia.

The United States did eventually intervene in Vietnam, but not to Ho's benefit. For US policymakers, communism and democracy were incompatible, and they refused to accept Ho and his comrades as legitimate voices for a reunified Vietnam. Ho, meanwhile, was left with a lingering distaste for American hypocrisy that only intensified as the US military became more involved in fighting the Viet Minh. The nationalist Vietnamese rejected American control just as they had rejected French and Japanese control. With regard to the French, the Statue of Liberty had figured symbolically in the Vietnamese sense of betrayal.

As a young kitchen aide on a French freighter, Ho had traveled to a few US cities, and he likely saw the Statue of Liberty when coming into New York Harbor. Most Americans had no idea that a smaller version of the French statue had stood in Hanoi for decades. Known to locals as the Statue of Madame Saux, Hanoi's copy in Lý Thái Tổ Park was moved by the French in 1890 to the top of sacred Turtle Tower (Tháp Rùa) on Hoàn Kiếm Lake, a controversial place to put a hypocritical symbol of the French colonial regime. Less than three meters tall even with her raised arm, the Statue of Madame Saux looked tiny and misplaced above the solid three-story arches of Turtle Tower. But symbolism mattered more than form. The irony of erecting a Statue of Liberty in a country without independence was not lost on the Vietnamese, and in 1945, when the short-lived Empire of Vietnam was established, the Statue of Madame Saux was removed and destroyed in an act of anti-imperialism against French rule. Empire and liberty, the Vietnamese made clear, could not co-exist, a truth that made the sculpted sign of freedom a sham and an insult.

IIIIIIIIIII

The United Nations responded to multiple calls against genocide around the globe, but one of the first petitions they received on those terms came from Blacks in the United States. "We Charge Genocide," presented by the Civil Rights Congress (CRC) in 1951, documented the systemic violence that Blacks had faced since the Civil War, especially lynchings. Using the United Nations' definition of genocide to make their case, the CRC claimed that the practice existed in the United States "as the result of the consistent, conscious, unified policies of every branch of government." Signed by Black intellectuals and activists, such as W. E. B. Du Bois, the document demanded a UN response. "If the General Assembly acts as the conscience of mankind and therefore acts favorably on our petition, it will have served the cause of peace."[16]

The CRC was quickly denounced as a communist organization, and its two delegates to the United Nations, Paul Robeson and William Patterson, were investigated by US officials for submitting the appeal. Paul Robeson, for one, did intone communist theories of liberation, and he traveled throughout the Soviet bloc. But the struggle for liberty, justice, and basic civil rights among most Black Americans and their supporters in the 1950s and 1960s did not spring from foreign sources. Civil rights activists were not asking for a centralized political system or a command economy. They wanted inclusion in the nation's democratic process and its economic opportunities.

Criticized for "attacking" the US government on a world stage, petitioner William Patterson defended his actions by saying, "It's your government. It's my country. I am fighting to save my country's democratic principles." The distinction was significant. Patterson believed the US government needed to be held accountable for its ongoing problems of democracy. His aims, he asserted, were toward perfecting democratic values, not accepting or excusing an imperfect US society. Though the appeal went unacknowledged by the United Nations, the incident revealed how Black Americans wielded a double-edged sword during the Cold War. From one angle, activists could leverage US rhetoric about the "free world" and "democracy" to highlight American hypocrisy and incentivize reforms; but in the Cold War context of "us versus them" thinking, they constantly had to deflect charges of communist influence in their fight for change.

Intelligence officials were aware of Soviet propaganda that exploited America's poor record on race. In a 1963 memo, Thomas Hughes reported on Soviet media, which "laid bare" "the hypocrisy of US claims to leadership of the free world" and treated "US racism" at home as "indicative of its policies toward colored peoples throughout the world."[17] The State Department took the report seriously and referred to the race issue as a national "crisis" that prompted President John F. Kennedy and, later, Lyndon Johnson, to champion civil rights legislation for the sake of America's international image.

But the Cold War was not always fought in the open. While civil rights reforms were made public to protect America's image, covert operations during the Cold War were kept secret for the same reason. The Central Intelligence Agency (CIA), created as a tool for communist containment, had its origins in World War II. The Office of Strategic Services (OSS) served as an intelligence arm for US commanders in the early 1940s, and though it was dissolved after the war, Truman reorganized it in 1947 as a permanent intelligence agency, which became the CIA. Subsequent presidents, however, relied on the CIA for more than spying and information. It was regularly used to thwart communist regimes without full military force by assisting local opposition groups in their overthrow of unwanted leaders. From Cuba to Guatemala to Chile and Afghanistan, US administrations over the four decades of the Cold War carried out insurgencies and assassinations through covert ops.

Eisenhower set a precedent in Iran where the CIA and British counterparts instigated a coup against the elected prime minister, Mohammad Mossadegh. While the Western powers feared possible Soviet influence in Iran, the coup had a lot to do with oil, an industry that Mossadegh nationalized at the expense of the Anglo-Iranian Oil Company (AIOC), a predecessor of British Petroleum (BP). Policymakers in the United States could empathize with the British on these interrelated issues of oil and national security. Earlier in the 1950s, the State Department had implemented the Mutual Defense Assistance Agreement with Saudi Arabia to formalize exclusive access to the Saudi oil industry through the US-Saudi joint company Aramco. The deal also allowed US arms trade to Saudi Arabia as well as military training facilities to counter Soviet incursions. As Eisenhower wrote in 1953, "the immediately increased ability of Saudi Arabia to defend itself is important to the preservation of the peace and security of the Near East area, and to the security of the United States."[18]

Eisenhower held similar beliefs about Iran, which Mossadegh threatened to close to Western interests. He and Winston Churchill decided that an Iranian regime without British or American involvement could not stand, and the two leaders orchestrated a CIA-directed overthrow of Mossadegh's government in favor of former Iranian monarch Mohammad Reza Pahlavi, who was returned to power as a pro-Western shah. The coup was not immediately successful, but Eisenhower eventually got what he wanted: a US ally and a guarantee from the British that they would share control of oil production in Iran with US companies. It took until the twenty-first century for the CIA to acknowledge their involvement in the overthrow of an elected leader, one of the most undemocratic actions of the Cold War. Empire, in this case, overrode liberty.

The shah ruled Iran as a dictator (albeit a noncommunist one) and a US ally until he was forced to flee the country during the 1979 Iranian Revolution. By that time, Islamicist networks spanned the Middle and Near East, including terrorist organizations like Al Qaeda, headed by Osama bin Laden. Bin Laden had been born in Saudi Arabia in 1957 during the Eisenhower administration, but during the Cold War, he developed an ideology that transcended US-Soviet bipolarity marked by a deep resentment of any outside interference into Arab states and Muslim governance. He considered all foreign powers harmful invaders that needed to be destroyed.

IIIIIIIIIII

Propaganda always accompanies war, and the Cold War was no exception. It was delivered through presidential rhetoric, anti-communist imagery, and foreign aid. Even Hollywood got caught in the cross fire. When *Invasion of the Body Snatchers* appeared in theaters in 1956, audiences lined up to see a sci-fi film about an extraterrestrial invasion of "pod people" in a quiet California town. Some viewers couldn't help but notice the Cold War allegory embedded in the plot's cautionary tale about dangerous influences that could be anywhere, infecting anyone. Released during the Red Scare, *Body Snatchers* and, later, *The Manchurian Candidate*, suggested that ordinary Americans had to be vigilant to prevent communist inside agents from taking over their towns and their country. Allusions to brainwashing and the loss of individualism also reflected concerns about the use of propaganda and scare tactics to create conformity across America.

Truman had called for "unity of purpose, unity of effort, and unity of spirit" in his 1948 message to Congress about Soviet threats, but unity for him meant supporting the government's Cold War agenda and participating in the effort to contain communism.[19] The Red Scare, fueled by Joe McCarthy's allegations of communist infiltration, divided Americans along lines of ideology, making anyone with left-leaning affiliations a suspected public enemy. Accused teachers, journalists, labor leaders, activists, and entertainers lost their jobs, careers, friendships, and reputations for the "crime" of exercising civil liberties, and they were often investigated by Congress or the FBI.

Homosexuals, believed to be morally corrupt and thus corruptible, were especially targeted as national security risks. Policymakers actively opposed the employment of those they called "lavender lads" in the State

Department and other agencies susceptible to Soviet incursion, and thousands lost their jobs because of loyalty laws such as Eisenhower's Executive Order 10450, effective in May 1953, which allowed firings for criminal, dishonest, or disgraceful conduct, drug addiction, and sexual perversion, among other broad rationales.[20]

Folk singer Pete Seeger invoked his civil liberties in 1955 when he was called to testify before the House Un-American Activities Committee (HUAC) about his communist connections. Refusing to answer "any questions as to my association, my philosophical or religious beliefs or my political beliefs, or how I voted in any election, or any of these private affairs," Seeger affirmed that "I love my country very dearly, and I greatly resent this implication that some of the places that I have sung and some of the people that I have known, and some of my opinions, whether they are religious or philosophical, or [that] I might be a vegetarian, make me any less of an American."[21] Seeger was sentenced to prison and blacklisted from performing.

Civil rights were central to the emerging New Left, a baby boomer generation of progressives distinct from Old Left labor organizers. New Leftists supported Black voting and education in the South and free speech on college campuses. At UC Berkeley, students such as Mario Savio spoke out against the university's suppression of liberties and the complicity in Cold War military research. Objecting to a university managed as a company or bureaucracy, Savio concluded that "the faculty are a bunch of employees and we're the raw material!" He named the university as part of the "machine" propelling the Cold War—an impersonal, inhumane, objectifying system of private-public hegemony that opposed civil liberties and dissent.[22]

To combat Cold War conformity, New Leftists emphasized the need for "participatory democracy" or full democratic inclusion in local, national, and international decision-making. But they clung to their hope for democracy from the edges of a profound disillusionment. "American virtue" and "American ideals," they realized, functioned more as "ruling myths than as descriptive principles." Democracy, they wrote, remained an "unfinished" project that no amount of economic prosperity or military supremacy could resolve.

The students who gathered during the summer of 1962 to draft the "Port Huron Statement" exposed the pervasive angst they believed most Americans felt beneath a veneer of confidence. "Some would have us believe that Americans feel contentment amidst prosperity," the New Leftists at Port Huron wrote, "but might it not better be called a glaze above deeply felt anxieties about their role in the new world?" As kids, they recalled, they had felt secure in "the wealthiest and strongest country in the world," which was poised to "distribute Western influence throughout the world." They believed in the primacy of American values that proclaimed "freedom and equality for each individual" and "government of, by, and for the people." As they grew older, however, their faith in democratic idealism faltered as they "began to see complicated and disturbing paradoxes in our surrounding America," notably racial injustice and a permanent war society that held human values hostage.

The Students for a Democratic Society (SDS), in their Port Huron Statement, exposed an uncomfortable condition of the Cold War era: Americans were not so sure of themselves, only pretending to be, as actions sparked by anxiety spoke louder than a rhetoric of hubris. Policymakers belied their faith in democratic institutions by foisting them upon foreign peoples. Domestically, limits on liberty and justice for all revealed a lack of faith in democratic inclusion. Idealistic youth could not help but notice the contradictions. As much as they wanted to believe in American democracy, they harbored doubts that the republic had ever truly existed or ever would emerge without radical change, a view reinforced by a cohort of historians like William Appleman Williams who analyzed the United States as an empire since its founding.

The Port Huron Statement also reinforced many of Mario Savio's points about the inhumane dysfunctions of Cold War America. "We oppose the depersonalization that reduces human beings to the status of things—if anything, the brutalities of the twentieth century teach that means and ends are intimately related." New Leftists acknowledged the complexities of "a world in upheaval," "testing the tenacity of our own commitment to democracy and freedom and our abilities to visualize their application." But they could not excuse their own nation's complicity in illiberal acts.[23]

While the New Left considered democracy a constant project, Cold Warriors saw authoritarianism as a constant threat. The irony that New Leftists highlighted, however, was the practice of authoritarianism in the United States. Millions of people living under oppressive communist regimes suffered from a lack of democracy, and many Americans shared their experience, especially racial minorities. The New Left's concern about civil and human rights later extended to the war in Vietnam, and their critique of American imperialism and the dehumanization of the Vietnamese people became increasingly strident over the course of the 1960s.

Yet New Leftists had their own blind spots. Though they claimed to recognize the rights of everyone, male activists assumed leadership roles and women often remained marginalized in the movement, relegated to menial tasks or objectified as sex objects. After experiencing gender discrimination in civil rights organizations, Casey Hayden and Mary King cowrote "Sex and Caste," calling attention to a system of discrimination that oppressed racial minorities *and* women. "Women seem to be placed in the same position of assumed subordination" in a "caste system which, at its worst, uses and exploits women," they wrote.

Since 1886, when suffragists had protested at the dedication of the Statue of Liberty, women in the United States had gained the right to vote but had not achieved freedoms equivalent to men. Hayden and King quoted from an article in *The Nation* that exemplified the public disregard for gender equity. "A woman should not aim for 'a second-level career' because she is a woman," the article argued; "from girlhood on she should recognize that, if she is also going to be a wife and mother, she will not be able to give as much to her work as she would if single."[24] Cultural change, Hayden and King insisted, had to come.

Realizing that political rights did little to alter society, women activists launched a new wave of protests in the mid-twentieth century to transform the prevailing, chauvinist culture, including the counterculture. The

1962 novel *One Flew Over the Cuckoo's Nest*, written by celebrity hippie Ken Kesey, reflected the gender stereotypes that Hayden and King had noticed in the New Left. Kesey's story about a maverick patient in a mental hospital challenging conformity was celebrated as an ode to liberty and individualism. But, in the book and film adaptation, women are portrayed as either uptight, sadistic matrons (Nurse Ratched) or sexual free spirits (Mac's girlfriends). Men, Kesey suggested, could break free from conventions to find their true selves. Women, however, could not escape the roles assigned to them.

IIIIIIIIIII

In 1952, Queen Elizabeth II ascended to the role assigned to her as monarch of the British Empire. Five years later, she visited the United States, and while in New York, she went to the top of the Empire State Building. The Waldorf-Astoria Hotel supplied a long red carpet to welcome Her Royal Highness and her husband Prince Philip from Thirty-Fourth Street into the lobby. Tiffany's jewelers gifted the queen a gold-plated replica of the skyscraper, and the mayor bestowed her with a Medal of Honor. When the queen finally reached the observatory deck, she complimented the view. She also spoke well of New York, calling it a "gateway" "through which have passed millions of people in search of a happier, freer and more prosperous life." "This is the city known as the financial capital of the United States but also known for its friendliness and hospitality," she said at a luncheon in her honor.[25]

Changes were afoot at the Empire State Building in the 1950s, starting with the death of its founder, John Raskob, and its sale to new owners. But the symbolism of the skyscraper was also undergoing renovation. When Al Smith opened the tallest building in the world back in 1931, he had pitched it as a marvel of ingenuity and a symbol of economic power. But in 1956, "Operation: Light Up the Sky," better known as the "Freedom Lights," revitalized the Midtown behemoth as a sign of liberty. Four bright beacons—so bright they interfered with astronomers—were placed below the building's TV tower to signify freedom shining in a dark world. The new directors also commissioned a poem, entitled "Empire State Lights," written by MacKinlay Kantor, who asked rhetorically, "What mark you, Lights? Our Nation's doorway," and alluded to the millions of Americans "who love this Land because they chose to come." Though the Cold War was a "strange new time," the Lights never showed "fear." "There is something more powerful," Kantor concluded, in "the heart and soul of all Mankind" that yearns for freedom.[26]

The publicist behind the lighting project, Ben Sonnenberg, knew he was co-opting the meaning of the Statue of Liberty's torch. He explained the update as an extension of Lady Liberty, which had greeted mostly arriving ships. In the 1950s, however, millions were arriving by airplane. As the *New York Times* described, quoting an unnamed source, the sweeping lights were intended as an "'air-age symbol of welcome and freedom' to supplement and not to supplant the Statue of Liberty." The author of the article accepted the logic but expressed "the sincere hope that they, as well as Bartholdi's copper statue, never become empty, meaningless symbols."[27]

At the dedication ceremony to ignite the Freedom beacons in May 1956, most of the speakers, including Empire State Building director Lester Crown, mentioned the Statue of Liberty. Crown assured the public that the skyscraper was an "assistant to the good lady" and hoped the two icons would "glow together with the spirit of freedom for many generations to come." Quoting Kantor's poem, Mayor Robert Wagner reaffirmed "America's Devotion" to "offer succor and asylum to oppressed and underprivileged peoples."[28] The Empire State Building, like its home New York City, now served dual functions, as Queen Elizabeth had recognized in her thank-you speech. It represented both empire and liberty.

Since the late nineteenth century, Americans had covered imperialism with the language of liberty, and during the Cold War, they brought the British under the same umbrella. At the queen's luncheon in 1957, Mayor Wagner referred to the British Empire as "a unique alliance of free people and independent states which embraces more than a quarter of the world's population." The queen, he said, acted as "the force which binds them and brings this remarkable unity out of diversity," ensuring "the stability of the entire world." The mayor also spoke of the United States and United Kingdom as united in purpose to maintain stability and defend liberty. "Today your people and ours stand closer together than ever before as a bulwark of democracy and freedom in a world beset by fears," he said, adding that the two major powers must have a "constructive influence upon other nations." The queen, too, emphasized the collaboration between "English-speaking countries" and agreed that "the future of the free world depends" on "the maintenance of understanding between us."[29]

Feted by her American hosts, Elizabeth was one of the few women on top of the world. Conflating monarchy and freedom, however, made an uneasy fit. As queen, the young royal ruled over dozens of foreign territories, including those vying for independence, and served as the head of state for Commonwealth nations that voluntarily remained tied to Great Britain. She stressed the point of "free association of fully independent states" when she appeared at the United Nations headquarters in New York. "Common ideals—not formal bonds—unite the members of the Commonwealth," she explained.[30] She did not mention the colonies that Great Britain maintained via suppression of rebellions. Like the United States, the United Kingdom had always employed soft- and hard-power techniques to keep countries within their sphere of influence, and during the Cold War, they rationalized their actions as safeguards against communism.

Soviet leaders also used euphemisms to describe their empire, which consisted of fifteen so-called "republics" and additional nations in Eastern Europe that had no say over decisions emanating from Moscow. Attempting to deny their imperialism, the Bolsheviks, early on, had referred to the territories of the Soviet Union as a "friendship of peoples," an array of ethnicities and nations coexisting voluntarily under the roof of communist authority. The Soviet anthem alluded to the concept with its lyrics "United forever in friendship and labor, our mighty republics will ever endure." Artwork, parades, and performances celebrated the diversity of multiple cultures—all forms of propaganda that put a benevolent spin on a brutal regime that enforced assimilation into the dominant Russian culture and its rule from Moscow. Stalin, during his time, implemented collective farming, which led to the removal of landowners as well as mass starvation when the agrarian changes failed to produce. He also eliminated over half a million perceived threats to his power through deportations, imprisonments, or murder. And he demanded the resettlement of millions of people as an effective tool to divide potential dissidents and punish nonconformists.

Though Nikita Khrushchev eased some of the restraints that he inherited from Stalin's era, the Soviet Union continued to impose Communist Party totalitarianism throughout its empire. In a 1963 speech celebrating Cuba's recent revolution, Khrushchev declared that "no matter how much imperialist reaction, headed by the United States, tries to stop or check the great revolutionary process of liberation of mankind, it is powerless to do so."[31] Yet Soviet critiques of Western imperialism (and racism) rang hollow in echo chambers resounding with the hypocrisy of their own rhetoric. All empires operated via illiberal means with varying forms of menace.

|||||||||||

Before he assumed the presidency in 1961, John F. Kennedy published two books about American exceptionalism. The first, *Profiles in Courage*, contained biographies of US senators who had put principles above public pressure. The second, *A Nation of Immigrants*, addressed a glaring problem of American liberty for all. Kennedy opened the book with Alexis de Tocqueville, the French traveler whose *Democracy in America* examined US political culture. "What [he] saw in America was a society of immigrants," Kennedy wrote, "each of whom had begun life anew, on an equal footing." Not every US citizen descended from immigrants. But the fact that much of the population could trace their family's immigrant origins prompted Kennedy to elevate the issue and call for reforms. Expressing his admiration for the multifaceted enrichments they brought to US society, Kennedy believed the "peculiarly American social revolution" of millions of migrants arriving on US shores deserved more attention and respect.

Kennedy, a member of a prominent Irish family, appreciated how his ancestors, especially, had "eased the way for other immigrant groups and speeded their assimilation" into English-speaking institutions such as schools and labor unions. He also listed the contributions of Italians, Germans, Scandinavians, and each successive ethnic group that made their mark on America. Those arriving from "the Orient," Kennedy noted, had received harsher treatment. "Our behavior toward these groups of newcomers represented a shameful episode in our relationships to those seeking the hospitality of our shores." Mexicans also bore the brunt of racist tendencies, and Puerto Ricans were unfairly shunned. "We often forget that Puerto Ricans are US citizens by birth and therefore cannot be considered immigrants," Kennedy reminded.

Despite discrimination, processes of assimilation and social mobility, he believed, offered a pathway for people seeking a better life. He mentioned the "melting pot" analogy that made many Americans willing to accept differences—so long as those differences became diluted by the dominant culture. Realizing he could do little to dislodge prejudice, Kennedy still favored a more "generous" immigration policy in the United States to align with a republican regard for liberty. "With such a policy, we can turn to the world, and to our own past, with clean hands and a clear conscience. Such a policy," he wrote, "would be but a reaffirmation of old principles."[32]

Like race issues, immigration reforms found their moment during the Cold War, when presidents had performative reasons to expand liberties. Lyndon B. Johnson, who succeeded Kennedy after the assassination of 1963, harnessed the momentum of his predecessor to pass the Civil Rights Act and the Voting Rights Act, as well as the Immigration and Nationality Act abolishing national origins quotas. President Johnson signed the last legislation on Liberty Island, replacing a system of discrimination that he said "violated the basic principle of American democracy." Emanuel Celler of New York, the immigrant advocate who had shepherded the bill through the House, also stood beneath the Statue of Liberty that day. Johnson acknowledged that the new law did not "add importantly to either our wealth or our power," but he considered it imperative for making America "truer to ourselves as a country and as a people." "It will strengthen us in a hundred unseen ways," he assured.

Rather than repeat the oft-used axiom "nation of immigrants," the president referred to a "nation of strangers," a phrasing that suggested the country had been built not by a "friendship of peoples" or easy allies, but by millions of newcomers learning to cooperate for a common cause. Johnson illustrated his point with the war in Vietnam, where, he said, men were fighting for democracy against enemies who "killed them" without inquiring where "their parents came from." In freedom's foxholes, he implied, there were no Mexicans, Chinese, Polish, or Italians. "They were all Americans," he stated.[33] Johnson had inherited the war in Vietnam from past presidents, including Kennedy, but his escalation of US involvement overshadowed domestic achievements like civil rights, immigration reform, and the social programs of his Great Society.

Johnson's handling of the war also sparked protests in the United States and across the globe. Critics believed US militance in Vietnam was illiberal and immoral. After the Tet Offensive, many doubted the war was even winnable. Americans were shocked that their economic and military superiority once again seemed unable to trounce communist guerrillas, and a crisis of confidence shook the nation and its commander in chief. When Johnson announced that he would not accept the nomination for another term as president in 1968, delegates in Chicago that summer weighed in for Vice President Hubert Humphrey, who ultimately lost to the Republican opponent, Richard Nixon, on issues of domestic and international order.

Nixon's vow to secure peace with honor in Vietnam may have helped him win over voters, but he also credited the so-called silent majority of quiet, conservative Americans who elected him to crack down on left-liberal chaos. Nixon's supporters did not stay silent for long. In the 1970s, they organized into political groups on issues of importance to them, including religion, traditional family values, fiscal conservatism, anti-abortion, crime, and race-based reforms like busing. The phenomenon known as "identity politics" developed on the left and the right of the political spectrum as people found common cause with those who didn't necessarily share the same ethnic background but held similar beliefs.

The Baptist university known as Liberty in Lynchburg, Virginia, for instance, was founded in 1971 by Jerry Falwell, who chose the name Liberty instead of Lynchburg to signify freedom, elide race associations (lynching), and align with the upcoming US Bicentennial. Bemoaning the lack of Christian influence in education and government, Liberty's leadership aimed to provide a "conservative" alternative to secular universities across the country affected by the New Left. As it grew over the decades to become the largest Christian fundamentalist institution in the country, Liberty University helped transform the "silent majority" into the "Moral Majority," a coalition of evangelicals and New Right activists who fused patriotism, piety, and free-market choice in their appeal to Americans through churches and televangelism.

The New Left had achieved gains throughout the 1960s by demanding civil rights and a voice for oppressed Americans. Conservatives took note and adopted an underdog language to defend their rights, even if they were wealthy, White, and well represented in positions of power. They sought to preserve or restore a society that seemed safer for them, a mission that US forces carried abroad. As Reinhold Niebuhr observed in the 1930s, "the intelligence of privileged groups is usually applied to the task of inventing specious proofs for the theory that universal values spring from, and that general interests are served by, the special privileges which they hold."[34] Liberties from this perspective are not infinitely expansive but zero sum, meaning that the rights of others detract from the rights of oneself. On the left and right, those who organized into special interest groups had a hard time accepting the opinions of anyone outside their narrow identity politics, making broad coalitions more difficult to build.

Few leaders were able to speak for identity and unity in the same breath. Martin Luther King Jr. was one of them. His "I Have a Dream" speech in 1963 objected to racial injustice, opening with a grievance that Black Americans "still languished in the corners of American society," as the United States continually "defaulted" on the "promissory note" of freedom for all its citizens. But King did not succumb to a narrow race identity. In fact, he warned against a militance of identity that divided people, arguing that all humans were bound together in "a beautiful symphony of brotherhood."

King's oratory may have sounded lofty, but it was not mere magniloquence. As a Christian, he believed the moral health of a nation was measured by the treatment and welfare of "the least of these"—those members of society whose unfortunate condition made a mockery of idealism and threatened to upend the republic. Oppression anywhere, in other words, affected everyone everywhere. This universal truth, King held, made identity-based rights, by definition, limited. His famous line, "I have a dream that my four little children will one day live in a nation where they will not be judged by the color of their skin but by the content of their character," sprung from his conviction that racial identifiers should not matter.

Drawing upon the gospels and passages such as Galatians 3:28, King rejected interpersonal distinctions as well as international borders that produced illusions of an "us" vs. "them" contest for power. His moral vision transcended all boundaries, as though he were seeing the world from the highest mountaintop, too far away to discern divisions, a world as it should be—united by freedom and fellowship, undivided by tribe, nation, or empire.[35]

|||||||||||

In the 1970s, protestors took their grievances to New York's Liberty Island more than once. A demonstration by women activists, reminiscent of the suffragists in 1886, took place at the base of Lady Liberty in 1970. Vietnam Veterans Against the War (VVAW) occupied the Statue of Liberty in 1971 and again in 1976. Puerto Rican nationalists went there in 1977, and Islamic fundamentalists took over the statue in 1979 in support of the Iranian Revolution.

The veterans hoped to gain publicity for their cause at Liberty Island in 1971, expecting to stay a few minutes before being arrested. Instead, they barricaded themselves inside the statue for three days. As VVAW member Don Bristow-Carrico remembered, "We had turned all the American flags upside down as a distress symbol. A reporter from France told us that if we took a flag up to the head, he would get it in every paper in the world. We put it up there and he did it! He rented a helicopter and got a great shot." The group got the attention of the media, but their message was simple. "We didn't have any demands," Carrico recalled. "We only had a statement that said, 'we support anyone who refuses to fight'—in hopes of extending the Christmas cease-fire."[36] The war did not formally end until 1973, when the United States signed peace terms with the North Vietnamese. Few Americans celebrated, even if they felt relief that the war was finally over. The conceit of US power had been tested and humbled, and the country's positive impact on the world was questionable.

America's relative wealth offered little comfort for a war-weary nation in need of confidence, especially during an economic slump. Back in 1959, Vice President Richard Nixon had taken pride in US consumer culture during the famous "Kitchen Debate" with Nikita Khrushchev, who dismissed American capitalism as empty. In the early 1970s, Nixon presided over an economy that had hollowed out considerably since those affluent years at midcentury. There were multiple causes of the 1970s recession and much confusion, as Americans grappled with an economic empire in apparent distress. Though the United States led the world in all international institutions and the GDP appeared strong, Americans were reeling from economic currents beyond their control.

In 1973, the Organization of the Petroleum Exporting Countries (OPEC) imposed an embargo on countries that had supported Israel in the Yom Kippur War over disputed territories. The United States, one of Israel's strongest supporters, was denied OPEC imports for a year, causing rations on fuel sources. Terrorism, such as the attack on Israeli athletes in the Munich Olympic Village and the hundreds of aircraft hijackings around the world, also raised concerns about the means of defense against nontraditional forms of militance.

There were moments of levity. In the summer of 1974, Frenchman Philippe Petit performed a stunning high-wire act between the recently opened Twin Towers in Lower Manhattan. Unauthorized and undercover,

Petit and his entourage snuck their equipment to the top of each building and strung a line across the 130-foot expanse between them. Petit spent nearly an hour walking across the wire a quarter mile above ground, on a misty morning, while onlookers took in the spectacle. Petit said later he felt "on top of the world" "dying of happiness."

One police officer who arrived at the scene to arrest him called it a "once in a lifetime" event, while New Yorkers from all walks of life seemed to appreciate the daring touch of grace and humanity that Petit brought to the cold Twin Towers. "As he was led away," a columnist wrote, "street-level spectators booed the police while construction workers tried to shake Mr. Petit's hand-cuffed hand." Criminal charges were later dropped on the condition that Petit would perform for children in New York City parks, and he was even granted a lifetime pass to the observatory deck of the World Trade Center. While Petit achieved notoriety, he helped the Twin Towers garner more favorable attention from a public awed, and not as offended, by their height. As one woman put it, "the image of him crossing them became the lasting icon of the World Trade Center."[37] The joy and sense of freedom that one individual brought to the Towers meant more to the public than any form of currency traded within them.

IIIIIIIIIII

Though the United States had two hundred years of history to celebrate, the Bicentennial in 1976 was shrouded by the recent past. The Vietnam War, protests, political violence, scandals, and economic uncertainty compelled reassessments of the nation's identity and its founding ideals. As Americans longed to redeem their exceptional purpose in the world, many embraced the image of the underdog that had animated eighteenth-century colonists fighting for independence against the most powerful empire in the world. At the lowest, most humble moment in modern American history, this underdog mentality helped Americans heal their Cold War wounds and forge a path toward superpower status.

The Bicentennial was about historical memory and national narrative. But more Americans than ever in the 1970s sought to contribute to the story, making an elitist interpretation of US exceptionalism much more difficult to promote than it had been during the Centennial of 1876. At first, the official American Revolution Bicentennial Administration (ARBA), funded by the federal government, tried to present a triumphalist version of the nation's past, focused upon democracy and liberty as mainstays of American identity. The commission immediately met with resistance. Some critics questioned the need to spend money on the extravagance of US pride. Others denounced the commercialism of a Bicentennial sold to patriotic consumers through commemorative trinkets or told as whitewashed history that marginalized the experiences of Black Americans. Corporate power was a prime target of protests. The Boston Oil Party of 1973, for instance, dumped oil barrels, not tea, into the harbor and hung an effigy of Nixon.

Instead of a centralized, unified series of events organized at the top, the Bicentennial became a grassroots effort by multiple groups and communities mining the American past to bolster their political viewpoints. The People's Bicentennial Commission, a New Left rival to the official committee, emphasized the revolutionary tradition that had secured independence and established the republic. Jeremy Rifkin, as director of the group, wrote "Red, White, and Blue Left," an essay that encouraged activists to embrace American radicalism rather than follow Lenin, Mao, or Castro. "For the American left to develop a strategy that can win popular support for programs that answer present grievances," he argued, "it must first gain a clear understanding of the role which the American heritage plays in the formation of American people's political attitudes and behavior."[38]

Though leftists faced an entrenched capitalist system, Rifkin enlisted the rebels of the 1770s as models for a "second American revolution" for economic equality in the 1970s. The equivalence did not stick for radicals aware of the elitism and slaveholding complicity of most of the nation's founders. But Rifkin was not summoning the revolutionary leaders for their records on race and class; he was drawing upon their dark horse determination to overcome power.

Race and class issues were not easily sidelined, as Black Americans spoke about the unfinished revolution of 1776 and the uncritical patriotism of 1976 that treated them as collateral damage. Comedian Richard Pryor won best comedy album of the year for *Bicentennial N____*, and Gil Scott-Heron's spoken-word poem "Bicentennial Blues" framed America as "home of the blues." The blues, the lyrics explained, had been "born on the slave man's auction block" and "grew up a slave." For over two hundred years, Scott-Heron reminded, the blues expressed the pain of second-class citizens "ripped off" and "violated by commercial corporations." The poem dismissed the Bicentennial as another "blues year" marked by "halfway justice, halfway liberty, halfway equality, it's a half-ass year."[39] Protest parades for July 4, 1976, took place in Philadelphia and DC as a coalition of Black Americans, Native Americans, Puerto Ricans, and various dissenters made their voices heard.

Despite these waves of disillusionment across the country, the Bicentennial provided an ocean of opportunity for Americans to recover from the Vietnam War and reassert patriotism. Millions focused on the bright side of US history, celebrating American virtues. Red, white, and blue floodlights illuminated the top of the Empire State Building, starting a tradition of using colored lighting patterns to mark special occasions. Little Liberty Bells and coins were popular items, while Queen Elizabeth II sent the city of Philadelphia the Bicentennial Bell, a full-size replica of the Liberty Bell from the same London foundry that created the original. Speechwriters for President Gerald Ford encouraged him to put the meaning of America in terms of an ongoing "experiment" that still represented the world's best hope for freedom. "Rebirth" and "renewal" were stated themes of administrators trying to lift the gloom and shift the mood of the nation.

In Philadelphia on the Fourth of July, Ford expressed "both pride and humility" as he harked back to Lincoln on the eve of the Civil War, "the cruelest national crisis of our 85-year history." Ford acknowledged the many crises and "hardships" that Americans had encountered over the centuries, but he reminded that faith in the republic and faith in God helped them endure. His entire speech, in fact, linked patriotism and religion, noting the biblical verse on the Liberty Bell, "Proclaim liberty throughout all the land unto all the inhabitants thereof," and claiming the "Founding Fathers knew their Bibles as well as their Blackstone." "It continues in a common conviction that the source of our blessings is a loving God," he averred.

By appealing to faith, Ford implied that Americans needed to uphold liberty and democracy as extensions of religious conviction, not only for US citizens but for all humanity. "The world knows where we stand," he said. "The world is ever conscious of what Americans are doing for better or for worse, because the United States today remains the most successful realization of humanity's universal hope." Yet the president did not call for more campaigns abroad; he asked his audience to set an example at home. "The establishment of justice and peace abroad will in large measure depend upon the peace and justice we create here in our own country, where we still show the way." For a nation chastened by recent war, Ford's words were balanced between humility and hope.[40]

Two popular movies that year also reflected a national mood in flux between darkness and hope. *Taxi Driver*, the story of unlovable loser Travis Bickle, presented a gritty allegory of US involvement in Vietnam. A more uplifting film released later in 1976 followed the journey of underdog Rocky Balboa, a boxer in Philadelphia determined to fight for his dignity against all odds.

In Martin Scorsese's New York drama *Taxi Driver*, Robert De Niro plays Bickle, a Vietnam War veteran struggling with post-traumatic stress disorder. Bickle takes a night job driving a cab around the city, a cesspool of sex and crime that he desperately wants to clean up. After failing to court a beautiful campaign worker, Bickle descends further into depression, and he sets himself to right the wrongs of the world by assassinating the politician whose staff let him down and by rescuing a teenage prostitute from the grips of her handler. Bickle's plans end in a bloodbath, but he returns to his taxi and reimagines himself as a hero, a commentary on the delusion of US machismo to police the world and apply vigilante justice to protect the innocent.

The film *Rocky* also resonated with Americans who felt on the ropes, but unlike *Taxi Driver*, it tendered an optimistic belief in the American spirit to overcome all challenges. Writer and actor Sylvester Stallone invoked Bicentennial themes through characters like Apollo Creed, a heavyweight champion eager to represent the American Dream in a showcase match. He chooses down-on-his luck Rocky Balboa, the "Italian Stallion," as his opponent to highlight the United States as a nation of underdogs only in need of a chance. As reviewer Arthur Knight wrote, "For the course of its two hours we learn that . . . America is still a place where a man can haul himself up by his own bootstraps provided he believes in himself and has the will to do so."[41]

Few if any characters in the film expected Rocky to win the exhibition fight, but he worked hard and refused to give up, going the distance against the best in the world, and losing on a technicality. However, Rocky never really failed. He transcended his modest circumstances and earned the love and respect of those around him, particularly his love interest, Adrian. He also inspired a nation. While some critics, including the *New York Times*, panned the film as unsophisticated "make-believe," Rocky became a sleeper hit that helped awaken Americans from their self-doubts.[42]

||||||||||

Americans had one more humiliation to suffer before the decade ended. In 1979, revolutionaries overthrew the government in Iran to establish an Islamic fundamentalist state under the authority of Ayatollah Khomeini. The US embassy in Tehran was one of their targets. Students seized the embassy in November and detained more than fifty American hostages, who were shown bound and blindfolded on international news for over a year. The United States, the Iranians charged, had supported the illegitimate shah and imposed Western depravity upon a devout Islamic nation. Islamic fundamentalists wanted nothing to do with an American culture that flaunted revealing clothing, open sexuality, women's rights, and secular education. They opposed both US empire and US liberty.

While students in Tehran stormed the US embassy, their Iranian counterparts in the United States occupied the Statue of Liberty in solidarity with the revolution. They hung a banner demanding punishment for the shah, who was hospitalized in exile in New York City, and chained themselves inside the statue for three hours. Demonstrations against the shah erupted elsewhere in the city and across the country.[43]

President Jimmy Carter, elected in the Bicentennial year, scrambled to deal with the crisis, which reinforced Republican allegations that he appeared weak on the world stage. His inability to rescue the hostages contributed to his loss in the 1980 election to Ronald Reagan. Carter's administration finally secured an agreement with the Iranians on January 19, 1981, and the hostages were released, unharmed, the next day, but the timing added only insult to injury for Democrats. The announcement of the freed Americans came minutes after the inauguration of the new president, creating a myth that Reagan's tough approach to foreign affairs had frightened the Iranians into submission. Reagan ran with the myth and crafted more during his presidency, including the notion that the United States was and always had been a superpower. The timing of the end of the Cold War in 1991 reinforced that idea and fused it with the American image well into the new millennium.

CHAPTER 7

EMPIRE AND LIBERTY UNDER ATTACK—2001

The Statue of Liberty had endured nearly one hundred years of daily weather, brutal storms, lightning strikes, war shrapnel, and tourism, but by the late twentieth century, the structure needed major restoration. In 1982, President Ronald Reagan appointed Lee Iacocca, chairman of the Chrysler Corporation, to raise private funds for a preservation project in conjunction with the National Park Service. They needed to implement the plans and reopen the island in time for the statue's Centennial celebration in October 1986.

Lady Liberty's proverbial facelift, Reagan hoped, would also uplift the patriotic spirit of Americans struggling to process the losses suffered during the Vietnam War. The national Bicentennial events had helped reassess a history shaped by republicanism and militarism, an odd amalgam that had led Americans into places like Vietnam. When the Vietnam Veterans Memorial opened in November 1982, millions made the trek to DC to see the long black wall etched with the names of fifty-eight thousand men and women who were killed over the course of the war. For many veterans and protestors, however, it was too soon to confront the emotions that the memorial was meant to trigger and salve.

The polished, granite wall was reflective—both literally and figuratively—and its positioning, descending below ground level and ascending into a wide V-shape or spearhead across a small park, symbolized a "wound that is closed and healing." As designer Maya Lin stated in her proposal, the wall was intended for private mourning. "Brought to a sharp awareness of such a loss, it is up to each individual to resolve or come to terms with this loss," she said. "For death, is in the end a personal and private matter, and the area contained with this memorial is a quiet place, meant for personal reflection and private reckoning."[1]

Of course, the wall also had a public impact. Critics condemned the dark, stark design, calling it a "tomb-stone," "trench," "gash of shame," or "black spot on American history," while Lin defended her minimalist style as democratic and inclusive, explaining, "I wanted to create a memorial that everyone would be able to respond to, regardless of whether one thought our country should or should not have participated in the war."[2] Lin received a positive reception from journalists like Elise T. Chisolm of the *Baltimore Evening Sun*, who praised its "beautiful design." "It does not smack you with machoism like many war memorials. Instead, it is tranquil and thoughtful."[3] Art critic Bernard Jacob also appreciated its originality, writing that until Lin's design "our democracy was unable to develop its own architectural expression. Instead it assimilated and reinterpreted classical models from Egypt, Italy and France." He encouraged Americans to visit the memorial as a "sobering and emotional experience."[4]

That somber tone came across to moviegoers in 1982 as well. Six years after playing underdog Rocky Balboa, Sylvester Stallone portrayed another American hero seeking redemption. *Rambo: First Blood* introduced audiences to John Rambo, a troubled former Green Beret in search of steady work and the soldiers he served with. While traveling through the Pacific Northwest, Rambo is arrested for vagrancy and harassed by local cops before escaping into the wilderness where he uses his combat skills to survive and evade recapture. When Rambo is finally confronted by his former commander, who convinces him to surrender, the distraught veteran breaks down into a tearful confession about the traumas of his military service and postwar life. The film brought attention to the maltreatment of veterans of the unpopular and unwinnable war that continued to haunt the psyche of a nation.

As the nation mourned, President Reagan grew more impatient to leave the past behind, at least the parts casting shadows on US glory. He drew backlash for failing to attend the dedication of the Vietnam Veterans Memorial in 1982, though he did comment on the statue that was placed near the wall two years later, saying, "I believe that in the decade since Vietnam the healing has begun, and I hope that before my days as Commander in Chief are over, the process will be completed."[5] Appearing at the Memorial again on Veterans Day in 1988, Reagan announced that "the night is over."[6] Throughout his presidency, Reagan exhorted his fellow Americans to recover from their collective depression and get back to reasserting American greatness. He did not regard this sense of stoicism as insensitive but as a matter of urgency in the context of the ongoing Cold War.

Reagan regularly reminded the public that the Cold War had not ended with the Vietnam War. Communism continued to spread, and the Soviet Union remained a pressing threat. He was particularly frustrated by the so-called Vietnam Syndrome, a reluctance on the part of Americans to send US soldiers into conflicts that might embroil them in another long-term losing battle. "For too long," the president said in 1980, "we have lived with the 'Vietnam Syndrome.'" Reagan dismissed US wariness as a false sense of shame about US imperialism, insisting that US military involvement, including Vietnam, was part of the "noble cause" the United States had undertaken to support democracy—a noble cause hindered only by a lack of confidence and will to win. "We dishonor the memory of 50,000 young Americans who died in that cause when we give way to feelings of guilt as if we were doing something shameful," he stated.[7]

During the 1980s, Reagan tested Americans' tolerance for foreign campaigns by sending troops to quell unrest in Lebanon and Grenada. These short-lived deployments, he hoped, would reignite the nation's fighting spirit. Reagan also acted behind the scenes without congressional consent or public knowledge as his administration carried out covert operations in places like Nicaragua, where a left-wing revolution had overthrown the Somoza dictatorship. The Iran-Contra scandal broke in 1986, exposing the web woven to funnel money from gun sales in Iran to the "freedom fighting" Contras trying to reclaim Nicaragua. While the means of thwarting communism or any left-leaning regime were often drastic and undemocratic, Reagan believed the United States had a responsibility to rid the world of socialistic systems that he equated with authoritarianism. Great Britain served, sometimes, as a sidekick, but to Reagan, it was a job best done with the ultimate leveraging of power, by a superpower. And the only superpower he recognized was the United States.

A former sports broadcaster and actor, Reagan rose to political prominence in the early 1960s after delivering his "A Time for Choosing" speech about limited government and laissez-faire economics, a direct challenge to lingering New Deal policies. He was elected governor of California in 1966 and made headlines as a "law and order" leader willing to crack down on New Left dissent across the state's campuses. Ten years later, Reagan made a run for the presidency calling for a balanced budget, individualism, and economic growth, but he made clear he wanted to channel more tax dollars into the military to enhance US power abroad. Opposed to the peace overtures of détente, which Nixon had offered the Soviets and Chinese, Reagan insisted in 1976 that "peace does not come from weakness or from retreat. It comes from the restoration of American military superiority."

Reagan read US history as an exceptional story of a "new breed" of people building democracy and bringing forth God's gift of freedom to the world. Since he harbored no doubts about the superiority of American values, and he was unapologetic about efforts to extend them internationally, he had a hard time understanding why Americans had lost their nerve in the wake of the Vietnam War. Expanding on the pithy slogan "Make America Great Again," which branded his election campaigns in 1980 and 1984, Reagan voiced his wish "to see the American spirit unleashed once again. To make this land a shining, golden hope God intended it to be."[8]

Even before becoming president in 1981, Reagan abhorred the bipolar Cold War assumption of Soviet parity with the United States. Referring to the many nations under communist control, he invited complacent

Americans to "ask them what it's like to live in a world where the Soviet Union is Number One. I don't want to live in that kind of world; and I don't think you do either."[9] Though Reagan lost his bid for the presidency in the 1976 election, he was able to align his 1980 candidacy with the patriotic spirit of the Bicentennial and appeal to Americans longing for a revitalization of national purpose. Reagan seemed sure of that purpose—guardians of liberty—but he failed to realize that as Americans embraced their role as a superpower after the collapse of the Soviet Union, they would take liberty increasingly for granted.

IIIIIIIIIII

Like many politicians before him, Reagan used Lady Liberty as a reference point for his political image, particularly when he spoke at Liberty State Park, New Jersey, in September 1980 while campaigning for the presidency. With the statue visible in the background, the Republican nominee lauded the millions of immigrants who had passed through America's "Golden Door," those who "helped to build that magnificent city across the river." As he put it, these immigrants and their offspring "spread across the land building other cities and towns and incredibly productive farms," all betting on the American Dream to build a better life. "They brought with them courage, ambition and the values of family, neighborhood, work, peace and freedom," he said. Critical of the Carter administration, Reagan vowed that his policies would restore not only economic vitality but unfettered freedom for people who wanted to make their way in the world. "We can make that dream that brought so many of us or our parents and grandparents to this land live once more."[10]

Reagan equated liberty with self-rule and self-reliance, enhanced but unencumbered by a limited government that left individuals mostly to their own devices. Believing that people should pull themselves up the social ladder through hard work and personal resources rather than federal aid, he opposed social welfare programs. He supported instead business enterprise, big and small, as self-help projects accumulating into a strong national economy. Internationally, however, Reagan did not preach

Gorbachev, Reagan, and Bush

self-reliance or self-determination for other countries. He saw them as dependent upon US aid to thwart communism and defend liberty.

Meanwhile, the Statue of Liberty was under construction in the mid-1980s as engineers worked to refurbish the exterior and reinforce the interior. As consultant Edward Cohen explained, "We found it wasn't just a matter of cosmetics. We just couldn't buy her a new dress and dab on some new makeup. We had to fix her internal problems." A few of the issues stemmed from her initial erection in 1886, including the misalignment of the upraised arm that Gustave Eiffel had designed to be supported by the central pylon. Instead, the arm was positioned eighteen inches out of place, causing the weight to rest upon less sturdy underpinnings. The head also sat off-center, and it had shifted over time, so that one of the spikes of the crown punctured through the "skin" of the right arm. The entire exterior needed cleaning as well, though it would remain covered by the corroded copper that had turned green from decades of weather-related damage. Additionally, renovators installed a new spiral staircase, elevators, and a heating and ventilation system for the comfort of visitors.[11]

While the project to revamp the Statue of Liberty continued into 1985, tourists could not visit the monument, but they were given opportunities to reflect on its meaning. A PBS documentary by Ken Burns captured the thoughts of scholars, artists, and political leaders, including writer and narrator David McCullough, who opened the film by observing that "the statue is only a symbol. . . . It's what it speaks to us about—what it makes us feel inside—that is so important." McCullough suggested that Americans could get closer to the Statue of Liberty by asking themselves first and foremost "What is liberty?" Speakers featured in the documentary gave a variety of answers to McCullough's question. One described it as "the absence of constraints" and another rejected abstract principles in favor of a simple act: the "freedom to be oneself." Black intellectual James Baldwin struggled to define the word, lamenting that those of his race had been excluded from the ideals laid out in the Declaration of Independence and other founding documents. He called the statue a "bitter joke" for Black Americans, suggesting the concept had little substance if its promise went perpetually unfulfilled.[12]

The documentary surveyed the history of the Statue of Liberty as an idea pitched by Laboulaye and built by Bartholdi, over years plagued by delays, until the triumphal opening in October 1886. The monument's initial purpose had nothing to do with immigrants per se, the filmmakers reminded, though immigrants projected their love of liberty onto the statue over time. New York governor Mario Cuomo spoke about the Statue of Liberty as a symbol that encouraged his Italian ancestors to pursue the American Dream in a nation they believed valued liberty. Such symbols were important, he said, to remind Americans of the "essence" of the country, namely the national spirit of freedom that was too easily suppressed by greed and fear and all the "temptations" to infringe upon liberty for the sake of power.

But as David McCullough mused, the Statue of Liberty invoked more than national pride for Americans. It communicated the transnational, universal message that French republicans sent across the Atlantic, a tribute to the yearning for freedom alive in all human hearts. Though the statue, physically, was made up of raw materials, its meaning was crafted by hopes and dreams. Immigrants to the United States certainly were not the only ones moved by the symbolism of the Statue of Liberty, but their efforts to seek opportunities in a new land made them a poignant, visible personification of its meaning. Grateful for their newfound freedoms, they regularly reinfused the Statue of Liberty with significance, and they often took it more seriously, and less for granted, than Americans accustomed to their civil rights. Polish American writer Jerzy Kosinski confessed that he had been "in love with her" long before he arrived in the United States in the mid-1950s, escaping communism.[13]

In the early 1980s, the National Park Service commissioned Maryland artist Phillip Ratner to reinforce the immigrant theme by crafting bronze sculptures representing immigrants as well as five statues depicting the "founders" of the Statue of Liberty: Bartholdi, Eiffel, Laboulaye, Pulitzer, and Emma Lazarus. Ratner crafted elongated, impressionistic-style figures, each standing about four-and-a-half-feet tall. Miniatures of Ratner's concept traveled around the country to raise money for the monument's renovation, and once completed, eight of his full-size "immigrant experience" sculptures, including a man, a woman, a couple, and children, were placed in the lobby of the Statue of Liberty, and the five "founders" were installed along a promenade behind her.

In later years, the immigration-themed pieces were moved to Ellis Island where thirty-three smaller Ratner statues had already been on display. "There's always been something desperately needed to remind people that a lot more happened here than just a statue," Ratner, the descendant of Jewish immigrants, told reporters in 1982, just after his pieces were placed on Liberty Island. Decades later, he said, "Telling the story of my grandparents coming to this country and making it their home—a story that connects many Americans—is a passion of mine."[14]

Immigration remained a hot topic in the 1980s, despite efforts to highlight the positive impact that ambitious arrivals had made on the country. On July 3, 1986, to mark the relighting of the Statue of Liberty's torch, Reagan repeated his praise of immigrants and named their collective love of liberty as the binding force of the nation. "What was it that tied these profoundly different people together?" he pondered. "Deep in our national consciousness," he answered, there exists "an abiding love of liberty." It was for liberty, Reagan claimed, that the Revolutionary War and US Civil War had been fought, that the western frontier had been "tamed," and that interventions into foreign lands were deemed valiant. "We are the keepers of the flame of liberty," he affirmed. But the president also felt the need to remind Americans that "liberty must never be taken for granted."[15]

Many Americans in the 1980s readily agreed with Reagan about the need to protect liberty, but they didn't necessarily share his positive view of immigrants. Since the 1965 law eliminating bans and quotas, immigration to the United States rose steadily, and by 1986, nearly a million migrants became new citizens each year. They did not come primarily from Europe, like in centuries past, but from regions labeled "Third World," including Asia and Latin America. Most controversially, many immigrants coming into the United States in the 1980s crossed the border from Mexico, and their increasing population in Southwest states like Texas and California sparked concerns and a call for restrictions on their entry and employment. The Immigration Reform and Control Act of 1986, passed by Congress and signed by Reagan, placed penalties on the hiring of illegal immigrants and offered amnesty and citizenship to those eligible.

A lengthy 1986 article in the *El Paso Times* analyzed the debate over immigration in light of the Statue of Liberty centennial. Calling the statue a "symbol of worldwide welcome" and the United States a "land of refuge," the editorial briefed readers on the history of immigration policy, noting that "ironically, the installation of the Statue of Liberty coincided with the beginning of an era of ethnic selectivity." Concerns about the race and ethnicity of new arrivals, they reported, continued into the late twentieth century as the "controversy about immigration policy" grew in proportion to the "larger numbers" coming into the country since the 1965 reforms.

There were a variety of reasons, the editorial listed, for opposing the influx. Many Americans feared increased competition for jobs and resources. But race remained a factor. "They say recent newcomers are different," the article reported, "that they are not being assimilated so readily as in the past and they pose a threat to cultural unity." Hispanics arriving to the United States via Mexico, a group making up about 40 percent of legal immigrants, were of particular concern for Americans who feared that culture in the United States would become drastically altered and liberties threatened.

On the opposite side of this argument, immigration advocates saw newcomers as a boon to culture, economics, and American ideals. As the article reported, supporters "contend the problem of illegal immigration has been exaggerated and say such enforcement measures are inconsistent with our tradition as an open society." Referring to the Lazarus poem at the base of the Statue of Liberty, the *El Paso Times* asked who gets to decide who or how many are welcome. "Keeping unwanted aliens from its shores is a difficult task for a nation of immigrants that has often managed to live up to its promise of offering shelter to huddled masses fleeing poverty or persecution in search of freedom," the paper stated. The article, accompanied by a cartoon depicting a distressed-looking Lady Liberty holding a tally book instead of the independence tablet, concluded by saying "the centennial celebration of the Statue of Liberty is an occasion not just to renew century-old ideals, but to recast them in a form appropriate to the 1980s."[16] Americans needed to redetermine the contours of liberty, whether expanded or limited, into the new millennium.

IIIIIIIIII

Immigrants arriving in the United States since the mid-1960s came from around the world, bringing non-European cultures and non-Christian forms of religion to a country that had considered itself a "city on the hill" destined to implement God's will for the world. Christian mission had undergirded the imperial unfolding of "Manifest Destiny" that served as a rationale for conquering the continent and spreading American influence internationally.

By the 1980s, the increasing number of Americans who practiced non-Christian religions, embraced secularism, lived nontraditional lifestyles, or considered themselves atheists made many evangelicals nervous. They had been taught to proselytize across the globe and gain converts, but they feared their "Moral Majority" status at home in the United States might become diluted in a sea of diversity and religious choice. Appalled by cultural liberation, Christian fundamentalists (also called Christian evangelicals, the Christian Right, or Christian nationalists) were willing to circumscribe the liberties afforded to other religions, including alternative Christian viewpoints, for the sake of tightening their grip on the levers of political influence. As Liberty University founder Jerry Falwell put it in his 1980 manifesto *Listen America*, "We must look for the answer to the highest places in every level of government." As for the separation of church and state, protected by the First Amendment of the Constitution, Falwell claimed that Christian leaders like him had a right to organize in their own interests to save a nation he considered imperiled.

Falwell appealed to Christian fundamentalists who believed the nation had strayed from traditional piety and family values. He and his supporters took issue with gay and lesbian rights, abortion, women's equality, and the modern tolerance for promiscuity and pornography, all "trends" that they wanted to see reversed. Falwell blamed US problems abroad and pandemics such as AIDS on cultural degeneracy and warned that the nation would suffer the wrath of God because it "has turned its back on God." "The hope of reversing the trends of decay in our republic now lies with the Christian public in America," he avowed.

Falwell twisted his arguments for restricting choice around the concept of liberty. "Let us never forget," he said, "that as our Constitution declares, we are endowed by our Creator with certain inalienable rights. It is only as we abide by those laws established by our Creator that He will continue to bless us with these rights. We are endowed with our rights to freedom and liberty and the pursuit of happiness by the God who created man to be free and equal." Constitutional law, in his opinion, depended on adherence to God's law, while citizens of a misaligned nation risked losing their liberties altogether, like misbehaved children deserving punishment. As Falwell warned, "I am listening to the sounds that threaten to take away our liberties in America." The word "our," however, was not inclusive. Falwell believed that liberty and justice for all impinged on the right of Christian fundamentalists to live in a Christian nation conformed to their worldview and way of life.

There were no compromises for fundamentalists like Falwell. While communism divided a bipolar world, he divided the nation along lines of race, gender, religion, and political party. Democrats, he claimed, were pernicious domestic enemies that had allowed freedom for the wicked to flourish. "We cannot expect help from the liberals," he wrote. "They certainly are not going to call our nation back to righteousness and neither are the pornographers, the smut peddlers, and those who are corrupting our youth." That left the Republican Party, and its candidate Reagan, to take up Falwell's cause.[17]

Reagan offered Christian fundamentalism and Falwell legitimacy before and during his presidency. He spoke at Liberty University in October 1980, a month before his election, and he addressed the National Association of Evangelicals in a 1983 speech, in which Reagan echoed Falwell's language about American liberty as contingent upon God's favor. "Freedom prospers only where the blessings of God are avidly sought and humbly accepted," he said. "The American experiment in democracy rests on this insight. Its discovery was the great triumph of our Founding Fathers."[18] Reagan erroneously enlisted William Penn, the founder of a haven for broad religious freedom, and liberal Deist Thomas Jefferson, who did not subscribe to biblical literalism. Both of these leaders believed that religious freedom required tolerance, a point that fundamentalists were unwilling to concede, making them poor choices for Reagan to reference.

By tracing the lineage of Christian nationalism back to the "Founding Fathers," Reagan was peddling revisionist history. Though revolutionaries in the eighteenth century spoke of "inalienable rights" ordained by God, they did so to transcend the king's authority and imbue republican values with universal, unconditional substance. Many of the founders, including Washington, Jefferson, and Hamilton, identified as Freemasons, Deists, agnostics, or even atheists. They found common cause in republicanism, but they did not share a Christian theology, and they did not build a new government based upon biblical doctrines. Religious freedom, in fact, had been written into the Constitution to protect religious conscience from the state, and to protect the state from theocracy. If Americans' rights were filtered through a particular version of God's law, they realized, then republicanism and democracy would no longer matter and would cease to exist. Reagan and Falwell turned the logic of that truism upside down.

In his speech to evangelicals, Reagan did not miss an opportunity to criticize the Soviet Union, particularly for the state-mandated atheism that Reagan and Falwell said sprang from Marxism. He exhorted his Christian followers to challenge the sins of an "evil empire" by refusing to compromise. Reagan, a Cold Warrior, would not accept peace without victory over the Soviets, and he used communism as a litmus test for determining allies and foes. Foreigners who did not support communism, including those from Islamic nations like Saudi Arabia or Afghanistan, were considered allies in the fight. That included Islamic guerrillas struggling to push the Soviets out of Afghanistan in the 1980s. By supplying them with money and weapons, the United States supported the mujahideen groups operating in Afghanistan, essentially empowering future members of the Taliban and Al Qaeda, including Osama bin Laden. Islamic extremists appeared as the lesser of evils to US leaders bent on defeating communism.

The long, costly, and ultimately unsuccessful invasion of Afghanistan did take its toll on the Soviet Union, which suffered from a poor economy and the subsequent weakening of its ability to keep people in Eastern Europe from achieving independence. When the Berlin Wall was brought down in 1989, not by Gorbachev or Reagan, but by Germans demanding freedom, it was difficult for Americans to process or determine how much American militarism had contributed to defeating the Soviets. Meanwhile, the newly formed Al Qaeda organization was consolidating in Pakistan to carry out jihad for the sake of establishing Islamic fundamentalist regimes across the Middle East.

Americans noticed the rise of Islam, the fastest growing global religion in the 1980s, with a mix of curiosity, ignorance, and alarm. For many, the image of the religion and its followers stemmed from international relations, including the OPEC embargo, conflicts between Israel and its Arab neighbors, and the Iranian Revolution. Americans heard Islamic hostilities toward the United States—Ayatollah Khomeini, for one, referred to the country as the "great Satan" for upholding a liberal, secular society.

Some observers, however, saw similarities between Islamic fundamentalism and Christian fundamentalism, especially in terms of rights. During the Iran hostage crisis in late 1980, Carter's secretary of health and human services, Patricia Robert Harris, told Princeton University students that Moral Majority evangelicals were "dangerous" for democracy because they wanted to impose a "moral absolutism" on the United States similar to Islamic "zealots" in Iran. Moorhead Kennedy, one of the Americans held hostage in Iran for 444 days, also raised flags about the "parallels" between Falwell's worldview and that of Khomeini. They were both, he said, "myopic, looking backwards, anti-women, and anti-progress." He especially highlighted patriarchy as common ground between them. Islamic leaders in Iran sought to "diminish very dramatically the gains that women had made in Iran under the shah," while Falwell too, he charged, valued the rights of men over women.[19]

A 1982 op-ed piece in the *Roanoke Times* voiced agreement. As its author J. F. Mays of Lynchburg wrote, Falwell, "like the radicals in Iran," "wishes to turn back the clock in America by using literalistic scripture." Mays gave the Moral Majority at least some credit, acknowledging that it "doesn't shoot its opposition," though he thought they intended to "rid America of liberals, the American Civil Liberties Union and secular humanists" by other means.[20]

A few days later, another op-ed appeared in *Roanoke Times*, arguing that "fundamentalist ideologies—be they Muslim, Christian or communist—have more in common than they have to distinguish themselves." The letter, penned by Baptist pastor Howard V. Pendley III, listed the similarities between Falwell and Khomeini, calling it "dangerous when one seeks to order an entire social structure—especially in a pluralistic society—upon an authority and an interpretation of that authority not shared by everyone else." As Pendley saw it, both Falwell and the Iranian leader were "extremists" guilty of "coercion to achieve their goals." Imposing one's religion on others, he recognized, is inherently irreligious because force obscures true faith. It is also un-American because conformity undermines true freedom.

The Christian and Islamic fundamentalists, Pendley continued, were alike in their advocacy of illiberal means and ends. "Both include . . . subjugation of women, stringent regulations regarding private behavior, and the imposition of severe penalties for non-conformity to the established moral codes." Pendley, an American Christian, could not support their agendas of patriarchy, conformity, and theocracy. "Quite frankly, I don't think I'd much like living in a society run by either Khomeini or Falwell," he concluded.[21]

The discourse surrounding religion in America in the 1980s was part of a larger contest over culture and the power to define or confine liberties. Many Americans took it for granted that freedoms achieved in past struggles could not be reversed or rolled back. But there were warnings against taking liberties for granted. Pundits reminded their fellow countrymen to be ever vigilant of seemingly small, harmless changes or policy proposals that authoritarians covered in the rhetoric of religion or patriotism. Once the Cold War ended, many Americans let their guard down, believing that the United States, its empire, and its system of democracy had emerged superior to all challengers. Symbolically, the Statue of Liberty and Empire State Building still stood, like the flag at Fort McHenry, to give them a semblance of proof.

||||||||||||

Popular culture helped shape perceptions of the Empire State Building and the Statue of Liberty over the decades as well as the meanings that Americans bestowed upon them. For decades, commentators had warned against cheapening Lady Liberty with overexposure in political ads and commercialism. Yet her image continued to be co-opted for a variety of causes. Illustrators drew her likeness into hundreds of cartoons over the years, depicting her as sad or angry about political policies that, it was implied, undermined liberty. In films and television, the landmark appeared in B-roll footage to establish location, while movies about immigrants arriving in New York featured her prominently. In *The Godfather Part II*, *Once Upon a Time in America*, and the animated film *An American Tail*, audiences saw immigrants looking at the Statue of Liberty with awe.

She was also used as a device in disaster films to conflate an attack on the statue as an attack on the nation. The sci-fi flick *Planet of the Apes* became famous for its twist ending, in which the protagonist, played by Charlton Heston, discovers the severed top of the statue awash on a beach and realizes that the "foreign" planet ruled by authoritarian apes is actually Earth. Outraged by the dystopian fate of the home he left lightyears ago, he shouts in agony: "We finally, really did it. You maniacs! You blew it up! Damn you! God damn you all to hell!" The sight of the broken Statue of Liberty in the scene signaled to audiences that human civilization had been destroyed. Heston's reaction made clear that such a sad fate had always been possible and preventable.

Threats to liberty were not confined to the realm of make-believe. The perceived nemesis of communism had made Americans aware of oppressive regimes around the world stifling freedom and democracy. But internal threats had always existed within the United States, feeding on ignorance or apathy. In the 1985 PBS documentary about the Statue of Liberty, screenwriter Milos Forman, born in Czechoslovakia, made a provocative observation about the complacency of Americans toward freedom. "I don't think anyone who was born in this country really cares," he stated. "You are born here, and you take everything for granted, and all you really see is what bothers you and what irritates you."

Former congresswoman Barbara Jordan agreed that apathy posed a danger. She identified the "greatest threat" to the American way as "the inattention of the people of this country to liberty." "If we don't attend to it," she warned, "if we take it for granted, and let people trample on it in even minute ways, it can gradually suffer an erosion just like the statue itself suffered some erosion." Scholar Vartan Gregorian made the case more pointedly. He blamed the American tendency to regard citizens as economic units rather than spiritual beings for lackadaisical attitudes about civil liberties. Opportunities to accumulate wealth, he believed, could reduce people to transactional terms or monetary value, an equation in which liberty and justice for all becomes far less relevant.[22]

Once the Soviet Union collapsed in the early 1990s, the United States emerged as a lone superpower suddenly reassured that, in the long run, freedom had prevailed. So had capitalism. Technology investment and production growth in the United States brought Americans relative prosperity after decades of slump. "Globalization was in full swing," the *Atlantic* recalled in a 2002 retrospective of the "Roaring 1990s," referring to the influence the United States was able to wield over global markets as the undisputed leader of organizations like the International Monetary Fund (IMF). American economists and neoliberals from both political parties confidently encouraged the rest of the world to follow their example. "The US model reigned supreme," wrote analyst Joseph Stiglitz. "There was even talk of a radical New Economy, in which incomes would soar and the very idea of a business cycle would be relegated to history."[23] But like in the 1920s, pride preceded the fall. Ambitious "wolves of Wall Street" like the fictional Gordon Gekko and the real-life Jordan Belfort carried the ruthless and reckless trading schemes of John Raskob into a new generation. Exploiting loopholes in a system insufficiently regulated, opportunistic investors shorted the American public and contributed to the recession of 2008.

Instead of the Empire State Building, the World Trade Center, in the 1990s, was seen as the most prominent symbol of US economic supremacy. "Within a short period of time at the end of the 20th century," explains the 9/11 Memorial and Museum, "the forces of globalization had made the towers the most familiar structures on the most familiar skyline in the world."[24] The Towers were more than symbolic; they bustled as an institution managing money around the world and integrating global markets into its hub of US hegemony. The Empire State Building, meanwhile, leased offices for more traditional forms of business. These operational differences made the older skyscraper seem antiquated in comparison.

Al Smith had marketed the Empire State Building in 1931 as a symbol of economic power, but it also projected beauty and romance since its opening. King Kong climbed the tower for the sake of love, Cary Grant and Deborah Kerr made plans to reunite and launch a life together in *An Affair to Remember*, and Meg Ryan's character contrived to meet her soulmate on the observation deck in *Sleepless in Seattle*. Into the late twentieth century, the landmark still stirred hearts, even as a new crop of skyscrapers dominated the city as bigger, bolder symbols of power. It was the Twin Towers, not the Empire State Building, that filmmakers featured in movies like *Wall Street* and *Bonfire of the Vanities* as epitomes of greed and decadence.

A 1985 op-ed in the *New York Times* expressed its favoritism by imagining how an onlooker might feel if the Empire State Building were suddenly "gone." The first three thoughts, the writer predicted, would be "I am going to miss it." "It was so beautiful that it's a wonder no one loved it enough to put up a fight and keep it." And "Why couldn't they have taken down the World Trade Center instead?" At the end of the piece, the author mused that architects might be "embarrassed" by the building. "That's understandable," he jested. It is "standing there as a constant reminder that a skyscraper doesn't have to be just another big arrogant, dim-witted glass bore."[25] According to the *Chicago Tribune*, the classic "Gotham landmark" in Midtown was, along "with the Statue of Liberty, the most visible symbol of the city."[26] In 1986, the skyscraper was officially designated a National Historic Landmark.

Romanticisms aside, the Empire State Building was also a status symbol in high-stakes real estate. In the summer of 1994, the *Tribune* announced that "Donald Trump has finally bought something that can house most of his ego—the 102-story Empire State Building." As Trump explained, he took a 50 percent interest in the skyscraper because it was a "great deal for me" and "it solidifies my position as New York's native son." However, reporters predicted trouble between Trump and his real estate rivals, Harry and Leona Helmsley, who operated the building along with partner Peter Malkin. They were right. "I wouldn't believe Donald Trump if his tongue were notarized," Leona quipped. Trump, for his part, called Leona "a disgrace to humanity" and a "vicious, horrible woman."[27]

Personal animosities boiled into battles over the building, which offered Trump prestige if not maximum profitability. Before Prudential Insurance sold Empire State in 1991, a few months after the skyscraper's sixtieth anniversary, it had arranged a 114-year lease of the entire office space to Malkin and the Helmsleys, meaning that annual earnings for any brick-and-mortar owners were contingent upon their management. According to Trump, it was more like mismanagement. The mold-prone interior was undergoing a $60 million renovation to make cosmetic and operational updates, including replacement windows, but Trump wanted to modernize the building under his own brand and whim. He suggested emblazoning his name on the facade and converting the upper levels into pricey condominiums. Malkin and the Helmsleys stood in his way, insisting that the historical integrity of the building must be preserved and rents fixed. Leona Helmsley accused Trump of seeking revenge against her for past slights. The press also suggested as much, framing the maintenance dispute as a petty feud between adversaries.

Trump's involvement in the building took a circuitous route. Back in 1991, when Prudential was looking for buyers, they did not expect high bids, but they received one from Japanese investor Hideki Yokoi, who "collected" iconic structures. Facing criminal charges in Japan that would eventually land him in prison, Yokoi allowed his daughter and her husband to negotiate the purchase of Empire State. The optics of the deal, however, mattered as much as money, and ultimately Prudential's concerns about the sale of the all-American Matterhorn to a man from Japan caused them to reject Yokoi's $41 million bid in favor of New Yorker Oliver Grace Jr.'s $39 million offer. Prudential believed they had avoided backlash by blocking the sale to Yokoi's company. Yokoi, however, arranged to buy the building through back channels, using Grace as a front. At least, that's what he thought.[28]

Yokoi's purchase remained secret for a couple of years until his daughter supposedly spilled the beans one day to a woman at a gym in New

York. The woman turned out to be Trump's wife, Ivana. When Trump heard about the Empire State Building's true owners, he set about courting them, eventually securing a deal with Yokoi's daughter, but not Yokoi himself, that gave Trump a 50 percent stake in the iconic property on the condition that he could somehow break the Malkin-Helmsley mandates and raise the return on investment.

The Japanese billionaires were gambling on Trump's notoriety to add value to the aging skyscraper. Trump certainly brought media attention and piqued the curiosity of journalists about the paper trail that had sealed the sale. Investigators in 1994 discovered a complicated shell game that led back to Yokoi, who apparently had no idea that his daughter had taken control of the building and given half of it to Trump. Yokoi hired lawyers to pursue the matter in New York, and lawsuits soon erupted among all parties—Yokoi, his daughter, Trump, Malkin, and the Helmsleys—for several years before Trump finally sold his share of the property in 2002 to Peter Malkin for a small profit.[29]

But the legality of who really "owned" the Empire State Building persisted, a confusion that prompted the *New York Daily News* to demonstrate how easy it was to claim the icon. Wagering that city clerks would not conduct thorough checks on their submitted paperwork, in 2008 the *Daily News* requested a deed transfer in the name of Fay Wray, the *King Kong* actress, and after coming clean about their ruse, they transferred it back. The publicity stunt unveiled the ease of shady dealings in the city, while the Yokoi-Trump ownership fiasco throughout the 1990s revealed the tangled web of international investments in an era of increasing globalization.

||||||||||

Globalization affected how the world perceived the Empire State Building and US imperialism. Traditionally, empires had been built on territorial acquisition (colonies) and resource control (mercantilism). In that model, geography mattered. The globalization that developed into the late twentieth century, however, went beyond borders and boots on the ground to include more subtle and insidious forms of soft power that the United States had been practicing for decades. The spread of American ideas, commercial brands, capitalist norms, and democracy around the world marked the 1990s as a new era of US influence that did not depend on acquiring more land but on opening and controlling more markets. The World Trade Center helped manage the money that made this new world go round, serving as a locale for investment and trade deals as well as an educational arm for integrating global markets and maximizing profits. But the architects of the World Trade Center framed their project's purpose in even loftier terms, insisting that world trade would bring world peace as countries learned to cooperate for their mutual benefit.

Not everyone wanted part of the US-led system. Osama bin Laden, who directed Al Qaeda's holy war against the United States, opposed Western influence, especially in Middle Eastern affairs. "The collapse of the Soviet Union made the US more haughty and arrogant and it has started to look at itself as a master of this world," he told a CNN journalist in 1997. The US government, he lambasted, had committed "hideous crimes" that "abandoned humanitarian feelings," more than "any imperialist power in the world."[30] Bin Laden and his network of jihadists devised plans to attack US symbols of power, using nonconventional warfare.

Terrorists singled out the Twin Towers not only because they symbolized US imperialism but because of their size, visibility, and vulnerability. The towers stood side by side at the lower end of Manhattan, far removed from the skyscrapers of Midtown. Nothing obstructed the airspace around them, creating an image of two lone, tall, sitting ducks. Al Qaeda took notice.

In February 1993, operatives affiliated with the terrorist group targeted the North Tower with a vehicle bomb detonated in the site's basement garage. The blast killed six people and injured a thousand more. But it did not make the impact the terrorists had planned. As perpetrator Ramzi Yousef admitted, he intended for the first tower to topple into the second tower, inflicting maximum casualties. And he claimed legitimate reasons for seeking revenge against the American people, who he alleged allowed their government to engage in imperialism and genocide. Before carrying out the act, Yousef sent letters to newspapers listing the reasons for attacking the US landmark, calling it retribution for US involvement in the Middle East, especially support for Israel and its violence against Palestinians. Though caught and convicted, the jihadists warned that attacks would continue until the United States conceded to their demands. In 2000, Al Qaeda took credit for the bombing of the USS *Cole* off the coast of Yemen, before setting their sights on New York again.

Outrage about US-Israeli relations also prompted Palestinian Ali Abu Kamal to attack bystanders on the observation deck of the Empire State Building in February 1997. Visitors that day remembered Abu Kamal asking them to point out the Statue of Liberty in the distance. "I love Americans, and I love America," he supposedly said. A few minutes later, he opened fire with a .380-caliber Beretta, killing one tourist before turning the gun on himself. Investigators found in his possession a suicide note that vowed revenge against "bitter enemies." The United States, along with Britain and France, he stated, were responsible for the "savage aggression" against Palestine, while the Empire State Building, in his mind, stood as a symbol of US imperialism. "I have decided to strike at their own den in New York, and at the very Empire State Building in particular," he wrote. News reports noted that it was the most violent incident at the skyscraper since the B-25 crash in 1945.[31]

Al Qaeda floated ideas about hijacking aircraft in the early 1990s, and US analysts even anticipated such an attack on New York buildings. Days after the 1993 bombing, John Skilling, the Twin Towers' structural engineer, told reporters that he and his colleagues had taken aircraft collisions into consideration when designing the structures. "We looked at every possible thing we could think of that could happen to the buildings, even to the extent of an airplane hitting the side," Skilling explained. "However, back in those days people didn't think about terrorists very much." The 1945 crash into the Empire State Building, he said, served as a cautionary tale. As the *Seattle Times* wrote, "Skilling's people did an analysis that showed the towers would withstand the impact of a Boeing 707," concluding that jet engine fuel could cause a massive fire but not topple the buildings.[32]

Eight years later, Ramzi Yousef's uncle, Khalid Sheikh Mohammed, orchestrated another version of the Al Qaeda plan, using hijacked commercial airlines to strike the Towers on September 11, 2001. That morning, several people working in the Empire State Building noticed the first plane approaching and crashing into the North Tower. They called out alarms to evacuate all floors, fearing the Midtown skyscraper might be next. The building's oldest tenant, jeweler Jack Brod, watched from the sixty-sixth floor. "I couldn't believe my eyes," he said later.[33] Most eyewitnesses in Manhattan recalled seeing the flames first, then bodies falling, the Towers collapsing, and thousands of people covered in ash walking uptown or crossing bridges into the boroughs. A few articles in the days that followed compared the event to the 1945 crash into the Empire State

September 11, 2001

Building; but the 9/11 attack was of much greater magnitude and caused much more destruction, killing nearly three thousand people in one day, and additional thousands who succumbed to health complications in subsequent years.

The terrorist act also affected the American psyche and the nation's sense of security as a superpower. As journalist R. W. Apple observed the next morning, "The whole nation—to a degree the whole world—shook as hijacked airliners plunged into buildings that symbolize the financial and military might of the United States. The sense of security and self-confidence that Americans take as their birthright suffered a grievous blow." In an op-ed entitled "America the Vulnerable," John F. Burns likewise opined, "Since the end of the cold war in the early 1990's, there have been two Americas, existing side by side: the America that is the world's only superpower, dwarfing every other nation in its economic and military might, and the America that learned in one deathly hour on Tuesday that no amount of power can provide protection against an enemy with limited means but a ruthless determination."[34] He referred to the ancient David and Goliath story as a metaphor for terrorists taking on the might of US empire.

Confusion abounded as Americans questioned how and why the attack had happened. In the aftermath, analysts devoted themselves to answering those inquiries, studying the ways in which US imperialism had sowed resentment around the world. Some foreigners, they explained, faulted the United States for intrusive acts that undermined liberty, while others detested American attempts to bolster liberalism against their authoritarian regimes. Islamic jihadists took issue with the United States on both counts. They rejected both American empire and liberty as pillars of a new world order they opposed.

After 9/11, Americans unaware of the negative image or extent of US imperialism awakened to it and weighed the costs. Some commentators suggested at least partial retreat into isolationism for the sake of safety. As one student argued in the University of Illinois campus newspaper, "as the empire expands, the United States becomes weaker. Money is spent on expansion instead of protecting the homeland." He worried that retribution against terrorist networks in Iraq and Afghanistan only exacerbated the problem of US vulnerability. "To avoid future catastrophic attacks, the only solution might be to shift US foreign policy," he concluded.[35] But the rise of terrorism also prompted Americans to rally around US empire and its military, believing that a more aggressive approach abroad was essential for protecting the homeland and the American way of life. Scholar Bruce Robbins noticed that "Americans have lost their shame about it." Historian Michael Adas agreed, saying that Americans were willing to give up domestic freedoms for "force overseas" and "an empire of preemptive military strikes."[36]

Americans demonstrated resilience in small ways. It took a few weeks for New York City to reopen after the attack, as residents struggled to overcome their anxieties, especially in tall buildings. The Empire State Building's twenty thousand workers returned to work after suffering through several bomb threats, and though some businesses initially announced they would break their leases and find quarters elsewhere, the building lost only four tenants as the year wound to a close.[37] The observation deck reopened to visitors on September 29, offering a drastically different, "disconcerting" view downtown. "It's like the city has reverted to 1972," a Manhattan resident remarked.[38]

After the Twin Towers were destroyed, the 1931 skyscraper became, again, the tallest building in New York and, as such, "the most obvious target." But, as one reporter reasoned, "this is precisely why it's the safest place to be. Security officials, like generals, are always fighting the last war, so they're primed for an attack like the one on the World Trade Center."[39] Americans also reassessed their appreciation for the classic landmark. "The Empire State Building is once again the tallest building in New York," wrote Fred Bernstein. "But its appeal goes deeper." As New York lawyer Paul Washington was quoted in Bernstein's piece, "'The Empire State Building is a reflection of who we were.'" Bernstein described his alarm in the weeks after 9/11 whenever he saw the top of his "old friend" shrouded in fog. "I panicked, imagining for a split second that the floors

I couldn't see were missing." He also felt uneasy when the lights at the crown of Empire State went dark at midnight. "Since then," he admitted, "I've been thinking of calling the building's owners and asking them to keep the lights on until dawn. Funny, I've never needed to sleep with a night light before."[40]

Liberty Island also began welcoming tourists again in late September, and the statue that stood across the harbor from the carnage of 9/11 gave Americans hope that their nation would endure. Christina Ray Stanton, a tour guide who regularly took groups to Liberty Island, recalled how she "never had to remind anyone to smile as they gathered beneath the massive statue that had welcomed millions of immigrants to our shores. Her beautiful green face and determined look," she said, "inspired me, no matter how often I visited." Lady Liberty became more poignant for Stanton on and after 9/11. She and her husband were in Battery Park that morning when they were picked up by a ferry that carried evacuees to safety in New Jersey. After months of mourning, Stanton returned to her work as a tour guide in March 2002. As she approached the island, Stanton "looked back across the Hudson River to the hole in the sky where the Twin Towers" once stood. "Then I turned back toward the Statue of Liberty," she wrote. "And I was assured for the first time in months that America's freedom and liberty would be upheld." Though terrorists could destroy buildings or monuments, even the Statue of Liberty itself, Stanton was confident that "they cannot take away the American spirit and our determination to overcome." Looking back twenty years after her experiences on 9/11, Stanton hoped that "our memories of how much we lost that terrible day" would "inspire us to work toward unity, mutual respect, and peace."[41] For her, the Statue of Liberty represented those ideals.

IIIIIIIIIII

Into the twenty-first century, the Statue of Liberty continued to serve as a lightning rod for opinions about American political culture, policy, and purpose, and minority groups highlighted the irony of the celebrated statue in a nation that oppressed large parts of its population. Activists for LGBTQ rights drew attention to their liberties, and the backlash against them, just as women and Black Americans had in the past. On a trip to Liberty Island in 2011, Catholic scholar Gabriel Torretta noticed National Park Service posters declaring Pride Month and mentioning areas of interest in New York related to LGBT history. However, Torretta was disappointed that "nowhere on the posters did a connection to the Statue of Liberty . . . appear at all." In fact, "the poster makers couldn't even be bothered to make a cheap linguistic attempt to connect LGBT . . . with liberty." Claiming the statue as a symbol of inclusive rights, Torretta concluded that "what's important is that the 3,000 daily visitors to the pedestal of the Statue of Liberty need to know that to be an American

Lady Liberty and Lady Justice

means celebrating and fighting for the ability of the LGBT community to do whatever they want," including getting married.[42]

Women and people of color had been making the same point for centuries. Like W. E. B. Du Bois said in the late nineteenth century, and journalist Claudia Jones observed in 1950, while she was awaiting deportation for her radicalism, Lady Liberty "stands with her back to" America and its injustices.[43] In the 1985 documentary on the landmark, James Baldwin concurred, referring to liberty's affliction at the hands of American power, arguing that it "is always contradicted by the necessities of the state."[44] The US government, in other words, prioritized efficiency in its quest for power, building an empire upon amoralities rather than respecting the rights of everyone encountered along the way.

In recent years, Christian nationalists have made political inroads that many Americans oppose as illiberal because of their restrictions on women's rights, immigrant rights, and workers' rights. Responding to evangelical Franklin Graham's assertion that he is apolitical, even as he publicly supports and advises certain Republicans, Rev. Dr. William Barber quipped on social media that "preachers don't get to opt out of politics. We are either chaplains of empire or prophets of God."[45] As Barber implied, preachers like Graham favored the reins of coercive power over a Christian ethics that demands the liberation of the poor and oppressed.

The dichotomy between liberty and empire, in fact, has compelled many Americans to feel forced to choose between them. Talk show host Jerry Springer reflected on coming to America as a Jewish immigrant from Europe in the late 1940s and seeing the Statue of Liberty for the first time. "This is not a country of bullies," he exhorted in a 2003 speech. "We are not an empire. We are the light. We are the Statue of Liberty."[46] Right-wing radio personality Rush Limbaugh, meanwhile, became incensed at any association of immigration with the monument, claiming that "the Statue of Liberty was never meant to be a symbol of immigration. It was meant to be a symbol of liberty and freedom." Refusing to acknowledge the multiple and mutable meanings that millions had bestowed upon the landmark, Limbaugh insisted that the statue should remain frozen in time, at its dedication in 1886, when it was limited to Bartholdi's ode to republican virtues. "The torch is not to light the way to the United States," Limbaugh continued. "It is to light the way to liberty to the rest of the world."[47] Yet the rest of the world weighed in, most democratically, on the statue's significance not only for a particular ideology but for all people, framing debates about the United States as a republic, a nation, and an empire.

Concepts of empire also changed over time. Back in the 1800s, Americans newly freed from their colonial origins aspired to cultivate the continent for personal empowerment and national survival. As scholar Bruce Robbins explained, the term "empire" in those days did not carry the negative connotations that it would acquire by the turn of the twentieth century when "imperialism" of the traditional model became a dirty word. "Until very recently," he said, "there was no way you could use the word 'empire' in any but a critical sense. It's been a very, very long American tradition to set ourselves apart from the European notion of empire. The American public wouldn't support imperialism." Regardless, the United States did maintain an empire over the course of its history—its people just preferred euphemisms and rationales. As historian Walter LaFeber put it, "Americans don't like the word 'empire.' We like the word 'democracy.'"[48] The American way of soft-power peddling, these scholars suggested, had sharpened considerably since 2001 when reliance upon the military increased.

In the name of democracy, divinity, liberty, or prosperity, Americans over the centuries have exported what they expected the rest of the world would want. Those assumptions and the means of delivery, however, often undermined the stated intent. The United States gave hope to millions and shattered the hopes of millions, especially when manipulating weaker parties for gain and manifesting a destiny muddied by racism and bloodied by war. No nation, of course, stands blameless on these terms, but the high idealism of the founding documents makes the hypocrisies glaring. Fear also drove imperialism, as generations of Americans kept alive the deep-seated paranoia that colonists and early Americans harbored about their precarious place in the world. Projecting power and controlling the environment, they reasoned, would protect their rights and opportunities.

Shifting views on empire have affected perspectives on the Empire State Building. Initially opened as a "cathedral of commerce," America's Art Deco flagship of economic and imperial power in 1931 appeared quaint by the new millennium. "The Empire State Building," wrote journalist Mitchell Pacelle in 2001, "has weathered the tempest of envy and greed that swirled around it for a decade with its allure intact." Though no longer a powerhouse, the skyscraper, he maintained, lived on as "a monument," "a sturdy lighthouse," and as "a symbol of New York's grandeur." Even "jaded Manhattanites long since deadened to the scale and brawn of the city," still looked to the building as a "rock-solid sentinel" shimmering "with power and glory." Unlike the newer, nondescript structures erected in the twenty-first century, the Empire State Building, he added, projected "heart and soul."[49]

In his October 2001 editorial, Fred Bernstein made a similar point. While the World Trade Center was "always distant (even from up close)," the Midtown skyscraper offered the comfort of "an intimate" or "old friend."[50] Today, a crop of taller towers dot the New York skyline, including 30 Hudson Yards, One Vanderbilt, and One World Trade Center, the single structure built on the grounds of the original Twin Towers that rises 1,776 feet in the air, a deliberate height-design to symbolize American freedom. The size and scale of these buildings suggest dominance, innovation, industry, and the endurance of an American empire.

American empire has prevailed since the 9/11 attack with over seven hundred military bases in at least eighty countries. Economic power has also outpaced rivals in the twenty-first century. Yet some critics argue that US empire is waning. They point to problems of climate change, national debt, political dysfunction, and the costs of constant warfare as signs of decline. As John Dewey once explained, the American empire was not built overnight; it was extended through countless individual and seemingly unconnected acts.[51] And scholars have written about the fall of empires, including Rome, occurring in a similar fashion. "The fall of an empire—the end of a polity, a socioeconomic order, a dominant culture, or the intertwined whole—looks more like a cascading series of minor, individually unimportant failures than a dramatic ending that appears out of the blue," wrote historian Patrick Wyman. "All empires think they're special, but all empires eventually come to an end. The United States won't be an exception." According to Wyman, the perception of decline depends upon a person's status in society, since the wealthy are more insulated from disaster for longer. But social stability also gets at the root of the problem—an empire falls when it can no longer keep its entire population safe and content.[52]

While the inquiry "Are we living through the end of the empire?" has been a topic of articles and social media posts in recent years, fewer people seem to be asking if they are living through the end of the republic, even as signs of that downward spiral are evident. The rise of authoritarianism and corruption in the twenty-first century and attempts to limit the rights of Americans, especially along lines of race, religion, and gender, present a threat to liberties and the stability of the republic. If power no longer resides primarily with the people, and if the president and an oligarchy of billionaires are allowed broad, unaccountable authority, then the US republic is already in peril and may no longer exist by definition or function. An empire, after all, can survive without democratic inclusion and a balance of power. A republic cannot.

The creators behind the Statue of Liberty (Édouard Laboulaye and F. Auguste Bartholdi), lionized republics. It framed their concept of the gift statue to the United States, which, they believed, would shine as the best hope for freedom in the world. From their experience living in France, they knew how fragile republican forms of government could be. Yet they put their faith in the United States to value and defend liberty, elevating it as a viable option for other nations to emulate. The Statue of Liberty was meant to remind Americans of their fortune to live in a republic and their duty to strive against all odds to preserve and improve it. As Laboulaye predicted in 1875 about the year 1976, "the centenary of independence will be celebrated again. We shall then be only forgotten dust. America . . . will be ignorant of our names. But this statue will remain."[53] The assignment to uphold her, the Frenchmen knew, would not be easy.

It is not easy because a republic is always at a crossroads, always struggling through crises that could upset its delicate poise. Present times are no different. Idealists and naysayers aside, American liberty may always be imperfect and US empire may never retreat, so we must live in the meantime with the inconsistencies and contradictions that lie between them. Though the contradictions usually seem irreconcilable, if the Empire State Building and Statue of Liberty are put in proverbial conversation with each other, we may temper the harsher realities with a more positive approach.

The "Golden Rule," doing unto others as you would have them to do you, offers a basic guideline for reconciling empire and liberty. Though usually applied to interpersonal relations, the "Golden Rule" can also work at national and international levels, reminding us to treat people at home and abroad as we would want to be treated. It serves as an equalizer for those tempted to assume that their rights trump the rights of others. It humanizes people who are different or foreign. It makes liberty a process of giving as much as taking.

In a speech announcing his withdrawal from the 2024 presidential election, Joe Biden referred to America as "an idea . . . the most powerful idea in the history of the world." He cited the Declaration of Independence as first forming the substance of American idealism and acknowledged that "we've never fully lived up to it—to this sacred idea, but we've never walked away from it either." President Biden, like many political leaders before him, was warning the nation that ideals are realized or squandered by actions. Oftentimes inaction. He illustrated the stakes for Americans in deciding the age-old question: "Do we still believe in freedom, justice, and democracy?" If so, he insisted, the American people needed to imbue and *enact* those ideas with "honesty, decency, and respect."[54]

The greatest achievements in history have come to fruition through cooperation and unity of purpose. The Statue of Liberty and the Empire State Building are testaments to the fact. They were built by hundreds of people of all backgrounds working together to create lasting emblems of human potential. But even after construction on these monuments ended, they were incomplete. Over the years, people from all over the world have collectively assigned these landmarks meaning and contested what they symbolize. Is the United States an "empire of liberty"? Do the two icons represent the best or the worst of Americans—or something in between? It remains indefinitely undecided. As Herman Melville once wrote, grand structures, "true ones, ever leave the copestone to posterity."[55] The Statue of Liberty and the Empire State Building are two of America's grandest structures, standing as monumental, open question marks about who we are and who we want to be.

ACKNOWLEDGMENTS

Foremost, I am grateful to my husband, Daniel Cook, for his never-ending support. He encouraged me in this project from start to finish and discussed it with me daily.

I am indebted to several scholars who reviewed chapters along the way. My deepest thanks go out to Daniel Hummel, Doug Rossinow, Ronald Angelo Johnson, and Michael Gambone. Their insights were invaluable for improving sections of the manuscript. I also want to thank Jeremi Suri, Karla Mullen, Joseph Frasnelli, and Jennifer Ratner-Rosenhagen for reading the earliest version of the book proposal and offering feedback that ultimately shaped the themes and arc of the book.

Thanks to those who helped me locate sources or discuss topics essential for writing parts of this book, including Deena Ecker, Britt Tevis, Torrey Tiedeman, and Dennis Trest. I appreciate the time and interest you took to assist me in small but no less meaningful ways.

I deeply appreciate Rachael Marks for believing in this book and shepherding it through publishing, as well as Becca Johnson, Teddy Turner, Susan Lumenello, Beth Collins, and all the staff at Beacon Press.

My grandfather, Peter Giannotti, also deserves acknowledgment, especially since he took me to Liberty Island for the first time when I was seven or eight years old. We had a disagreement about whether to make the climb to the statue's crown. I wanted to do it, but he explained that there were hundreds of narrow, winding stairs, and I started to imagine a rickety apparatus with ropes and pulleys, missing steps, and perhaps even rats. I decided my grandfather was probably right. It took me until the fall of 2024 to make the trip to the top. I am pleased to report, there were no rats.

FURTHER READING

Anbinder, Tyler. *City of Dreams: The 400-Year Epic History of Immigrant New York*. Houghton Mifflin Harcourt, 2016.

Bacevich, Andrew. *American Empire: The Realities and Consequences of US Diplomacy*. Harvard University Press, 2002.

———. *Limits of Power: The End of American Exceptionalism*. Metropolitan Books, 2008.

Baldwin, Neil. *Henry Ford and the Jews: The Mass Production of Hate*. PublicAffairs, 2001.

Barber, William J., II. *Third Reconstruction: Moral Mondays, Fusion Politics, and the Rise of a New Justice Movement*. Beacon Press, 2016.

Bayor, Ronald H. *Race and Ethnicity in America: A Concise History*. Columbia University Press, 2003.

Berenson, Edward. *The Statue of Liberty: A Transatlantic Story*. Yale University Press, 2012.

Bergen, Peter L. *Holy War, Inc.: Inside the Secret World of Osama bin Laden*. Free Press, 2001.

Berlowitz, Leslie, Denis Donoghue, and Louis Menand, eds. *America in Theory*. Oxford University Press, 1988.

Blanchet, Christian, and Betrand Dard. *Statue of Liberty: The First One Hundred Years*. Trans Bernard Weisberger. Houghton Mifflin, 1985.

Bon Tempo, Carl J., and Hasia R. Diner. *Immigration: An American History*. Yale University Press, 2022.

Borgwardt, Elizabeth. *New Deal for the World: America's Vision for Human Rights*. Belknap Press of Harvard University Press, 2005.

Boutelle, R. J. *The Race for America: Black Internationalism in the Age of Manifest Destiny*. University of North Carolina Press, 2023.

Buhle, Paul. *History and the New Left: Madison, Wisconsin, 1950–1970*. Temple University Press, 1990.

Conroy-Krutz, Emily. *Missionary Diplomacy: Religion and Nineteenth-Century American Foreign Relations*. Cornell University Press, 2024.

Cowie, Jefferson. *Stayin' Alive: The 1970s and the Last Days of the Working Class*. New Press, 2010.

Debouzy, Marianne, ed. *In the Shadow of the Statue of Liberty: Immigrants, Workers, and Citizens in the American Republic, 1880–1920*. University of Illinois Press, 1992.

DiAngelo, Robin. *White Fragility: Why It's So Hard for White People to Talk About Racism*. Beacon Press, 2018.

Dicker, Rory C. *A History of U. S. Feminisms*. Seal Press, 2016.

Dillon, Wilton S., and Neil G. Kotler, eds. *The Statue of Liberty Revisited*. Smithsonian Institution Press, 1994.

Dinnerstein, Leonard. *Antisemitism in America*. Oxford University Press, 1995.

Du Mez, Kristin K. *Jesus and John Wayne: How White Evangelicals Corrupted a Faith and Fractured a Nation*. Liveright Publishing, 2020.

Dunbar-Ortiz, Roxanne. *An Indigenous Peoples' History of the United States*. Beacon Press, 2014.

———. *"Not a Nation of Immigrants": Settler Colonialism, White Supremacy, and a History of Erasure and Exclusion*. Beacon Press, 2021.

Farber, David. *Everybody Ought to Be Rich: The Life and Times of John J. Raskob, Capitalist*. Oxford University Press, 2013.

Ferguson, Niall. *Colossus: The Rise and Fall of the American Empire*. Penguin Books, 2004.

Foner, Eric. *Battles for Freedom: The Use and Abuse of American History*. I. B. Tauris & Co., 2017.

Fox, Nancy Jo. *Liberties with Liberty: The Fascinating History of America's Proudest Symbol*. E. P. Dutton, 1985.

Fukuyama, Francis. *The End of History and the Last Man*. Free Press, 1992.

Gambone, Michael D. *Small Wars: Low-Intensity Threats and the American Response Since Vietnam*. University of Tennessee Press, 2013.

Go, Julian. *Patterns of Empire: The British and American Empires, 1688 to the Present*. Cambridge University Press, 2011.

Gobat, Michel. *Empire by Invitation: William Walker and Manifest Destiny in Central America*. Harvard University Press, 2018.

Grandin, Greg. *Empire's Workshop: Latin America, The United States, and the Making of an Imperial Republic*. Picador Press, 2021.

———. *The End of the Myth: From the Frontier to the Border Wall in the Mind of America*. Metropolitan Books, 2019.

Gray, Walter D. *Interpreting American Democracy in France: The Career of Edouard Laboulaye*. University of Delaware Press, 1994.

Hahn, Steven. *Illiberal America: A History*. W. W. Norton & Co., 2024.

Hartman, Andrew. *A War for the Soul of America: A History of the Culture Wars*. University of Chicago Press, 2019.

Hartmann, Thom. *The Hidden History of American Oligarchy: Reclaiming Our Democracy from the Ruling Class*. Berrett-Koehler, 2021.

Higham, John. *Strangers in the Land: Patterns of American Nativism, 1860–1925*. Rutgers University Press, 1955.

Hofstadter, Richard. *Paranoid Style in American Politics*. Knopf, 1965.

———. *Social Darwinism in American Thought*. Beacon Press, 1955.

Howe, Daniel Walker. *What Hath God Wrought: The Transformation of America, 1815–1848*. Oxford University Press, 2007.

Immerman, Richard. *Empire for Liberty: A History of American Imperialism from Benjamin Franklin to Paul Wolfowitz*. Princeton University Press, 2010.

Immewahr, Daniel. *How to Hide an Empire: A History of the Greater United States*. Farrar, Straus & Giroux, 2019.

Joseph, Peniel E. *The Third Reconstruction: America's Struggle for Racial Justice in the Twenty First Century*. Basic Books, 2022.

Khan, Yasmin Sabina. *Enlightening the World: The Creation of the Statue of Liberty*. Cornell University Press, 2010.

LaFeber, Walter. *The New Empire: An Interpretation of American Expansion, 1860–1898*. Cornell University Press, 1963.

Lears, Jackson. *Rebirth of a Nation: The Making of Modern America, 1877–1920*. HarperCollins, 2009.

Lee, Erika. *The Making of Asian America: A History*. Simon & Schuster, 2015.

Lepore, Jill. *These Truths: A History of the United States*. Recorded Books, 2018.

Lerner, Gerda. *The Creation of Feminist Consciousness: From the Middle Ages to Eighteen Seventy*. Oxford University Press, 1994.

Levy, Jonathan. *Ages of American Capitalism: A History of the United States*. Random House, 2022.

Marable, Manning. *Race, Reform, and Rebellion: The Second Reconstruction in Black America, 1945–1982*. University Press of Mississippi, 2007.

Mayer, Jane. *Dark Money: The Hidden History of Billionaires Behind the Rise of the Radical Right*. Doubleday, 2016.

Mazower, Mark. *Hitler's Empire: How the Nazis Ruled Europe*. Penguin Press, 2008.

McGranahan, Carole, and John F. Collins, eds. *Ethnographies of U.S. Empire*. Duke University Press, 2018.

Menand, Louis. *The Free World: Art and Thought in the Cold War*. Farrar, Straus & Giroux, 2021.

Miller, James. *"Democracy Is in the Streets": From Port Huron to the Siege of Chicago*. Simon & Schuster, 1987.

Mitchell, Elizabeth. *Liberty's Torch: The Great Adventure to Build the Statue of Liberty*. Atlantic Monthly Press, 2014.

Morgan, Edmund S. *American Slavery, American Freedom*. W. W. Norton & Co., 1975.

Pacelle, Mitchell. *Empire: A Tale of Obsession, Betrayal, and the Battle for an American Icon*. John Wiley, 2001.

Pearl, Christopher R. *Declarations of Independence: Indigenous Resilience, Colonial Rivalries, and the Cost of Revolution*. University of Virginia Press, 2024.

Plummer, Brenda Gayle. *Rising Wind: Black Americans and US Foreign Affairs, 1935–1960*. University of North Carolina Press, 1996.

———. *Window on Freedom: Race, Civil Rights, and Foreign Affairs, 1945–1988*. University of North Carolina Press, 2003.

Reynolds, David. *Waking Giant: America in the Age of Jackson*. HarperCollins, 2009.

Rodgers, Daniel T. *Age of Fracture*. Belknap Press of Harvard University Press, 2011.

Rosenberg, Emily S. *Spreading the American Dream: American Economic and Cultural Expansion, 1890–1945*. Hill and Wang, 1982.

Rossinow, Doug. *Reagan Era: A History of the 1980s*. Columbia University Press, 2015.

———. *Visions of Progress: The Left-Liberal Tradition in America*. University of Pennsylvania Press, 2008.

Rutland, Robert Allen. *The Ordeal of the Constitution: The Antifederalists and the Ratification Struggle of 1787–1788*. Northeastern University Press, 1983.

Sargent, Daniel J. *Superpower Transformed: The Remaking of American Foreign Relations in the 1970s*. Oxford University Press, 2015.

Slayton, Robert A. *Empire Statesman: The Rise and Redemption of Al Smith*. Free Press, 2001.

Steger, Manfred B., et al., eds. *Globalization: Past, Present, Future*. University of California Press, 2023.

Suri, Jeremi. *Civil War by Other Means: America's Long and Unfinished Fight for Democracy*. PublicAffairs, 2022.

———. *Liberty's Surest Guardian: American Nation-Building from the Founders to Obama*. Free Press, 2011.

———. *Power and Protest: Global Revolution and the Rise of Détente*. Harvard University Press, 2003.

Tauranac, John. *The Empire State Building: The Making of a Landmark.* Cornell University Press, 2014.

Trachtenberg, Marvin. *The Statue of Liberty.* Penguin Books, 1976.

Westad, Odd Arne. *Global Cold War: Third World Interventions and the Making of Our Times.* Cambridge University Press, 2007.

Westbrook, Robert. *John Dewey and American Democracy.* Cornell University Press, 1991.

Wilentz, Sean. *Age of Reagan: A History, 1974–2008.* Harper, 2008.

Wilkerson, Isabel. *Caste: The Origins of Our Discontents.* Random House, 2020.

Williams, William Appleman. *The Tragedy of American Diplomacy.* Dell, 1962.

Willis, Carol, ed. *Building the Empire State.* W. W. Norton & Co., 1998.

Wineapple, Brenda. *Ecstatic Nation: Confidence, Crisis, and Compromise, 1848–1877.* HarperCollins, 2014.

Wood, Gordon. *Creation of the American Republic, 1776–1787.* University of North Carolina Press, 1969.

———. *Empire of Liberty: A History of the Early Republic, 1789–1815.* Oxford University Press, 2009.

———. *Radicalism of the American Revolution.* Knopf, 1992.

Yang, Jia Lynn. *One Mighty and Irresistible Tide: The Epic Struggle over American Immigration, 1924–1965.* W. W. Norton & Co., 2020.

Zinn, Howard. *A People's History of the United States.* Longman, 1980.

———. *The Politics of History.* Beacon Press, 1970.

IMAGE CREDITS

Page xiii, Liberty in fog: Dec. 3, 2017, Creative Commons Attribution-Share Alike. Photographer unknown.

Page 32, Construction in Paris: *Construction of the Statue of Liberty*. Wikimedia Commons. Photographer unknown.

Page 32, Liberty's Face: *Construction of the Statue of Liberty*. Wikimedia Commons. Photographer unknown.

Page 34, Al Smith campaign button, 1928, Heritage Auction Archives.

Page 52, Empire State Building under construction: Irving Underhill, *Empire State Building, 5th Ave. & 34th St., N.Y.C. Empire State Building Under Construction*, ca. 1930, https://www.loc.gov/item/2003678138/.

Page 58, Sky boys: Lewis Hine, *Icarus*, Ford Motor Company Collection, Gift of Ford Motor Company and John C. Waddell, 1987.

Page 72, Statue of Liberty dedication day: H. O'Neill, New York, Oct. 28, 1886, Wikimedia Commons.

Page 91, 1899 cartoon, US imperialism: Originally printed in *Philadelphia Inquirer*. Scanned by Infrogmation from reprint in 1899 book *War in the Philippines*.

Page 105, Empire State Building: Angelo Rizzuto, *The Empire State Building*, 1952, https://www.loc.gov/item/2020635807/.

Page 139, World War II war bonds poster: National Archives and Records Administration, catalogued under the National Archives Identifier (NAID) 515293, taken between 1941 and 1945. Artist unknown.

Page 205, Gorbachev, Reagan, and Bush: National Archives and Records Administration, catalogued under the National Archives Identifier (NAID) 198595, taken Dec. 7, 1988. Photographer unknown.

Page 222, September 11, 2001: Photograph by the National Park Service, September 11, 2001. Photographer unknown.

Page 226, Lady Liberty and Lady Justice: Quinn Dombrowski, June 30, 2013, Creative Commons Attribution-Share Alike.

NOTES

CHAPTER 1: LIBERTY ENLIGHTENING THE WORLD

1. Willadene Price, *Bartholdi and the Statue of Liberty* (Rand McNally, 1959), 29.

2. Edouard Laboulaye to John Bigelow, Mar. 30, 1865, in John Bigelow, *Retrospections of an Active Life, 1863–1865, vol.* 2 (Baker & Taylor, 1909).

3. Frederic Auguste Bartholdi, *The Statue of Liberty Enlightening the World* (North American Review, 1885), 13.

4. Laboulaye to Bigelow, Apr. 29, 1865, in Bigelow, *Retrospections of an Active Life.*

5. French Committee of Emancipation to President Andrew Johnson, May 1, 1865, in Bigelow, *Retrospections of an Active Life.*

6. See John Bigelow to Mary Todd, Dec. 7, 1866, Abraham Lincoln Papers, Series 3, General Correspondence, 1837–1897, Library of Congress, www.loc.gov.

7. Abraham Lincoln, "Gettysburg Address," November 19, 1863.

8. Edouard Laboulaye, *Paris en Amerique* (Charpentier, 1863), vii–viii.

9. Edouard Laboulaye, preface, *Questions constitutionnelles* (Charpentier, 1872).

10. John Bigelow, *Some Recollections of the Late Edouard Laboulaye* (G. P. Putnam's, 1889), 3–5.

11. William Edward Johnston [Malakoff, pseud.], "Interesting from Paris," dispatched May 2, 1865, *New York Times*, May 16, 1865.

12. Bartholdi, *The Statue of Liberty Enlightening the World*, 36.

13. Bartholdi, *The Statue of Liberty Enlightening the World*, 14.

14. Marquis de Lafayette and Samuel Lorenzo Knapp, *Memoirs of General Lafayette* (E. G. House, 1824), 16–18.

15. Lafayette and Knapp, *Memoirs of General Lafayette*, 18.

16. George Washington to James Duane, Apr. 10, 1785, National Archives, Founders Online, Washington Papers, letter, Apr. 10, 1785, footnote 1. See also Library of Congress, George Washington Papers.

17. Lafayette and Knapp, *Memoirs of General Lafayette*, 13.

18. Lafayette to Washington, Feb. 5, 1783, in Marquis de Lafayette, *Lafayette in the Age of the American Revolution: Selected Letters and Papers, 1776–1790*, part 1, ed. Stanley J. Idzerda (Cornell University Press, 1983), 91.

19. Washington to Lafayette, May 10, 1786, *The Writings of George Washington from the Original Manuscript Sources, 1745–1799, Vol. 28, December 5, 1784–August 30, 1786* (US Government Printing Office, 1938), 420–25.

20. *The Records of the Federal Convention of 1787*, ed. Max Farrand, vol. 2 (Yale University Press, 1911), 10.

21. Washington to Lafayette, Feb. 7, 1788.

22. Bartholdi, travel journal, June 21, 1871, Bartholdi Collection, New York Public Library.

23. Bartholdi, journal, July 22, 1871.

24. Bartholdi, *The Statue of Liberty Enlightening the World*, 20.

25. Bartholdi, *The Statue of Liberty Enlightening the World*, 16–17.

26. Bartholdi, letter to mother, June 24, 1871, Bartholdi Collection, New York Public Library.

27. Bartholdi, journal, June 28, 1871.

28. Bartholdi, letter to mother, July 28, 1981.

29. Bartholdi, letters to mother.

30. Bartholdi, journal.

31. Bartholdi, letter to mother, Sept. 24, 1871.

32. Bartholdi, journal, Sept. 29, 1871.

33. Washington to Lafayette, Feb. 7, 1788.

34. Washington to Duane, Apr. 10, 1785.

35. Thomas Jefferson to George Rogers Clark, Dec. 25, 1780.

36. Lafayette and Knapp, *Memoirs of General Lafayette*, 14, 61–62.

37. Edouard Laboulaye, *L'État et ses limites* (Charpentier, 1863), 391.

38. Laboulaye, *Paris en Amerique*, vii.

39. Alexis de Tocqueville to his mother, May 9, 1831. See Alexis de Tocqueville, *Letters from America*, ed. Frederick Brown (Yale University Press, 2012).

40. Tocqueville to his mother, May 14, 1831, in *Alexis de Tocqueville and Gustave de Beaumont in America: Their Friendship and Their Travels*, ed. Olivier Zunz, trans. Arthur Goldhammer (University of Virginia Press, 2010), 9.

41. Tocqueville to Ernest de Chabrol, May 18, 1831. See *Alexis de Tocqueville and Gustave de Beaumont in America*, 24.

42. Alexis de Tocqueville, *Democracy in America*, trans., ed. Harvey C. Mansfield and Delba Winthrop (University of Chicago Press, 2000), 528.

43. Tocqueville, *Democracy in America*, 235, 244–45.

44. Tocqueville, *Democracy in America*, book 1, chapter 2.

45. Laboulaye, *Paris en Amerique*, vii–viii.

46. Bigelow, *Some Recollections of the Late Edouard Laboulaye*, 22.

47. Laboulaye, *L'État et ses limites*, v–vi.

48. Tocqueville, *Democracy in America*, 265.

49. Frederick Jackson Turner, "The Significance of the Frontier in American History," 1893. See Annual Report of the American Historical Association, 1893, and Frederick Jackson Turner, *The Frontier in American History* (Henry Holt & Co., 1920).

50. Turner, "The Significance of the Frontier in American History," 322.

51. Laboulaye, *L'État et ses limites*, 320.

52. John L. O'Sullivan, "Annexation," *United States Magazine and Democratic Review* (July 1845); John L. O'Sullivan, "Who Will Set Limits to Our Onward March?" *United States Magazine and Democratic Review* (1839).

53. Alexander Hamilton, Final Version of the Second Report on the Further Provision Necessary for Establishing Public Credit (Report on a National Bank), December 13, 1790.

54. Bartholdi, letter to mother, June 24, 1871.

55. Elizabeth Cady Stanton, Declaration of Sentiments (1848).

56. Susan B. Anthony, "On Women's Right to Vote" (1872).

57. *New York Times*, June 1, 1871–Oct. 31, 1871.

58. Frederick Douglass, "What to a Slave Is the Fourth of July?" (1852).

59. Bartholdi, journal, July 18, 1871.

60. Edouard Laboulaye to *New York Tribune*, Oct. 15, 1875, American Committee of the Statue of Liberty records, Archives of American Art, Washington, DC, and New York Public Library, New York.

61. Bartholdi, *The Statue of Liberty Enlightening the World*, Appendix, Note A.

62. Bartholdi, *The Statue of Liberty Enlightening the World*, Appendix, Note B.

63. Bartholdi to Butler, American Committee of the Statue of Liberty records.

64. "Statue of Liberty," *New York Times*, Nov. 28, 1882.

65. "A Gift Statue," *New York Times*, Dec. 26, 1883.

66. Bartholdi, *The Statue of Liberty Enlightening the World*, 38–39, 48–49.

67. Bartholdi to Butler, Feb. 1, 1884, American Committee records.

68. Bartholdi to Butler, July 21, 1885, 6.

69. Bartholdi, *The Statue of Liberty Enlightening the World*, 32.

CHAPTER 2: BUILDING AN EMPIRE BUILDING

1. Herbert Hoover, "Principles and Ideals of the United States Government," Madison Square Garden, Oct. 22, 1928. See National Constitution Center, constitutioncenter.org.

2. Hoover, "Principles and Ideals of the United States Government."

3. Recounted in Richard O'Connor, *The First Hurrah: A Biography of Al Smith* (G. P. Putnam's Sons, 1970).

4. S. J. Woolf, "Al Smith at 60 Recalls Old New York," *New York Times*, Dec. 31, 1933.

5. Woolf, "Al Smith at 60 Recalls Old New York."

6. S. J. Woolf, "Raskob Takes Off His Coat for Smith," *New York Times*, Sept. 30, 1928.

7. "Stocks Up in 'Smith Market' as Raskob Tells Business It Need Not Fear the Governor," *New York Times*, June 17, 1928.

8. Woolf, "Raskob Takes Off His Coat for Smith."

9. Samuel Crowther, "Everybody Ought to Be Rich: An Interview with John J. Raskob," *Ladies' Home Journal* (August 1929).

10. Empire State Inc., *Empire State: A History* (1931), 13.

11. Robert A. Slayton, *Empire Statesman: The Rise and Redemption of Al Smith* (Simon & Schuster, 2001).

12. George Washington to James Duane, letter, Apr. 10, 1785; Milton M. Klein, *The Empire State: A History of New York* (Cornell University Press, 2001), xix, xx.

13. "General Harrison in New York," *Telegraph*, Alton, IL, Oct. 1836. See also Jenna Flannigan, "A History of NYC Nicknames," *TimeOut New York*, Jan. 18, 2011.

14. See, for one, *New York Evening Post*, July 9, 1822.

15. "Empire State Tower, Tallest in World," *New York Times*, May 2, 1931, 1, 7.

16. "Empire State Tower," *New York Times*.

17. William Howard Taft, "Dollar Diplomacy," Annual Message of the President (1912). See Office of the Historian, US Department of State.

18. Taft, "Dollar Diplomacy."

19. John Dewey, "Imperialism Is Easy," *New Republic* 50 (Mar. 23, 1927).

20. Dewey, "Imperialism Is Easy."

21. John Dewey, "Democracy and America," in *Freedom and Culture* (G. P. Putnam's Sons, 1939).

22. Dewey, "Democracy and America."

23. See Library of Congress, images, Udo Keppler prints.

24. Emma Goldman, *Living My Life* (Alfred Knopf, 1934), 11, 717.

25. Robert Russa Moton, "Address at the Dedication of the Lincoln Memorial," May 30, 1922. See Library of Congress, Robert Russa Moton Papers.

26. "How Shall 'Miss Liberty's' Toilet Be Made?" *New York Times*, July 29, 1906.

27. "Today Is 54th Birthday of Statue of Liberty," *New York Times*, Oct. 28, 1940.

28. David A. Reed, "America of the Melting Pot Comes to an End," *New York Times*, Apr. 27, 1924.

29. Paul S. George, "Brokers, Binders, and Builders: Greater Miami's Boom of the Mid-1920s," *Florida Historical Quarterly* 65, no. 1 (1986): 37.

30. See "Rethinking Raskob," *Forbes*, Oct. 9, 2000.

31. See Great Depression Facts, Franklin D. Roosevelt Presidential Library and Museum, fdrlibrary.org; see also The Gilder Lehrman Institute of American History, gilder lehrman.org; and federalreservehistory.org.

32. "Smith to Help Build Highest Skyscraper," *New York Times*, Aug. 30, 1929, 1, 9.

33. Robert C. Brown, handwritten memo, File 743, John Raskob Papers, Hagley Museum and Library, Wilmington, DE.

34. John Raskob to Gertrude Bradley, Oct. 10, 1929, file 219, Raskob Papers. See also in David Farber, *Everybody Ought to Be Rich: The Life and Times of John J. Raskob, Capitalist* (Oxford University Press, 2013), 266.

35. William Starrett, *Skyscrapers and the Men Who Build Them* (Charles Scribner's Sons, 1928). See also reprinting in Carol Willis, ed. *Building the Empire State* (W. W. Norton & Co., 1998), 12.

36. "Smith Skyscraper Has a Novel Design," *New York Times*, Jan. 8, 1930; "Empire State Wins Architects' Award," *New York Times*, Apr. 22, 1931.

37. Paul Starrett, *Changing the Skyline: An Autobiography* (Whittlesey House, 1938), 284.

38. "The International Jew: The World's Problem," *Dearborn Independent*, May 22, 1920.

39. Adolf Hitler, "German Alliance Policy After the War," chap. 13, in *Mein Kampf*, trans. Ralph Manheim, vol. 2 (1926; Houghton Mifflin, 1943), 639. See also "Berlin Hears Ford Is Backing Hitler," *New York Times*, Dec. 20, 1922, 2.

40. See "Nuremberg Trial Proceedings," vol. 14, May 23, 1946, at Lillian Goldman Law Library, Yale Law School.

41. "Americans Invest 7 Billions Abroad," *New York Times*, Nov. 25, 1930.

42. Russell Owen, "Lindbergh Leaves New York at 7:52 A.M.," *New York Times*, May 21, 1927.

43. C. G. Poore, "The Riveter's Panorama of New York," *New York Times*, Jan. 5, 1930.

44. Starrett Brothers and Eken, "The Fascination of Speed," in *Notes on the Construction of the Empire State Building*, 40.

45. Tony Tekaroniake Evans, "How Mohawk 'Skywalkers' Helped Build New York City's Tallest Skyscrapers," History.com, May 13, 2021.

46. Poore, "The Riveter's Panorama of New York."

47. Poore, "The Riveter's Panorama of New York."

48. "Workers Raise Flag 1,048 Feet Above Fifth Ave as Steel Frame of Smith Building Is Finished," *New York Times*, Sept. 20, 1930.

49. "Smith Acts to End 25-Year Labor Row," *New York Times*, Apr. 3, 1930.

50. *Empire State: A History*, promotional pamphlet, May 1, 1931.

51. Willis, *Building the Empire State*, 11.

52. Starrett, *Changing the Skyline*, 308.

53. Willis, *Building the Empire State*, 12. See also Starrett, *Skyscrapers and the Men Who Build Them*.

54. Starrett & Ekens, *Notes on the Construction of Empire State Building*, 77. Reprinted in Willis, *Building the Empire State*.

55. Dorothea Lange and Daniel Dixon, "Photographing the Familiar," *Aperture* 1, no. 2 (1952): 15.

56. Dorothea Lange, "The Assignment I'll Never Forget," *Popular Photography* 46 (Feb. 1960). Reprinted in *Lange: Migrant Mother* (New York: Museum of Modern Art, 2018), 40–41.

57. "What Does the 'New Deal' Mean to This Mother and Her Children?" *San Francisco News*, Mar. 11, 1936.

58. Margaret Bourke White, *At the Time of the Louisville Flood*, Jan. 1937, published in *Life* magazine Feb. 1937.

59. Ida B. Wells, "Lynching, Our National Crime," National Negro Conference, 1909.

60. Obituary, *Oakland Tribune*, Apr. 5, 1931; Obituary, *Chicago Defender*, Mar. 28, 1931.

61. Ad, *New York Times*, May 1, 1981.

62. Paul Goldberger, "A Symbol of Grace Unsullied by Age," *New York Times*, Apr. 23, 1981.

CHAPTER 3: LIBERTY LIMITED

1. "France's Gift Accepted: Liberty's Statue Unveiled on Bedlow's Island," *New York Times*, Oct. 29, 1886, 1–2.

2. "France's Gift Accepted," and "The Statue Unveiled," *New York Times*, Oct. 29, 1886, 1–2; "World-Lighting Liberty," *New-York Tribune*, Oct. 29, 1886, 1; "The Bartholdi Orations," *New-York Tribune*, Oct. 29, 1886, 7. See also multiple articles covering the event from the Oct. 29, 1886, issues.

3. Sally Roesch Wagner, *Matilda Joslyn Gage: She Who Holds the Sky* (Sky Carrier Press, 1998), 28; Angelica Shirley Carpenter, *Born Criminal: Matilda Joslyn Gage, Radical Suffragist* (South Dakota Historical Society Press, 2018), 155–58; "They Enter a Protest," *New York Times*, Oct. 29, 1886, 8.

4. National Woman Suffrage Association, "Statement of Protest" (1876).

5. *New York Times*, Oct. 29, 1886; *New York Herald*, Oct. 28, 1886.

6. Grover Cleveland, speech, Statue of Liberty dedication ceremony, Oct. 28, 1886.

7. Blake quote, "The Americans Who Saw Lady Liberty as a False Idol of Broken Promises," *Smithsonian*, May 28, 2019.

8. See, for example, the 1830 painting by Delacroix, *Liberty Leading the People*.

9. "France's Gift Accepted," *New York Times*, Oct. 29, 1886.

10. *Cleveland Gazette*, Nov. 27, 1886, 2. See Library of Congress, *The Cleveland Gazette* archive, 1883-1892, loc.gov.

11. John Boyle O'Reilly, "Liberty Enlightening the World," *Boston Daily Globe*, Oct. 29, 1886.

12. "Statue of Liberty," *New York Times*, May 6, 1883.

13. Henry R. Searle, *Washington Monument: Monograph* (Gibson Brothers, 1847), 3; Jennifer Barger, "Why the Washington Monument Was Once a National Embarrassment," *National Geographic*, Feb. 17, 2023.

14. "The Statue of Liberty," *New York Times*, Nov. 28, 1882.

15. *New York World*, Mar. 16, 1885.

16. Joseph Pulitzer, "The College of Journalism," *North American Review* 178, no. 570 (May 1904): 641.

17. "A Gift Statue," *New York Times*, Dec. 26, 1883.

18. Elizabeth Mitchell, *Liberty's Torch: The Great Adventure to Build the Statue of Liberty* (Atlantic Monthly Press, 2014), 237.

19. Emma Lazarus, "The New Colossus," *The Norton Introduction to Literature*, ed. Kelly J. Mays, 14th ed. (W.W. Norton, 2022), 752.

20. Emma Lazarus, "Admetus," in *Admetus and Other Poems* (Hurd and Houghton, 1871).

21. Emma Lazarus, "The New Ezekiel" (1882) and "The Banner of the Jew" (1882), *The Poems of Emma Lazarus*.

22. Christian Blanchet and Betrand Dard, *Statue of Liberty: The First One Hundred Years*, trans Bernard Weisberger (Houghton Mifflin, 1985), 111, 116.

23. Chauncey M. Depew, "Oration," Oct. 28, 1886, 34.

24. "The Bartholdi Statue," *St. Louis Globe-Democrat*, Oct. 29, 1886.

25. Unidentified artist, "Welcome to the Land of Freedom," *Frank Leslie's Illustrated Newspaper*, 1887, Library of Congress, Prints and Photographs.

26. See demographic data at NYC.gov and data.census.gov.

27. James D. Phelan, "Why the Chinese Should Be Excluded," *North American Review* 173 (Nov. 1901).

28. Saum Song Bo, "A Chinese View of the Statue of Liberty," *New York Sun*, June 30, 1885.

29. Eileen Putman, "Lady Liberty Welcomed Immigrants," *The Oklahoman*, June 1, 1986.

30. Blanchet and Dard, *Statue of Liberty*, 113–14.

31. Jocelyn Cohen and Daniel Soyer, eds., *My Future Is in America: Autobiographies of Eastern European Jewish Immigrants* (New York University Press, 2006), 148.

32. Putman, "Lady Liberty Welcomed Immigrants."

33. Putman, "Lady Liberty Welcomed Immigrants."

34. *Jewish Messenger*, Oct. 29, 1886, 4.

35. "Our Country's Future," *Chicago Tribune*, Sept. 28, 1864.

36. Frederick Jackson Turner, "The Significance of the Frontier in American History," American Historical Association, Chicago, 1893. See Annual Report of the American Historical Association, 1893, and Frederick Jackson Turner, *The Frontier in American History* (Henry Holt & Co., 1920).

37. Theodore Roosevelt, preface, *The Winning of the West, Vol. 1, From the Alleghanies to the Mississippi, 1769–1776* (1900).

38. Theodore Roosevelt, "Inaugural Address," 1905. See Theodore Roosevelt Association, theodoreroosevelt.org.

39. Theodore Roosevelt, "The Strenuous Life," speech, Apr. 10, 1899. See Theodore Roosevelt Association, theodoreroosevelt.org.

40. Roosevelt, "The Strenuous Life."

41. "Merely a Suggestion," *Puck*, July 10, 1907. For more on cartoons featuring Liberty, see Blanchet and Dard, *Statue of Liberty*, 1985.

42. Theodore Roosevelt, "Conservation as a National Duty," May 13, 1908. See Voices of Democracy: The US Oratory Project, voicesofdemocracy.umd.edu.

43. Turner, "The Significance of the Frontier in American History."

44. See Gerald Nash, "The Census of 1890 and the Closing of the Frontier," *Pacific Northwest Quarterly* 71, no. 3 (July 1980): 98–100.

45. Turner, "The Significance of the Frontier in American History."

46. Theodore Roosevelt, "The Liberty of the People," 1912 campaign speech. See History Matters, historymatters.gmu.edu.

47. Theodore Roosevelt, "Citizenship in a Republic," Apr. 23, 1910. See Theodore Roosevelt Association, theodoreroosevelt.org.

48. Turner, "The Significance of the Frontier in American History," and Roosevelt, "The Strenuous Life," para. 5.

49. John L. Stevens to John Foster, letter, February 1, 1893, in Foreign Relations of the United States (FRUS), Appendix II, Affairs in Hawaii, 1894.

50. Grover Cleveland, "Message Regarding Hawaiian Annexation," Dec. 18, 1893. See Miller Center, Presidential Speeches, millercenter.org.

51. Cleveland, "Message Regarding Hawaiian Annexation."

52. William James, "The Philippine Question," 1903. See The American Yawp Reader, americanyawp.com.

53. Carl Schurz to Jacob G. Schurman, May 8, 1902, in *Speeches, Correspondence and Political Papers of Carl Schurz* (G. P. Putnam's Sons, 1913), 290.

54. Carl Schurz, "For Truth, Justice and Liberty" (1900), in *Speeches, Correspondence and Political Papers of Carl Schurz*, 216, 235; Carl Schurz, "The Issue of Imperialism" (1899), in *Speeches, Correspondence and Political Papers of Carl Schurz*, 35.

55. Schurz, "The Issue of Imperialism," 35.

56. Carl Schurz, "Woman Suffrage," *Harper's Weekly*, June 16, 1894, 554.

57. William McKinley, "Interview," *Christian Advocate*, Jan. 22, 1903, 17.

58. Rudyard Kipling, "The White Man's Burden," *The Times* (London), Feb. 4, 1899; *The New York Sun*, Feb. 5, 1899.

59. Benjamin Tillman, "Address to the US Senate," Feb. 7, 1899. See National Humanities Center, nationalhumanitiescenter.org.

60. W. E. B. Du Bois, *The Autobiography of W. E. B. Du Bois: A Soliloquy on Viewing My Life from the Last Decade of Its First Century* (1961; Oxford University Press, 2007), 114.

61. Du Bois, "The Study of the Negro Problems," *Annals of the American Academy of Political and Social Science*, vol. 11 (1898).

62. Du Bois, *The Autobiography of W. E. B. Du Bois*, 98.

63. W. E. B. Du Bois, "The Present Outlook for the Dark Races of Mankind" (1900); "The Talented Tenth" (1903). See *The Oxford W. E. B. Du Bois Reader*, ed. Eric J. Sundquist (Oxford University Press, 1996).

64. W. E. B. Du Bois, "Strivings of the Negro People," *Atlantic Monthly* 80 (1897).

65. Du Bois, "The Study of the Negro Problems" (1898).

66. Ida B. Wells, *Southern Horrors: Lynch Law in All Its Phases* (1892) and *The Red Record* (1895).

67. Reprinted in Wells, *Southern Horrors*.

68. Ida B. Wells, *Crusade for Justice: Autobiography* (1970; University of Chicago Press, 2020), 358.

69. PBS, American Experience, "The Gilded Age," online, pbs.org.

70. Josiah Strong, *Our Country: Its Possible Future and Its Present Crisis* (Baker & Taylor, 1885).

71. Walt Whitman, "The Tramp and Strike Questions," 1879 (published 1882). See The Walt Whitman Archive, whitmanarchive.org.

72. Joseph Pulitzer, "A Danger to the Republic," speech, Oct. 9, 1880, reprinted in *St. Louis Post-Dispatch*, Dec. 13, 1903.

73. Joe Hill, "Workers of the World, Awaken" (1910). See Zinn Education Project, zinnedproject.org.

74. "Suffrage 'Bombs' for Wilson," *New York Times*, Dec. 2, 1916.

75. Bartholdi to Butler, letters, American Committee records, New York Public Library.

76. "Peace Can Come Only with Liberty," *New York Times*, Dec. 3, 1916.

77. Woodrow Wilson, statement to British envoy William Tyrrell, November 1913.

78. Woodrow Wilson, speech to Congress, Apr. 2, 1917. See National Archives, Milestone Documents, archives.gov.

79. "France's Gift Accepted," *New York Times*, Oct. 29, 1886; Chauncey Depew, "Oration," Oct. 28, 1886, 30–31.

80. Alexandra Kollontai, "The Statue of Liberty: The End of 1916," in *Selected Articles and Speeches*, ed. I. M. Dazhina et al., trans. Cynthia Carlile (New York: International Publishers, 1984), 112–15.

81. Woodrow Wilson, "Liberty Speech," *New York Times*, Dec. 3, 1916.

CHAPTER 4: EMPIRE AND LIBERTY IN CRISIS

1. "Roosevelt Calls Hoover and Regime Reactionary," *New York Times*, May 1, 1931.

2. "Smith Opens Empire State Building, World's Tallest," *New York Daily News*, May 2, 1931; "Tallest Building Opened by Hoover," *New York Times*, May 1, 1931.

3. "Curious Scientific Comparison of the Tower of Babel with the Tallest Building on Earth," *Ogden Standard-Examiner*, June 7, 1931.

4. "Tools Made Here Were Used in Constructing Empire State Building, Hoover Dam," *Pensacola News Journal*, Aug. 9, 1932.

5. Empire State Inc., "Dedication," in *Empire State: A History* (1931), 1.

6. "Smith Opens Empire State Building, World's Tallest," *New York Times*, May 2, 1931.

7. W. F. Bullock, "Higher and Higher in New York," *Daily Mail*, Nov. 13, 1930.

8. Helen Keller to Dr. John Finley, Jan. 13, 1932. American Foundation for the Blind, afb.org; see also "The New York That Helen Keller 'Sees;' Sightless, She Discerns in the Skyscrapers Symbols of Man's Great Achievements," *New York Times*, Jan. 31, 1932.

9. "World's Tallest," *New York Times*, May 2, 1931.

10. Ed Garcia Conde, "The Bronx Italian Immigrant Who Helped Construct the Empire State Building," Welcome2TheBronx, May 1, 2015.

11. *Ogden Standard-Examiner*, June 7, 1931.

12. W. F. Bullock, "Taking the Lift to the Sun," *Daily Mail*, May 29, 1931.

13. Edmund Wilson, "The Empire State Building Comes to New York City," *New Republic*, May 20, 1931.

14. Bullock, "Taking the Lift to the Sun."

15. "Picture of the Week," *Life*, May 12, 1947, 42–43; Ben Cosgrove, "'The Most Beautiful Suicide': A Violent Death, an Immortal Photo," *Time*, Mar. 19, 2014.

16. Mary Jane Kroll, "One Christmas Present for Two," *Daily News*, Feb. 14, 1931.

17. Fay Wray, *New York Times*, Sept. 21, 1969.

18. Patricia Winters, "To Oldest Tenant, Empire State a Jewel," *Chicago Tribune*, July 17, 1994.

19. Empire State Inc., *Empire State: A History*, 7.

20. "All Bedloe Island Soon to Become Park," *New York Times*, Dec. 29, 1933.

21. Walter B. Hayward, "Our Harbor Goddess in a New Radiance," *New York Times*, Nov. 15, 1931.

22. Newsreel, British Pathé, 1932, YouTube.com.

23. John Reed, "The Traders' War" (1914). See Marxist Internet Archive, marxists.architexturez.net.

24. "Is Hull Home a Socialist Center," *Nebraska Daily News-Press*, Sept. 17, 1903.

25. "Jane Addams—Facts," NobelPrize.org, Nobel Prize Outreach.

26. Jane Addams, *Peace and Bread in Time of War* (Macmillan, 1922), 4–5.

27. "Calls Jane Addams 'Truest American,'" *Springfield (MA) Daily Republican*, May 3, 1935, 26. The statement was reprinted in multiple newspapers after Addams's death.

28. Addams, *Peace and Bread in Time of War*.

29. Empire State Inc., *Empire State*, 10.

30. Franklin D. Roosevelt, First Inaugural Address, Mar. 4, 1933. See FDR Presidential Library & Museum, fdrlibrary.org.

31. *New York Times*, May 2, 1931.

32. Albert Einstein to W. E. B. Du Bois, Oct. 29, 1931, reprinted in *The Crisis* magazine, 1931.

33. Jane Addams, *The Second Twenty Years at Hull House* (Macmillan, 1930), 396–401.

34. John Dewey, *A Common Faith* (Yale University Press, 1934), 27, 51–52, 79, 71.

35. John Dewey, "Liberty and Social Control," *Later Works*, vol. 2, 1935–37 (Southern Illinois University Press, 1987), 360–63.

36. Henry Ford, *Ford News*, back cover, Oct. 1934.

37. Francis Scott Key, "Defense of Fort McHenry" (1814). See Media Rich Learning, mediarichlearning.com.

38. Craig Thompson, "Airship Like a Giant Torch on Darkening Jersey Field," *New York Times*, May 7, 1937.

39. Roosevelt to Hitler, letter, May 1937. See "Roosevelt Sends Hitler Message of Sympathy," *New York Times*, May 7, 1937, 19.

CHAPTER 5: EMPIRE AND LIBERTY AT WAR

1. Franklin D. Roosevelt, First Inaugural Address, Mar. 4, 1933.

2. Al Smith, "Betrayal of the Democratic Party," Liberty League Dinner, Washington, DC, Jan. 25, 1936. See Teaching American History, teachingamericanhistory.org.

3. Al Smith, "Smith Says Hitler Reflects People," *New York Times*, June 3, 1933.

4. Franklin Roosevelt, "Address on the Occasion of the 50th Anniversary of the Statue of Liberty," Oct. 28, 1936; "Roosevelt's Address at the Statue of Liberty," *New York Times*, Oct. 29, 1936.

5. "French Here Hail Statue of Liberty," *New York Times*, Oct. 29, 1944.

6. Al Smith, "Text of Smith's Address Urging Change in Neutrality Act," *New York Times*, Oct. 2, 1939.

7. Franklin D. Roosevelt, "Address at Chautauqua, NY," August 14, 1936.

8. "Report to the Secretary on the Acquiescence of This Government in the Murder of the Jews," US Treasury, Jan. 13, 1944, Morgenthau Diaries, FDR Library.

9. L. Frank Baum, *Aberdeen Saturday Pioneer*, Dec. 20, 1980; L. Frank Baum, *Aberdeen Saturday Pioneer*, Dec. 20, 1980; for uncensored transcription, see A. Waller Hastings, "L. Frank Baum's Editorials on the Sioux Nation," Northern State University (website), archived Aug. 13, 2008, at the Wayback Machine.

10. Baum, *Aberdeen Saturday Pioneer*, Jan. 3, 1891.

11. "The Senate's Declaration of War," *Japan Times and Mail*, Apr. 19, 1924.

12. "Lights Go on Briefly on Empire State," *New York Times*, Feb. 12, 1944; William H. Shriver, "Tall Buildings as Targets," *New York Times*, July 21, 1942; "War Agencies to Combine in Empire State Offices," *New York Times*, June 12, 1943.

13. "Ex-Sailor Dies in Leap From 86th Floor of Empire State," *New York Times*, Dec. 17, 1943; "The General in His New Command," *New York Times*, Dec. 5, 1944.

14. Upton Sinclair, "To Solve the German Problem—A Free State?" *New York Times Magazine*, Aug. 15, 1943, 6, 34.

15. Adolf Hitler, "Subject and Citizens," chap. 3, in *Mein Kampf*, vol. 2 (1926; Houghton Mifflin, 1943), 440-41.

16. S. J. Woolf, "Raskob Takes Off His Coat for Smith," *New York Times*, Sept. 30, 1928, 5.

17. Adolf Hitler, "Nation and Race," chap. 11, in *Mein Kampf*, vol. 1 (1925; Houghton Mifflin, 1943), 286.

18. See "Ask a Historian: How Many Japanese Americans Were Incarcerated During WWII?" at densho.org.

19. "Refugee Ship," *New York Times*, June 8, 1939, 24.

20. Franklin D. Roosevelt, "Message to Congress on Repeal of the Chinese Exclusion Laws," October 11, 1943. See The American Presidency Project, presidency.ucsb.edu.

21. Roosevelt, "Address on the Occasion of the 50th Anniversary of the Statue of Liberty," Oct. 28, 1936. See The American Presidency Project, presidency.ucsb.edu.

22. Roosevelt, "Four Freedoms Speech," Jan. 6, 1941. See FDR Presidential Library & Museum, fdrlibrary.org.

23. Roosevelt, "Lend-Lease Speech," Mar. 11, 1941. See Miller Center, millercenter.org.

24. Roosevelt, "Four Freedoms Speech."

25. Roosevelt, "Four Freedoms Speech."

26. Roosevelt, "Four Freedoms Speech."

27. Franklin Roosevelt and Winston Churchill, "Atlantic Charter," Aug. 1941. See FDR Presidential Library & Museum, fdrlibrary.org.

28. A. Philip Randolph, "Call to Negro America to March on Washington," *Black Worker* 14 (May 1941).

29. A. Philip Randolph, speech in Detroit, 1942. See UH Digital History, digitalhistory.uh.edu.

30. "Jersey City Raises Statue of Liberty," *New York Times*, Apr. 12, 1943; "City Jumps Gun in War Bond Drive," *New York Times*, Nov. 18, 1944; "Nazi 'Statue of Liberty' Projected for Hamburg," *New York Times*, Mar. 15, 1945; "Briton Urges US Erect Gold Statue of Liberty," *New York Times*, July 27, 1942.

31. Franklin D. Roosevelt, First Inaugural Address, Mar. 4, 1933.

32. Herbert Hoover, "This Challenge to Liberty," Oct. 30, 1936. See Hebert Hoover Library and Museum, hoover.archives.gov.

33. Al Smith, "Betrayal of the Democratic Party," Liberty League Dinner, Washington, DC, Jan. 25, 1936.

34. Hoover, "This Challenge to Liberty."

35. "'Double V' Campaign Attracts High and Low," *New Pittsburgh Courier*, Apr. 4, 1942.

36. Medgar Evers, WLBT radio address, May 20, 1963.

37. Woody Guthrie, *Bound for Glory: Autobiography* (1943; Plume, 1983), 251.

38. Henry Wallace, "The Price of Free World Victory," address transcript (May 8, 1942); Henry Luce, "The American Century," *Life* (Feb. 1941).

39. Dwight MacDonald, *Henry Wallace: The Man and the Myth* (Vanguard Press, 1948), 32, 12.

40. Wallace," *Christian Century* (Apr. 23, 1941).

41. Learned Hand, "The Spirit of Liberty," May 21, 1944. See Foundation for Individual Rights and Expression (FIRE), thefire.org.

42. John Adams, "Liberty and Knowledge," in *A Dissertation on the Canon and Feudal Law*, 1765.

43. "Alfred E. Smith Dies Here at 70; 4 Times Governor," *New York Times*, Oct. 4, 1944.

44. "Lights of Liberty Statue to Welcome Troops Home," *New York Times*, June 8, 1945.

45. Carl Beck, "Miss Liberty as World Symbol," letter to the editor, *New York Times*, May 23, 1944.

46. "Miss Liberty Lure for More Visitors," *New York Times*, Dec. 4, 1944.

47. "Colonel's Wife Had Feeling of Disaster Before Takeoff," *Evening Star*, July 29, 1945.

48. "Army Bomber Crashes Empire State Building in Dense Fog, Killing 13 and Injuring 20," *Knoxville Journal*, July 29, 1945.

49. Charles E. Harner, "Empire State Occupant Says Crash Was Like Earthquake," *Evening Star*, July 29, 1945.

50. *Knoxville Journal*, July 29, 1945.

51. Oscar Fraley, "Office Where 20 Worked for Mercy Now Scene of Death and Destruction," *Knoxville Journal*, July 29, 1945.

52. "Empire State Building Crash Death Toll May Exceed 15," *Evening Star*, July 29, 1945.

53. *Knoxville Journal*, July 29, 1945.

54. Patricia Winters, "To Oldest Tenant, Empire State a Jewel," *Chicago Tribune*, July 17, 1994.

55. "Colonel's Wife Had Feeling of Disaster Before Takeoff," *Evening Star*, July 29, 1945.

CHAPTER 6: FREEDOM LIGHTS IN THE COLD WAR ERA

1. "Jackhammers Bite Pavement to Start Trade Center Job," *New York Times*, Aug. 6, 1966.

2. Frank J. Prial, "Governors Dedicate Trade Center Here; World Role Is Cited," *New York Times*, Apr. 5, 1966.

3. Prial, "Governors Dedicate Trade Center Here."

4. Michael T. Kaufman, "World Trade Institute Is Labeled 'Heart' of Center," *New York Times*, Apr. 5, 1973.

5. Ada Louise Huxtable, "Big but Not So Bold: Trade Center Towers Are Tallest, but Architecture Is Smaller Scale," *New York Times*, Apr. 5, 1973. See additional commentary on the WTC in Karl Haskell, "Before & After: Talking of the Towers," *New York Times*, Sept. 16, 2001.

6. Robert A. Jones, "Highest Building—for Now—Debuts in N.Y.," *Los Angeles Times*, Apr. 5, 1973.

7. Nadja Sayej, "Facts You Didn't Know About the Original World Trade Centers," *Architectural Digest*, Sept. 10, 2021.

8. Harry S. Truman, "Special Message to the Congress on the Threat to the Freedom of Europe," Mar. 17, 1948. See Harry S. Truman Presidential Library and Museum, trumanlibrary.gov.

9. J. B. West, *Upstairs at the White House: My Life with the First Ladies* (1973; Open Road Integrated Media, 2016), 105–7.

10. West, *Upstairs at the White House*, 107.

11. Ho Chi Minh, "Declaration of Independence of the Democratic Republic of Vietnam," Sept. 2, 1945. See Ho Chi Minh, *Selected Writings, 1920-1969* (Foreign Languages Publishing House, Hanoi, 1977), 53.

12. Ho Chi Minh, "Letter to Secretary of State Robert Lansing," June 18, 1919. See National Archives Catalog, Record Group 256, Records of the American Commission to Negotiate Peace.

13. Ho Chi Minh, "The Path Which Led Me to Leninism," 1960. See *Selected Writings*, 250.

14. Ho Chi Minh, "Lenin and the Colonial Peoples," *Pravda*, Jan. 27, 1924. See also *Selected Writings*, 37.

15. Ho Chi Minh, "Letter to President Harry Truman," Feb. 28, 1946. See National Archives Catalog, Record Group 226, Records of the Office of Strategic Services, NAID 305263.

16. Civil Rights Congress, "We Charge Genocide: The Crime of Government Against the Negro People," Dec. 17, 1951. See Veterans of the Civil Rights Movement, crmvet.org.

17. Thomas Hughes, "Memo on Soviet Media Coverage of Current US Racial Crisis," US Department of State Bureau of Intelligence and Research, June 14, 1963, John F. Kennedy Presidential Library and Museum.

18. "Memorandum by the President to the Director for Mutual Security," Mar. 14, 1953, Foreign Relations of the United States (FRUS), 1952-1954, The Near and Middle East, vol. 9, part 2, no. 1451, Office of the Historian, history.state.gov.

19. Harry S. Truman, "Special Message to the Congress on the Threat to the Freedom of Europe," Mar. 17, 1948, Harry S. Truman Library & Museum, National Archives.

20. Executive Order 10450, 1953. See National Archives, Office of the Federal Register (OFR), archives.gov.

21. "Testimony of Pete Seeger before the House Un-American Activities Committee," Aug. 18, 1955. See History Matters, George Mason University, historymatters.gmu.edu.

22. Mario Savio, "Sit-In Address on the Steps of Sproul Hall," University of California at Berkeley, Dec. 2, 1964. See *The Essential Mario Savio: Speeches and Writings that Changed America*, ed. Robert Cohen (University of California Press, 2014).

23. "Port Huron Statement" (1962). See Center for American Progress.

24. Casey Hayden and Mary King, "Sex and Caste: A Kind of Memo," November 18, 1965. Published in *Liberation* magazine, April 1966.

25. "Visit of Queen Elizabeth to City," *New York Times*, Oct. 22, 1957.

26. See Tauranac, *The Empire State Building*, 343.

27. "New Lights," *New York Times*, Feb. 28, 1956.

28. Milton Bracker, "Empire State Building Becomes Lighthouse as Four Beacons Go On," *New York Times*, May 4, 1956.

29. "Visit of Queen Elizabeth to City."

30. "Visit of Queen Elizabeth to City."

31. Nikita Khrushchev, "Speech on the Cuban Crisis," May 23, 1963.

32. John F. Kennedy, *A Nation of Immigrants* (HarperCollins, 1958).

33. "Remarks at the Signing of the Immigration Bill, Liberty Island," New York, Oct. 3, 1965, American Presidency Project, presidency.ucsb.edu.

34. Reinhold Niebuhr, *Moral Man and Immoral Society: A Study in Ethics and Politics* (Charles Scribner's Sons, 1932).

35. Martin Luther King Jr., "I Have a Dream," Aug. 28, 1963. See npr.org.

36. Don Bristow-Carrico, "Seizing the Statue of Liberty 1971: Three Days with a Lady," *The Veteran* 29, no. 1 (1999): 15.

37. *Man on a Wire*, film, Magnolia Pictures, 2008; Grace Lichtenstein, "Stuntman, Eluding Guards, Walks a Tightrope Between Trade Center Towers, *New York Times*, Aug. 8, 1974; "Tightrope Walk Between the Twin Towers Is Recalled," *New York Times*, Aug. 7, 2005.

38. Jeremy Rifkin, "The Red, White, and Blue Left," People's Bicentennial Commission, in *The Progressive*, Madison, WI, 1971.

39. Gil Scott-Heron, "Bicentennial Blues." See YouTube.com.

40. Gerald Ford, "Bicentennial Celebration," July 4, 1976. See Gerald R. Ford Presidential Library, fordlibrarymuseum.gov.

41. Arthur Knight, "*Rocky* Review," *Hollywood Reporter*, Nov. 5, 1976.

42. Vincent Canby, "Film 'Rocky' Pure 30's Make-Believe," *New York Times*, Nov. 22, 1976.

43. Robert D. McFadden, "Iranians in Protest at Liberty Statue," *New York Times*, Nov. 5, 1979.

CHAPTER 7: EMPIRE AND LIBERTY UNDER ATTACK

1. Maya Lin, Vietnam War Memorial Proposal.

2. Maya Lin, "Making the Memorial," *New York Review*, Nov. 2, 2000.

3. Elise T. Chisolm, *Baltimore Evening Sun*; reprinted in *Detroit Free Press*, Feb. 7, 1982.

4. Bernard Jacob, "Vietnam Memorial Adds Subtlety Among Nation's Major Monuments," *Star Tribune*, May 28, 1983.

5. Ronald Reagan, "Remarks at the Dedication Ceremonies for the Vietnam Veterans Memorial Statue," Nov. 11, 1984. See Ronald Reagan Presidential Library & Museum, reaganlibrary.gov.

6. Reagan, "Remarks at the Dedication Ceremonies for the Vietnam Veterans Memorial Statue."

7. Ronald Reagan, "Address to the Veterans of Foreign Wars Convention," Chicago, Aug. 18, 1980. See The American Presidency Project, presidency.ucsb.edu.

8. Ronald Reagan, "To Restore America," 1976. See Ronald Reagan Presidential Library & Museum, reaganlibrary.gov.

9. Reagan, "To Restore America."

10. Ronald Reagan, "Labor Day Speech at Liberty State Park," Sept. 1, 1980. See Ronald Reagan Presidential Library & Museum, reaganlibrary.gov.

11. Calvin Sims, "Engineers Fix Original Defects in the Statue," *New York Times*, Dec. 17, 1985.

12. *Statue of Liberty*, PBS, 1985.

13. *Statue of Liberty*, PBS, 1985.

14. Michael Brenson, "Art People," *New York Times*, Sept. 24, 1982; Sarah Cascone, "Jewish History Museum Acquires Sculpture Models," Artnet, July 27, 2017.

15. Ronald Reagan, "Remarks on the Lighting of the Torch of the Statue of Liberty in New York," July 3, 1986.

16. "Immigration: A Commitment or a Problem?" *El Paso Times*, Nov. 9, 1986.

17. Jerry Falwell, *Listen, America* (Bantam, 1980).

18. Ronald Reagan, "Remarks at the Annual Convention of the National Association of Evangelicals in Orlando, FL," March 8, 1983. See Ronald Reagan Presidential Library & Museum.

19. "Moral Majority Worries Former Iranian Hostage," *Chicago Tribune*, July 23, 1981.

20. J. F. Mays, "Falwell and Islam," *Roanoke Times*, Apr. 12, 1982.

21. Howard V. Pendley, "Likening Falwell to Khomeini," *Roanoke Times*, Apr. 15, 1982.

22. *Statue of Liberty*, PBS, 1985.

23. Joseph Stiglitz, "The Roaring Nineties," *The Atlantic*, Oct. 2002.

24. "World Peace Through World Trade," 9/11 Memorial & Museum.

25. Russell Baker, "Curtains for the Empire," *New York Times*, Nov. 16, 1985.

26. "Clashing Empires," *Chicago Tribune*, July 17, 1994.

27. "Clashing Empires."

28. Mitchell Pacelle, *Empire: A Tale of Obsession, Betrayal, and the Battle for an American Icon* (John Wiley and Sons, 2001).

29. Pacelle, *Empire*.

30. Peter L. Bergen, *Holy War, Inc.: Inside the Secret World of Osama bin Laden* (Free Press, 2001), 19–20.

31. Robert D. McFadden, "Shots Send Empire State Crowd Fleeing," *New York Times*, Feb. 24, 1997, 1; Matthew Purdy, "Empire State Gunman's Note: Kill 'Zionists,'" *New York Times*, Feb. 26, 1997, 1.

32. Eric Nalder, "Twin Towers Engineered to Withstand Jet Collision," *Seattle Times*, Feb. 27, 1993.

33. "Empire's Elder," *New York Daily News*, July 2, 2004.

34. R. W. Apple Jr., "Awaiting the Aftershocks," *New York Times*, Sept. 12, 2001; John F. Burns, "America the Vulnerable Meets a Ruthless Enemy," *New York Times*, Sept. 12, 2001.

35. Zachary Schuster, "American Empire," *Daily Illini*, Sept. 20, 2004.

36. Julia Keller and Marja Mills, "'Empire' Losing Evil Association," Deseret News, *Chicago Tribune*, April 27, 2003; "Americans Wary of What's in a Name," *Hartford Courant*, Apr. 27, 2003, A14, reprinted article, Julia Keller and Marja Mills, "Empire Image Undergoes a Makeover, *Chicago Tribune*.

37. Charles V. Bagli, "Too Tall? Not at All, Tenants Say," *New York Times*, Nov. 5, 2001.

38. Fred Bernstein, "Drawing Closer to an Old Friend," *New York Times*, Oct. 11, 2001, 82.

39. John Tierney, "The Big City; Best Defense? Don't Get Defensive," *New York Times*, Oct. 9, 2001.

40. Bernstein, "Drawing Closer to an Old Friend," *New York Times*, Oct. 11, 2001.

41. "Opinion: How the Statue of Liberty Revived My Confidence After I Survived the 9/11 Attacks," *Des Moines Register*, Sept. 5, 2021.

42. Gabriel Torretta, "Queering the Statue of Liberty," *First Things*, July 18, 2011.

43. Du Bois, *The Autobiography of W. E. B. Du Bois*, 114; Claudia Jones, letter to editor, *Daily Worker*, Nov. 8, 1950.

44. *Statue of Liberty*, PBS, 1985.

45. Rev. Dr. William J. Barber, X platform, Nov. 8, 2017.

46. Jerry Springer, July 4, 1986; see also speech Jan. 2003, aired on *This American Life*, ep. 258, Jan. 30, 2004.

47. Rush Limbaugh, "It's the Statue of Liberty, Not the Statue of Immigration," *The Rush Limbaugh Show*, July 1, 2010.

48. "Americans Wary," *Hartford Courant*, Apr. 27, 2003.

49. Pacelle, *Empire*, 306–7, 2, 9.

50. "Drawing Closer," *New York Times*, Oct. 11, 2001.

51. Dewey, "Imperialism Is Easy."

52. "How Do You Know If You're Living Through the Death of an Empire?" *Mother Jones*, July/Aug. 2020.

53. Frederic Auguste Bartholdi, *The Statue of Liberty Enlightening the World* (North American Review, 1885), Note C, 57.

54. Joseph Biden, "Remarks by President Biden in Statement to the American People," July 24, 2024, White House.

55. Herman Melville, *Moby Dick*, 1851.

INDEX